DEATH

the high cost of living

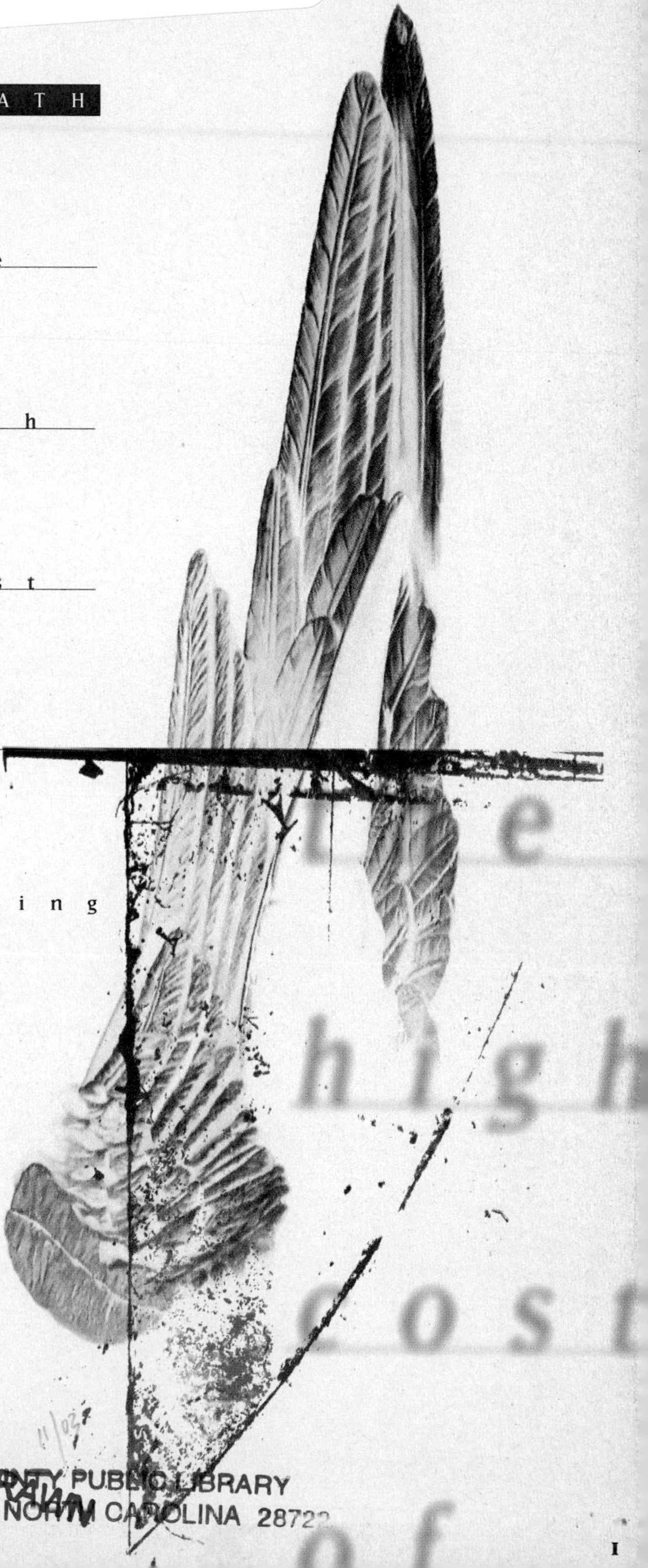

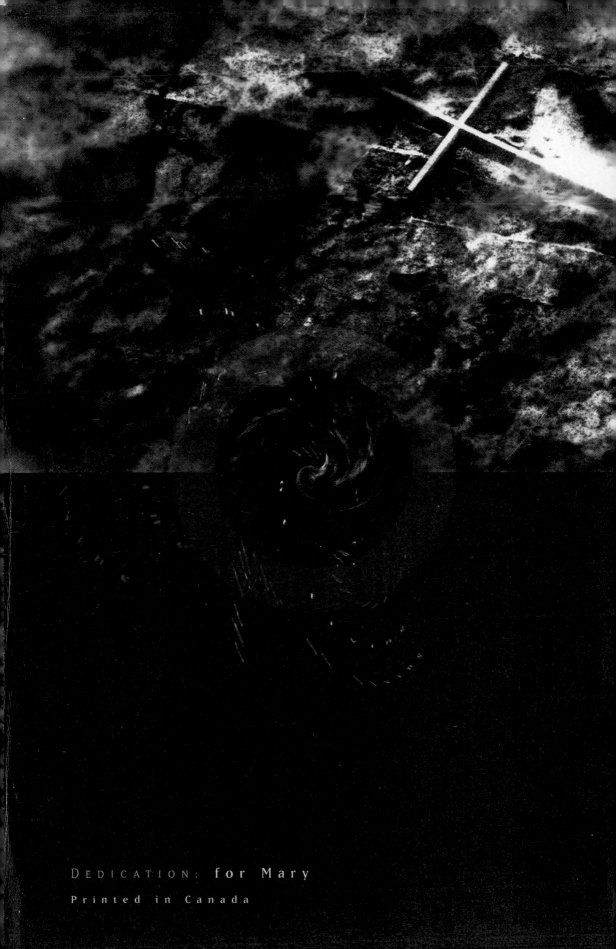

DEDICATION: for Mary

Printed in Canada

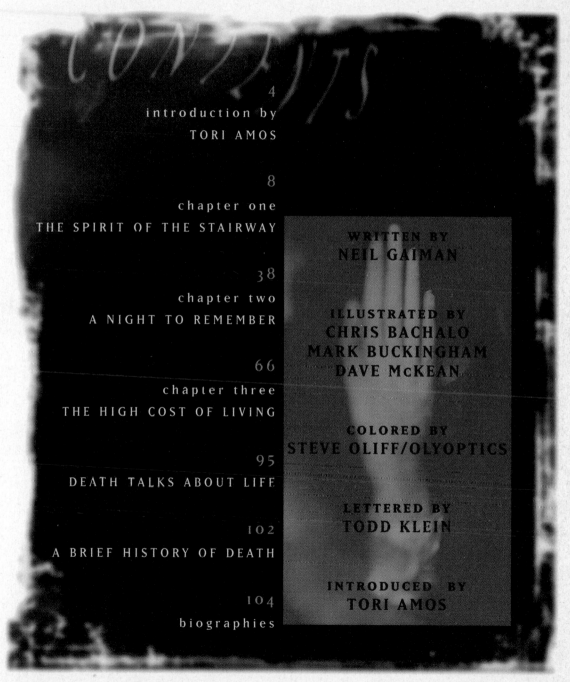

CONTENTS

WRITTEN BY
NEIL GAIMAN

ILLUSTRATED BY
CHRIS BACHALO
MARK BUCKINGHAM
DAVE McKEAN

COLORED BY
STEVE OLIFF/OLYOPTICS

LETTERED BY
TODD KLEIN

INTRODUCED BY
TORI AMOS

DEATH CREATED BY NEIL GAIMAN AND MIKE DRINGENBERG

3

introduction

TORI AMOS

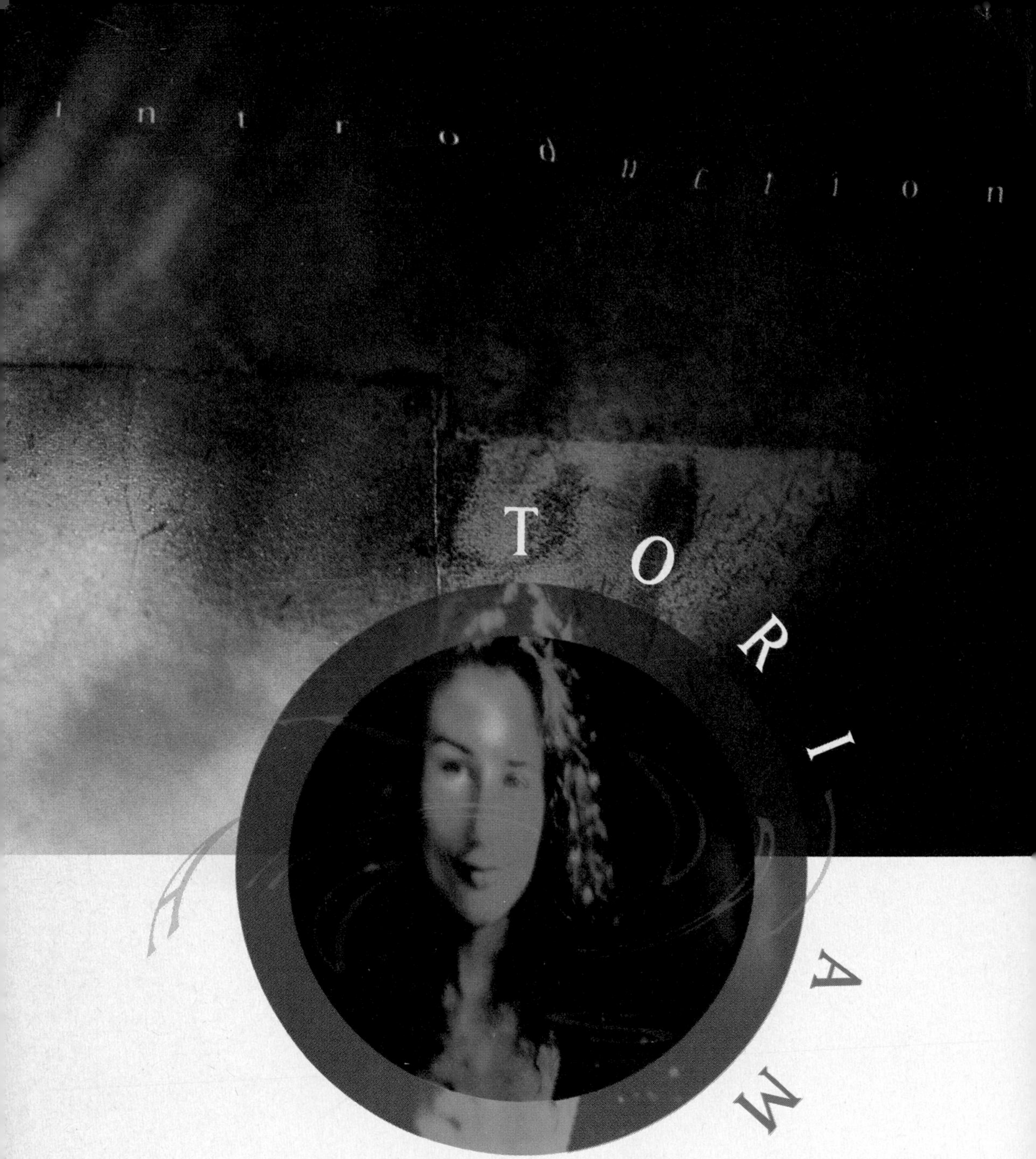

It's funny but on good days I don't think of her so much.

In fact never. I never just say hi when the sun is on my tongue and my belly's all warm. On bad days I talk to Death constantly, not about suicide because honestly that's not dramatic enough. Most of us love the stage and suicide is definitely your last performance and being addicted to the stage, suicide was never an option - plus people get to look you over and stare at your fatty bits and you can't cross your legs to give that flattering thigh angle and that's depressing. So we talk.

She says things no one else seems to come up with, like let's have a hotdog and then it's like nothing's impossible. She told me once there is a part of her in everyone, though Neil believes I'm more Delirium than Tori, and Death taught me to accept that, you know, wear your butterflies with pride. And when I do accept that, I know Death is somewhere inside of me. She was the kind of girl all the girls wanted to be, I believe, because of her acceptance of "what is." She keeps reminding me there is change in the "what is" but change cannot be made till you accept the "what is."

Like yesterday, all the

recording machines

were br

down again.

We almost lost a master take and the band leaves tomorrow and we can't do anymore music till we resolve this. We're in the middle of nowhere in the desert and my being wants to go crawl under a cactus and wish it away. Instead, I dyed my hair and she visited me and I started to accept the mess I'm in. I know that mess spelled backwards is ssem and I felt much better armed with that information. Over the last few hours I've allowed myself to feel defeated, and just like she said if you allow yourself to feel the way you really feel, maybe you won't be afraid of that feeling anymore.

When you're on your knees you're closer to the ground.
Things seem nearer somehow.

If all I can say is I'm not in this swamp, I'm not in this swamp then there is not a rope in front of me and there is not an alligator behind me and there is not a girl sitting at the edge eating a hot dog and if I believe that, then dying would be the only answer because then Death couldn't come and say Peachy to me anymore and after all she has a brother who believes in hope.

t o r i a m o s

(Tori Amos has been playing the piano since she was 2 years old. She was accepted into the Peabody Conservatory at the age of 5. She was kicked out for irreconcilable differences at the age of 11.

At 13 she was playing bars in Georgetown, Washington D.C. chaperoned by her father, a Methodist Minister. She continued playing in bars 5-6 nights a week for 11 years, until the release of "Y Kant Tori Read," recorded on Atlantic Records.

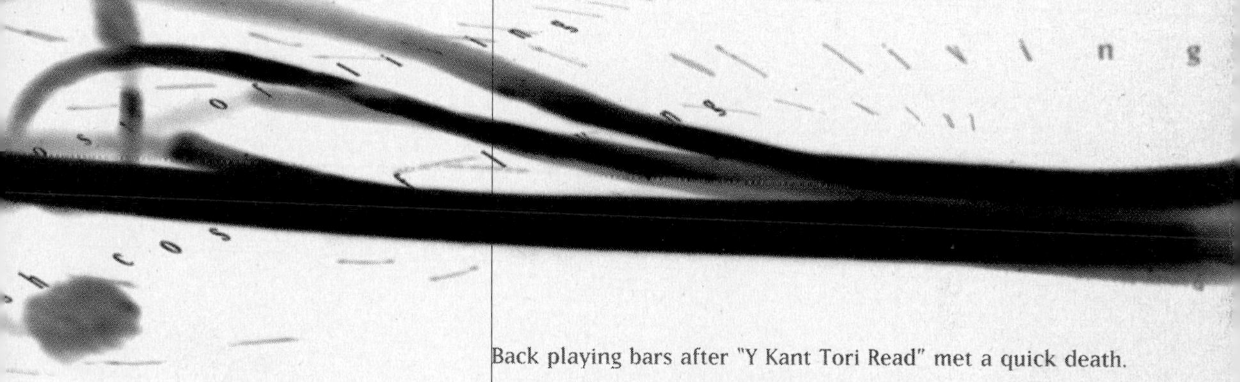

Back playing bars after "Y Kant Tori Read" met a quick death. Realizing the piano was "her thing," Tori started writing again at the piano. The songs written during this period became the basis for "little Earthquakes."

Tori moved to London, playing clubs alone at her piano. "Me and a Gun," an EP containing "Me and a Gun and "Silent All These Years" was released in October, 1991 in the UK and caused quite a stir.

"Little Earthquakes" was initially released in the UK in January, 1992 and worldwide release followed. A 1992 world tour gave Tori a chance to eat lots of good food! She played over 200 cities worldwide alone at her piano.

Currently, she is happy that recording is almost finished with her new project. The album is due for release in early 1994 and will be supported by a world tour of her and her piano.)

DEATH: THE HIGH COST OF LIVING

Published by DC Comics. Cover, introduction and compilation copyright © 1994 DC Comics. All Rights Reserved.

Originally published in single magazine form as DEATH: THE HIGH COST OF LIVING 1-3 and DEATH TALKS ABOUT LIFE. Copyright © 1993 DC Comics. All Rights Reserved. Vertigo and all characters, their distinctive likenesses and related indicia featured in this publication are trademarks of DC Comics. The stories, characters, and incidents featured in this publication are entirely fictional. DC Comics does not read or accept unsolicited submissions of ideas, stories or artwork.

DC Comics, 1700 Broadway, New York, NY 10019
A division of Warner Bros. - An AOL Time Warner Company
Printed in Canada. Sixth Printing.
ISBN: 1-56389-133-6

Cover and publication design by Dave McKean

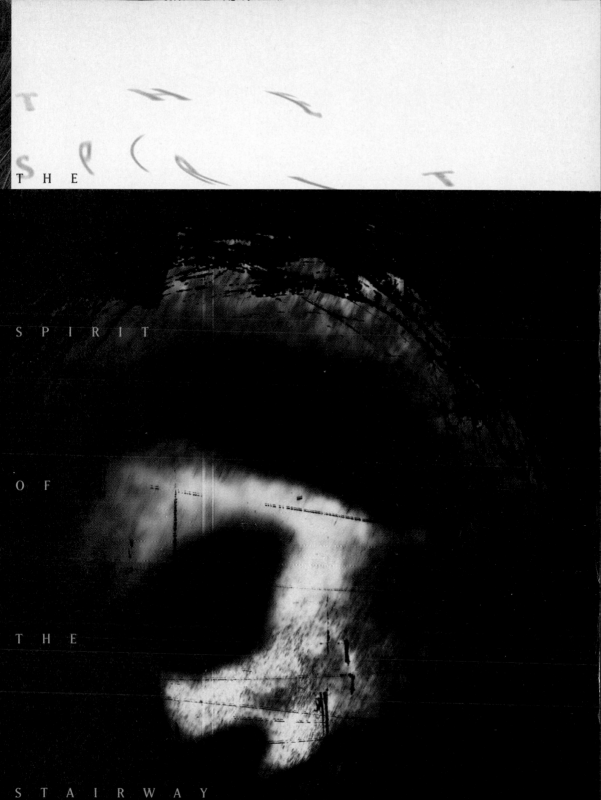

THE SPIRIT OF THE STAIRWAY

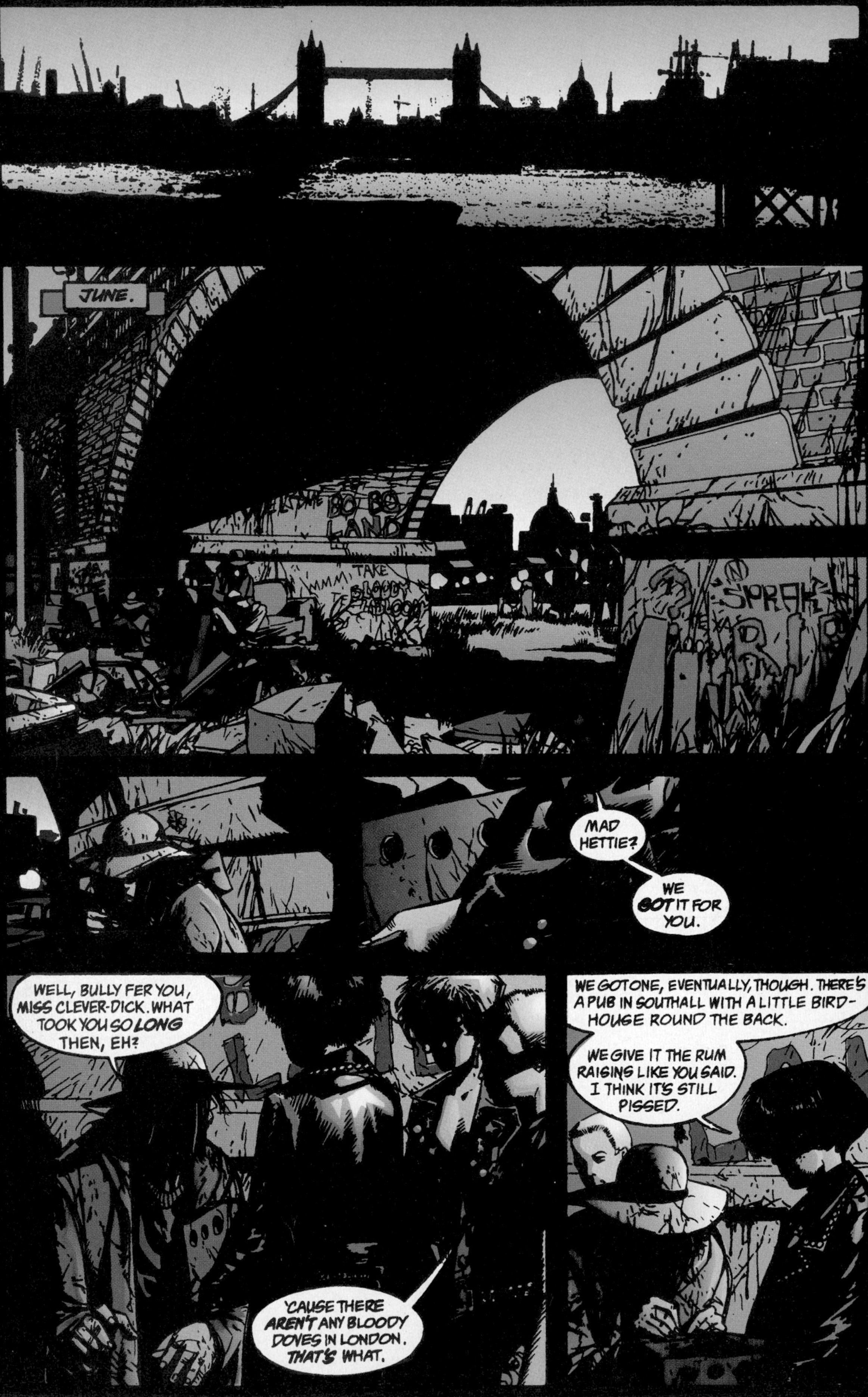

JUNE.
MAD HETTIE?
WE GOT IT FOR YOU.
WELL, BULLY FER YOU, MISS CLEVER-DICK. WHAT TOOK YOU SO LONG THEN, EH?
'CAUSE THERE AREN'T ANY BLOODY DOVES IN LONDON. THAT'S WHAT.
WE GOT ONE, EVENTUALLY, THOUGH. THERE'S A PUB IN SOUTHALL WITH A LITTLE BIRD-HOUSE ROUND THE BACK.
WE GIVE IT THE RUM RAISINS LIKE YOU SAID. I THINK IT'S STILL PISSED.

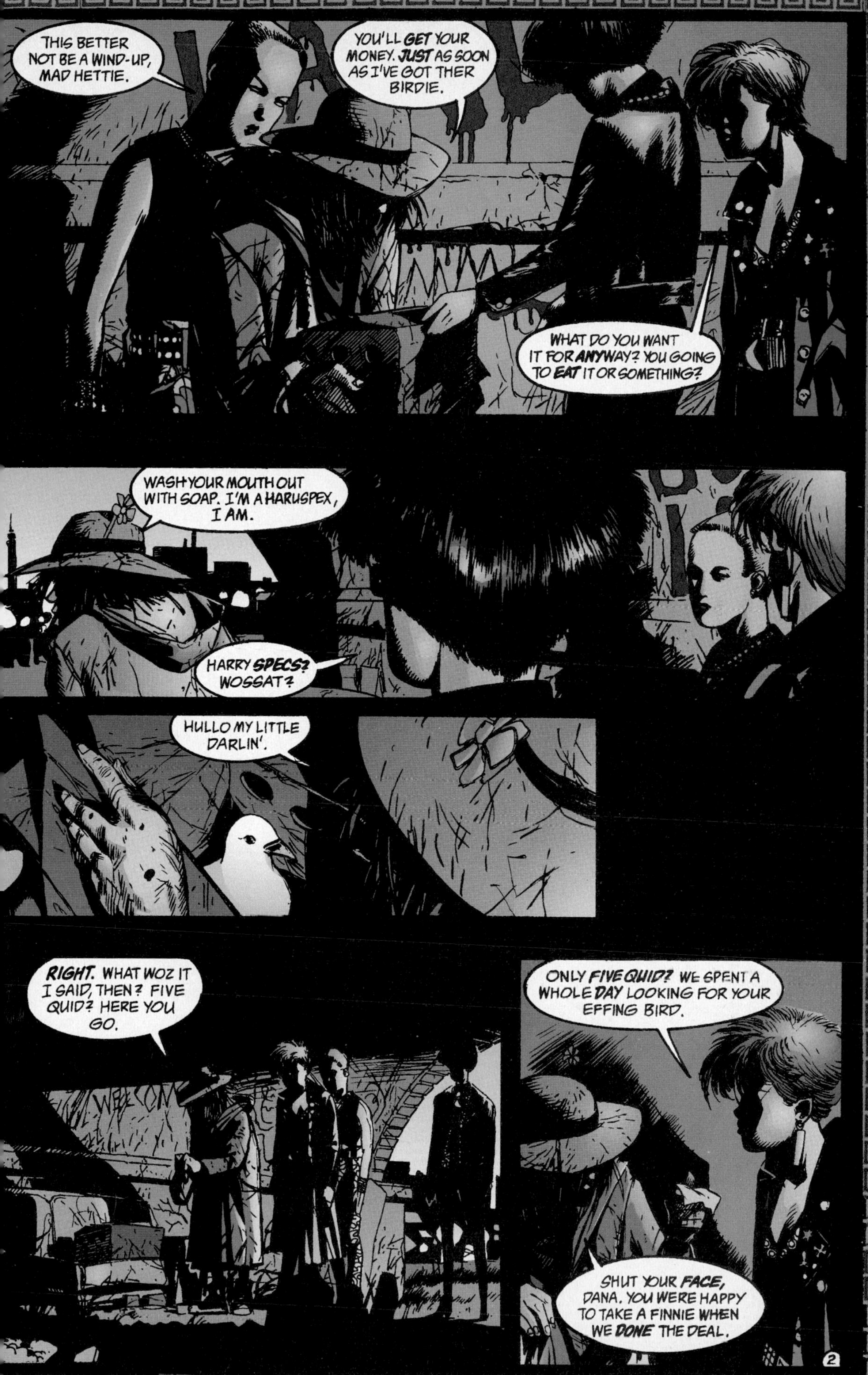
THIS BETTER NOT BE A WIND-UP, MAD HETTIE.
YOU'LL GET YOUR MONEY. JUST AS SOON AS I'VE GOT THER BIRDIE.
WHAT DO YOU WANT IT FOR ANYWAY? YOU GOING TO EAT IT OR SOMETHING?
WASH YOUR MOUTH OUT WITH SOAP. I'M A HARUSPEX, I AM.
HARRY SPECS? WOSSAT?
HULLO MY LITTLE DARLIN'.
RIGHT. WHAT WOZ IT I SAID, THEN? FIVE QUID? HERE YOU GO.
ONLY FIVE QUID? WE SPENT A WHOLE DAY LOOKING FOR YOUR EFFING BIRD.
SHUT YOUR FACE, DANA. YOU WERE HAPPY TO TAKE A FINNIE WHEN WE DONE THE DEAL.

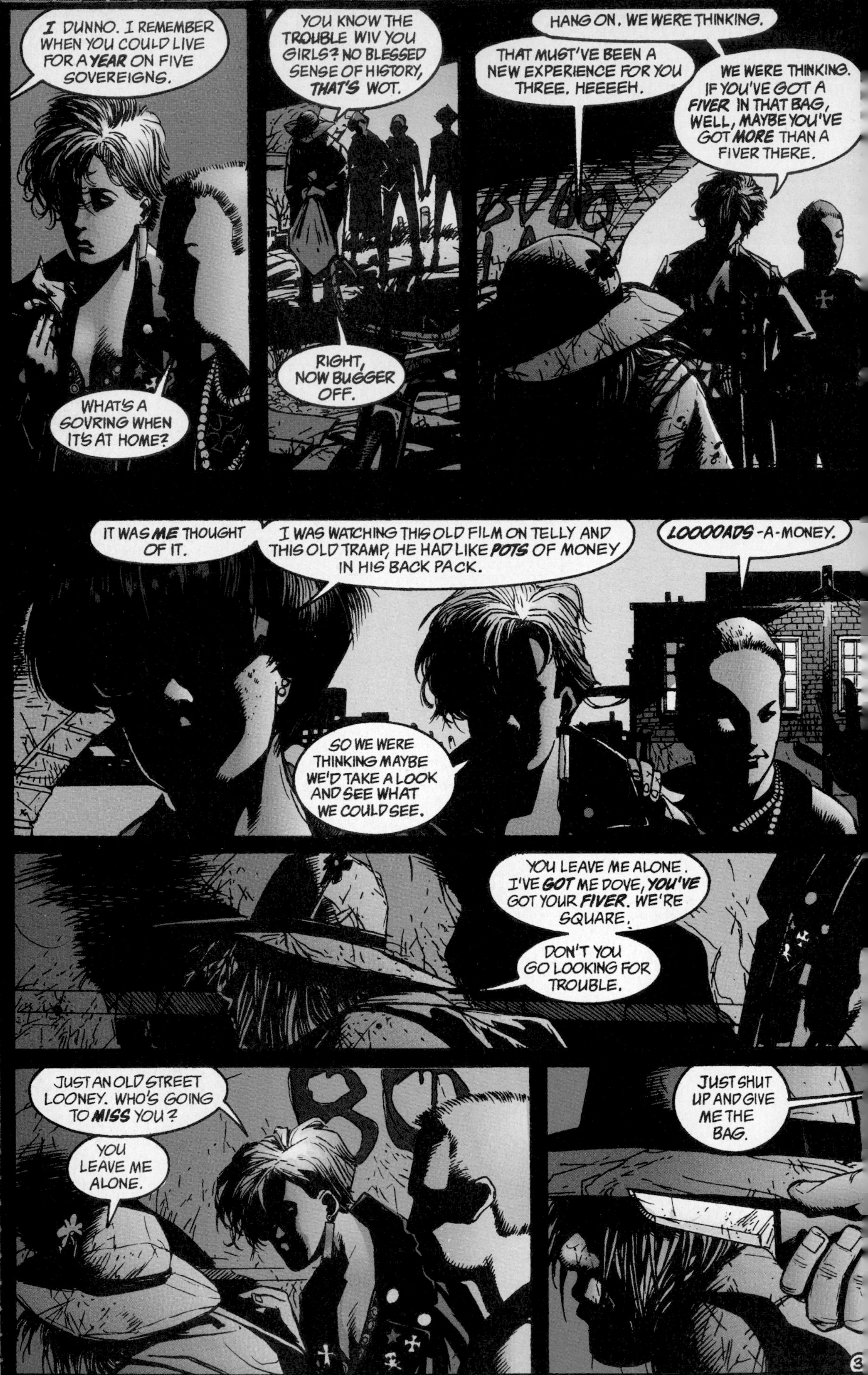

I DUNNO. I REMEMBER WHEN YOU COULD LIVE FOR A YEAR ON FIVE SOVEREIGNS.
WHAT'S A SOVRING WHEN IT'S AT HOME?
YOU KNOW THE TROUBLE WIV YOU GIRLS? NO BLESSED SENSE OF HISTORY, THAT'S WOT.
RIGHT, NOW BUGGER OFF.
HANG ON. WE WERE THINKING.
THAT MUST'VE BEEN A NEW EXPERIENCE FOR YOU THREE. HEEEEH.
WE WERE THINKING. IF YOU'VE GOT A FIVER IN THAT BAG, WELL, MAYBE YOU'VE GOT MORE THAN A FIVER THERE.
IT WAS ME THOUGHT OF IT.
I WAS WATCHING THIS OLD FILM ON TELLY AND THIS OLD TRAMP, HE HAD LIKE POTS OF MONEY IN HIS BACK PACK.
LOOOOADS-A-MONEY.
SO WE WERE THINKING MAYBE WE'D TAKE A LOOK AND SEE WHAT WE COULD SEE.
YOU LEAVE ME ALONE. I'VE GOT ME DOVE, YOU'VE GOT YOUR FIVER. WE'RE SQUARE.
DON'T YOU GO LOOKING FOR TROUBLE.
JUST AN OLD STREET LOONEY. WHO'S GOING TO MISS YOU?
YOU LEAVE ME ALONE.
JUST SHUT UP AND GIVE ME THE BAG.

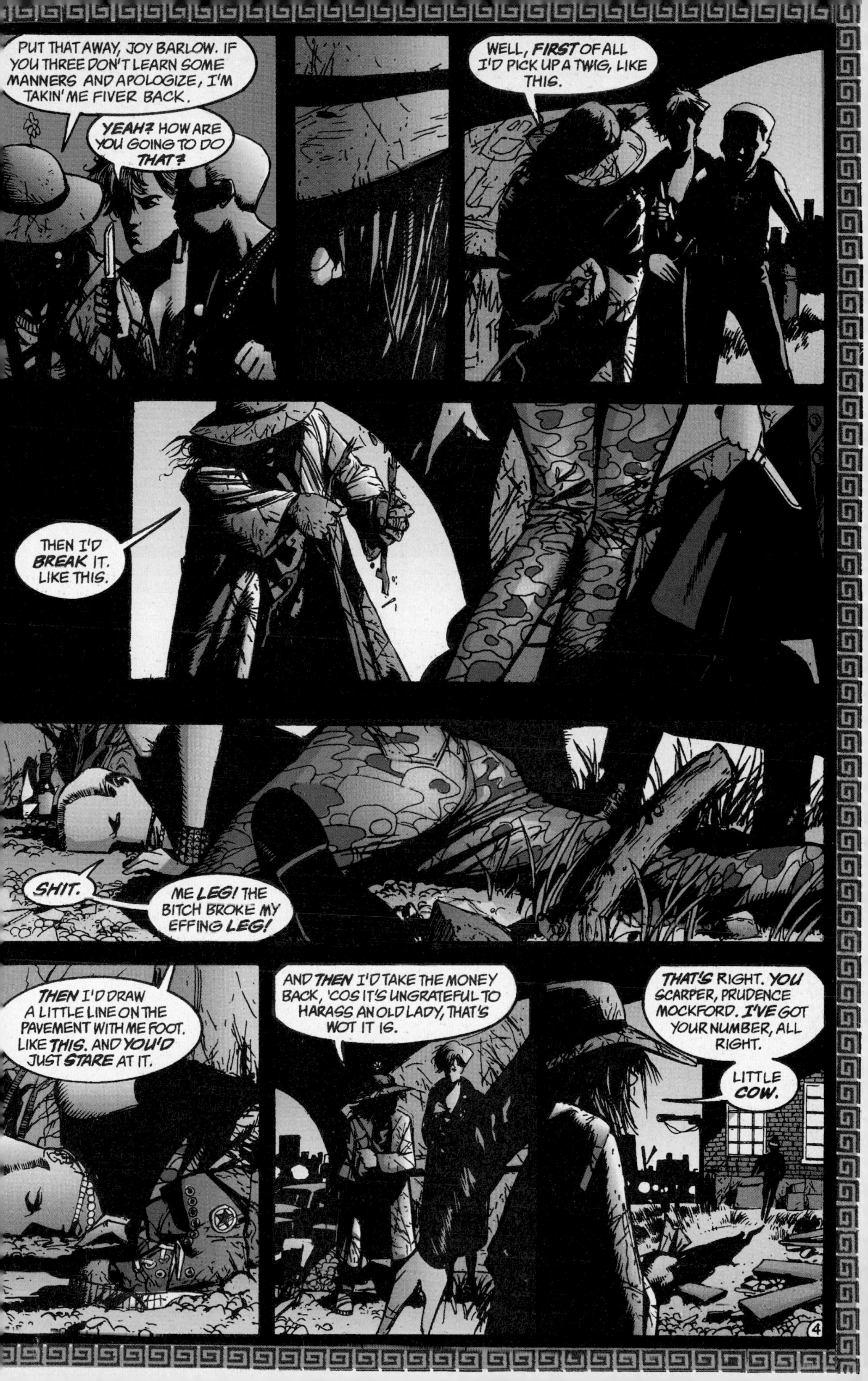
PUT THAT AWAY, JOY BARLOW. IF YOU THREE DON'T LEARN SOME MANNERS AND APOLOGIZE, I'M TAKIN' ME FIVER BACK.
YEAH? HOW ARE YOU GOING TO DO THAT?
WELL, FIRST OF ALL I'D PICK UP A TWIG, LIKE THIS.
THEN I'D BREAK IT. LIKE THIS.
SHIT.
ME LEG! THE BITCH BROKE MY EFFING LEG!
THEN I'D DRAW A LITTLE LINE ON THE PAVEMENT WITH ME FOOT. LIKE THIS. AND YOU'D JUST STARE AT IT.
AND THEN I'D TAKE THE MONEY BACK, 'COS IT'S UNGRATEFUL TO HARASS AN OLD LADY, THAT'S WOT IT IS.
THAT'S RIGHT. YOU SCARPER, PRUDENCE MOCKFORD. I'VE GOT YOUR NUMBER, ALL RIGHT.
LITTLE COW.
4

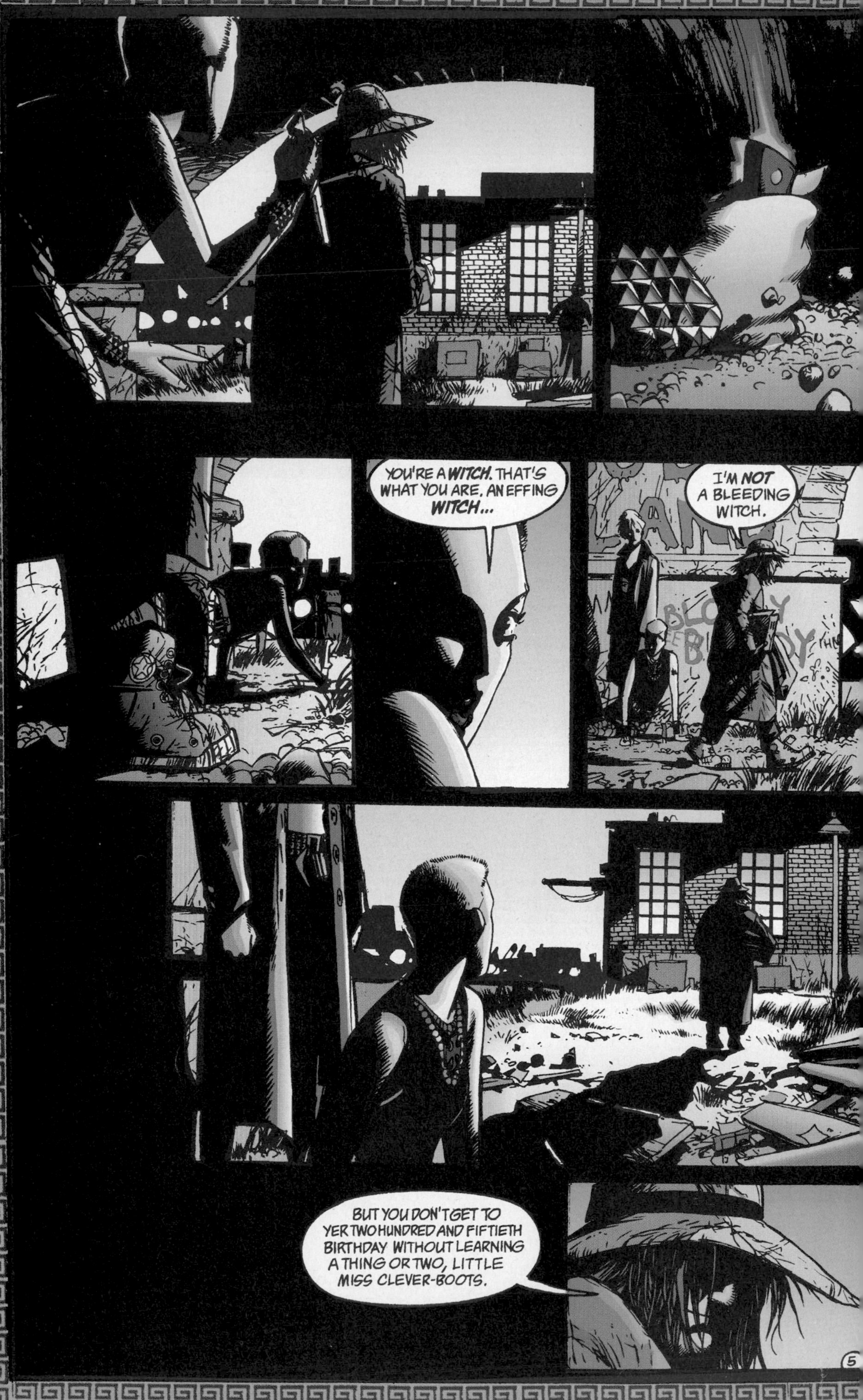
YOU'RE A WITCH. THAT'S WHAT YOU ARE, AN EFFING WITCH...
I'M NOT A BLEEDING WITCH.
BLOODY
BUT YOU DON'T GET TO YER TWO HUNDRED AND FIFTIETH BIRTHDAY WITHOUT LEARNING A THING OR TWO, LITTLE MISS CLEVER-BOOTS.

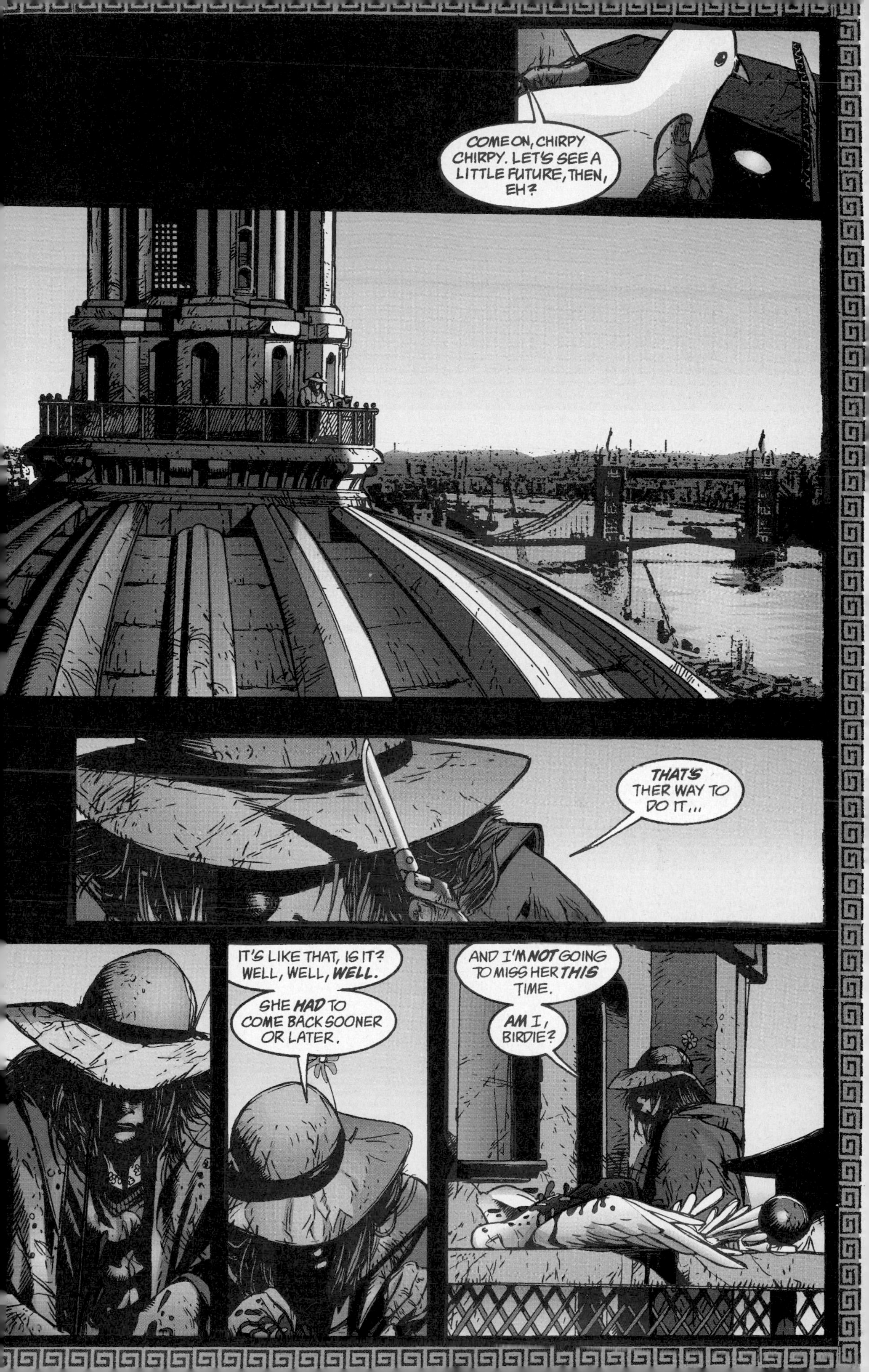
COME ON, CHIRPY CHIRPY. LET'S SEE A LITTLE FUTURE, THEN, EH?
THAT'S THER WAY TO DO IT...
IT'S LIKE THAT, IS IT? WELL, WELL, WELL.
SHE HAD TO COME BACK SOONER OR LATER.
AND I'M NOT GOING TO MISS HER THIS TIME.
AM I, BIRDIE?

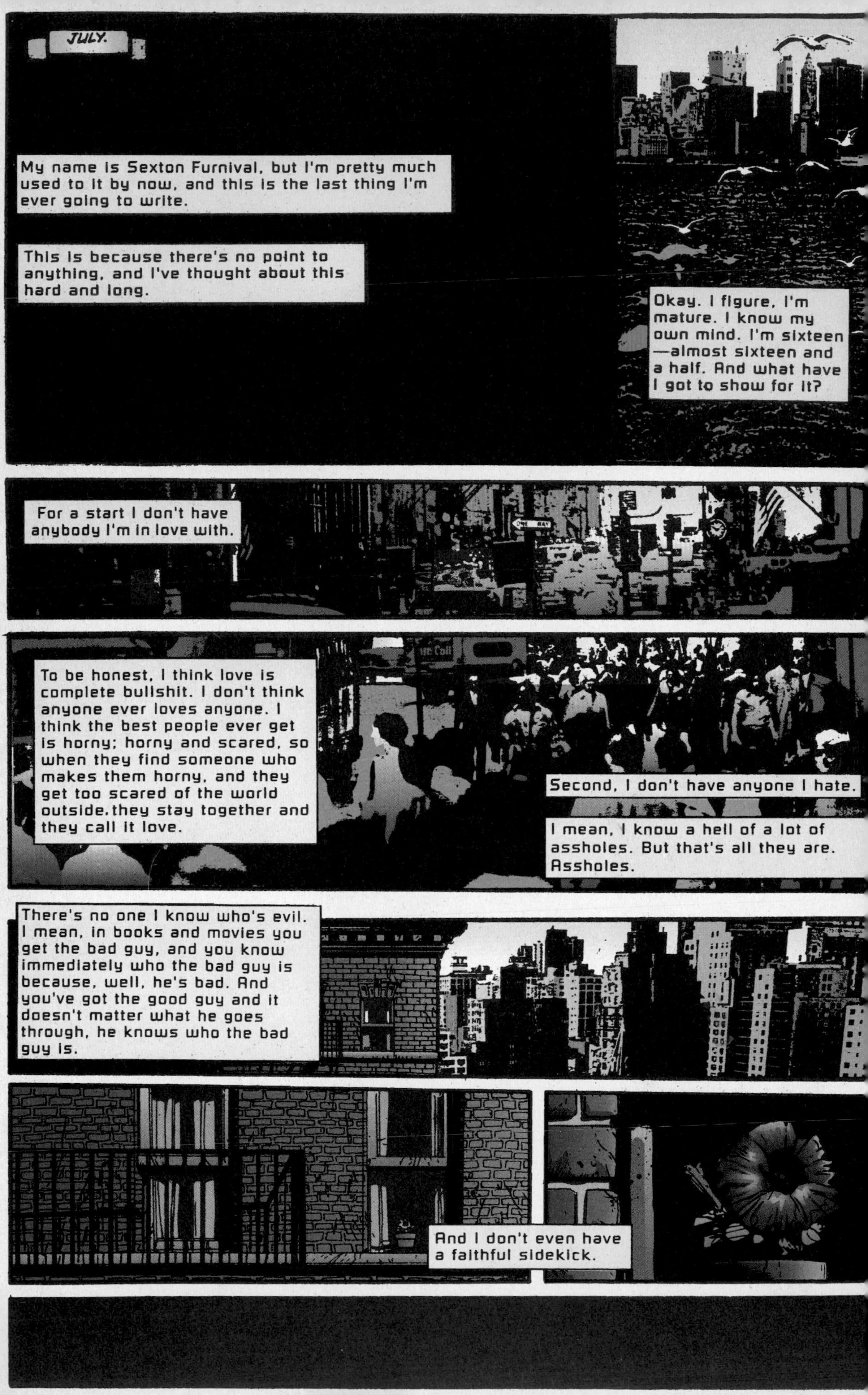

JULY.

My name is Sexton Furnival, but I'm pretty much used to it by now, and this is the last thing I'm ever going to write.

This is because there's no point to anything, and I've thought about this hard and long.

Okay. I figure, I'm mature. I know my own mind. I'm sixteen —almost sixteen and a half. And what have I got to show for it?

For a start I don't have anybody I'm in love with.

To be honest, I think love is complete bullshit. I don't think anyone ever loves anyone. I think the best people ever get is horny; horny and scared, so when they find someone who makes them horny, and they get too scared of the world outside, they stay together and they call it love.

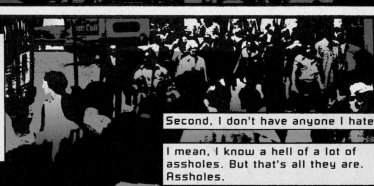

Second, I don't have anyone I hate.

I mean, I know a hell of a lot of assholes. But that's all they are. Assholes.

There's no one I know who's evil. I mean, in books and movies you get the bad guy, and you know immediately who the bad guy is because, well, he's bad. And you've got the good guy and it doesn't matter what he goes through, he knows who the bad guy is.

And I don't even have a faithful sidekick.

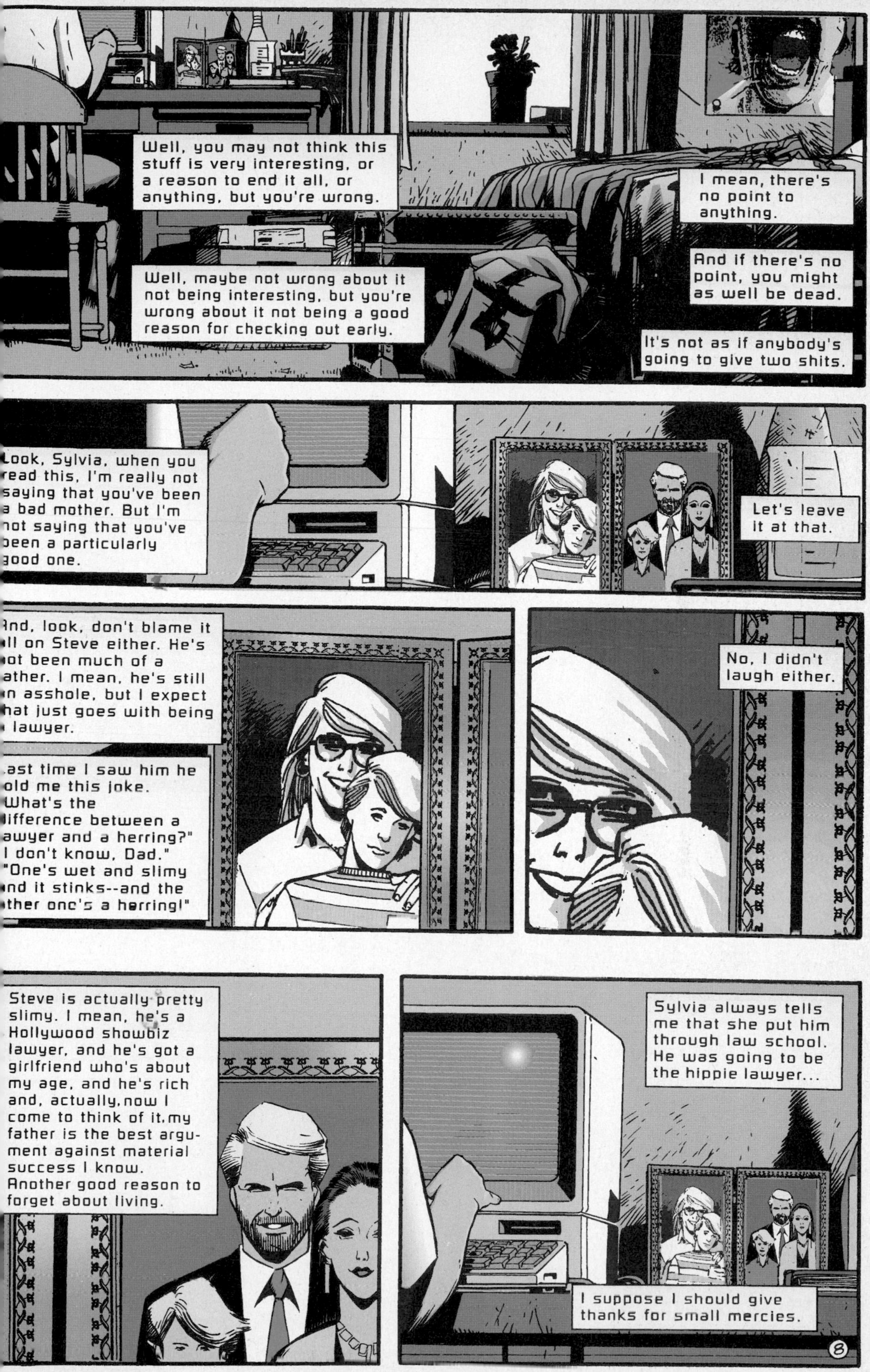

Well, you may not think this stuff is very interesting, or a reason to end it all, or anything, but you're wrong.
Well, maybe not wrong about it not being interesting, but you're wrong about it not being a good reason for checking out early.
I mean, there's no point to anything.
And if there's no point, you might as well be dead.
It's not as if anybody's going to give two shits.
Look, Sylvia, when you read this, I'm really not saying that you've been a bad mother. But I'm not saying that you've been a particularly good one.
Let's leave it at that.
And, look, don't blame it all on Steve either. He's not been much of a father. I mean, he's still an asshole, but I expect that just goes with being a lawyer.
ast time I saw him he old me this joke. What's the ifference between a awyer and a herring?" I don't know, Dad." "One's wet and slimy nd it stinks--and the ther one's a herring!"
No, I didn't laugh either.
Steve is actually pretty slimy. I mean, he's a Hollywood showbiz lawyer, and he's got a girlfriend who's about my age, and he's rich and, actually, now I come to think of it, my father is the best argument against material success I know. Another good reason to forget about living.
Sylvia always tells me that she put him through law school. He was going to be the hippie lawyer...
I suppose I should give thanks for small mercies.

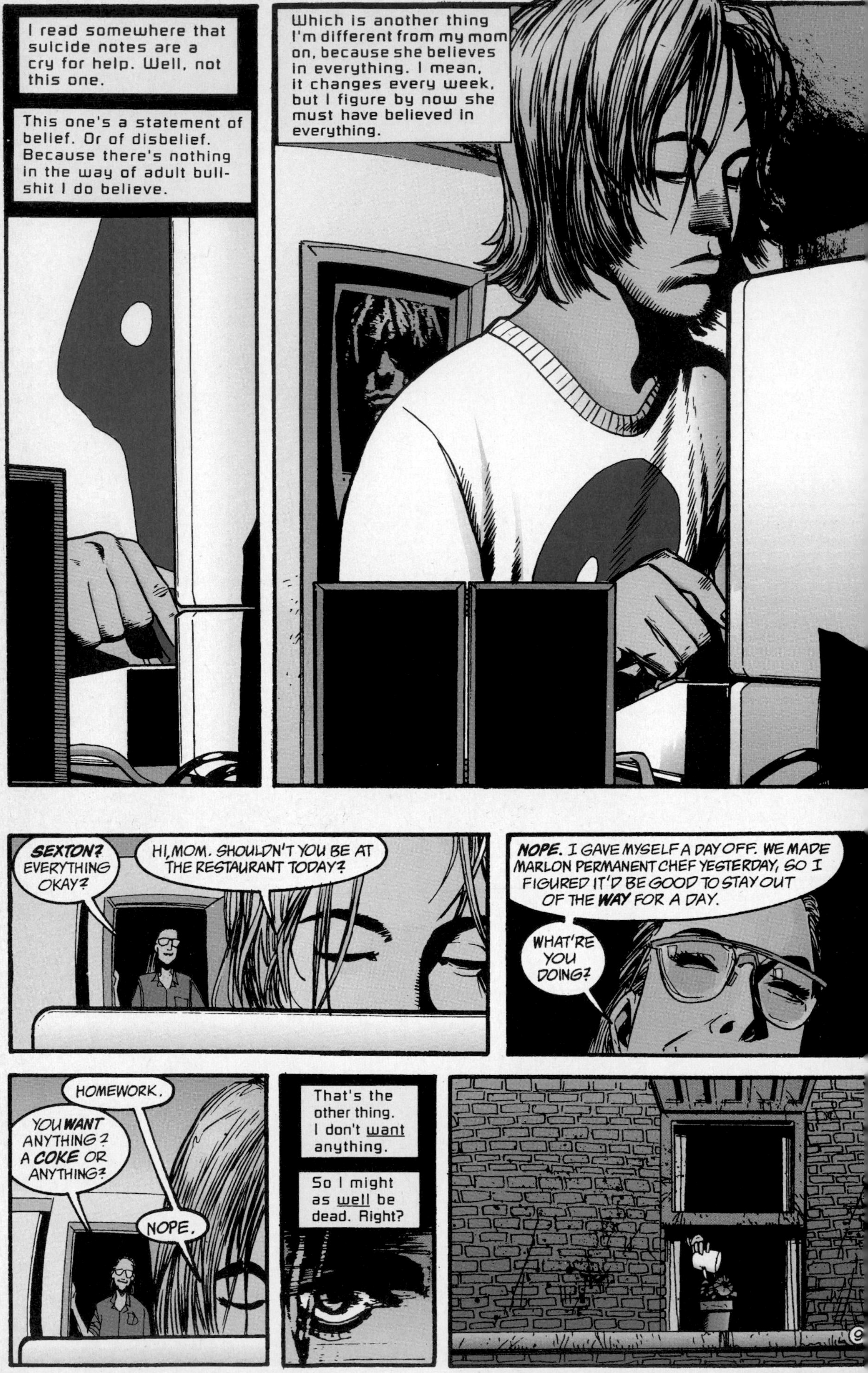
I read somewhere that suicide notes are a cry for help. Well, not this one.
This one's a statement of belief. Or of disbelief. Because there's nothing in the way of adult bull-shit I do believe.
Which is another thing I'm different from my mom on, because she believes in everything. I mean, it changes every week, but I figure by now she must have believed in everything.
SEXTON? EVERYTHING OKAY?
HI, MOM. SHOULDN'T YOU BE AT THE RESTAURANT TODAY?
NOPE. I GAVE MYSELF A DAY OFF. WE MADE MARLON PERMANENT CHEF YESTERDAY, SO I FIGURED IT'D BE GOOD TO STAY OUT OF THE WAY FOR A DAY.
WHAT'RE YOU DOING?
HOMEWORK.
YOU WANT ANYTHING? A COKE OR ANYTHING?
NOPE.
That's the other thing. I don't want anything.
So I might as well be dead. Right?
9

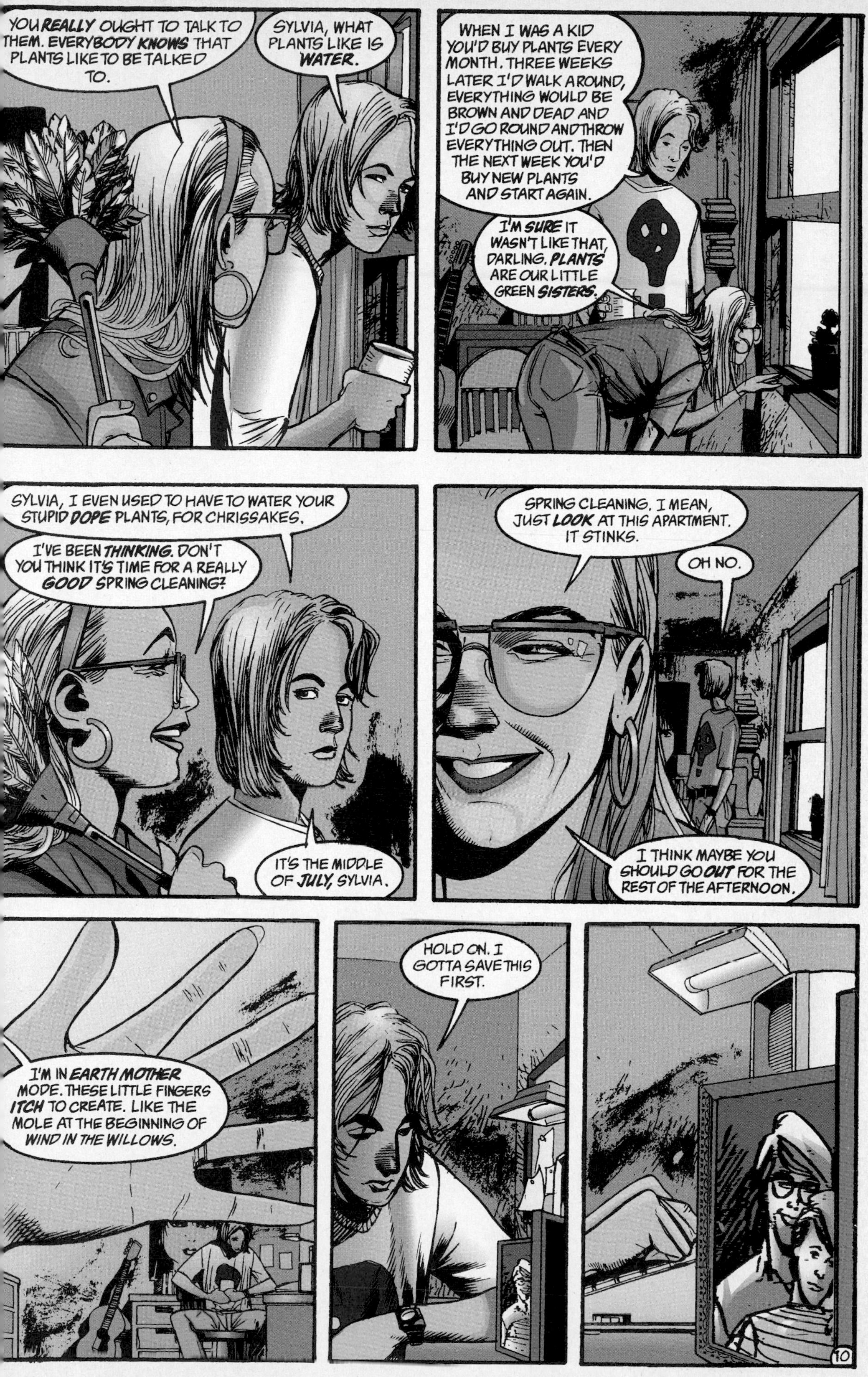
YOU REALLY OUGHT TO TALK TO THEM. EVERYBODY KNOWS THAT PLANTS LIKE TO BE TALKED TO.
SYLVIA, WHAT PLANTS LIKE IS WATER.
WHEN I WAS A KID YOU'D BUY PLANTS EVERY MONTH. THREE WEEKS LATER I'D WALK AROUND, EVERYTHING WOULD BE BROWN AND DEAD AND I'D GO ROUND AND THROW EVERYTHING OUT. THEN THE NEXT WEEK YOU'D BUY NEW PLANTS AND START AGAIN.
I'M SURE IT WASN'T LIKE THAT, DARLING. PLANTS ARE OUR LITTLE GREEN SISTERS.
SYLVIA, I EVEN USED TO HAVE TO WATER YOUR STUPID DOPE PLANTS, FOR CHRISSAKES.
I'VE BEEN THINKING. DON'T YOU THINK IT'S TIME FOR A REALLY GOOD SPRING CLEANING?
IT'S THE MIDDLE OF JULY, SYLVIA.
SPRING CLEANING. I MEAN, JUST LOOK AT THIS APARTMENT. IT STINKS.
OH NO.
I THINK MAYBE YOU SHOULD GO OUT FOR THE REST OF THE AFTERNOON.
I'M IN EARTH MOTHER MODE. THESE LITTLE FINGERS ITCH TO CREATE. LIKE THE MOLE AT THE BEGINNING OF WIND IN THE WILLOWS.
HOLD ON. I GOTTA SAVE THIS FIRST.

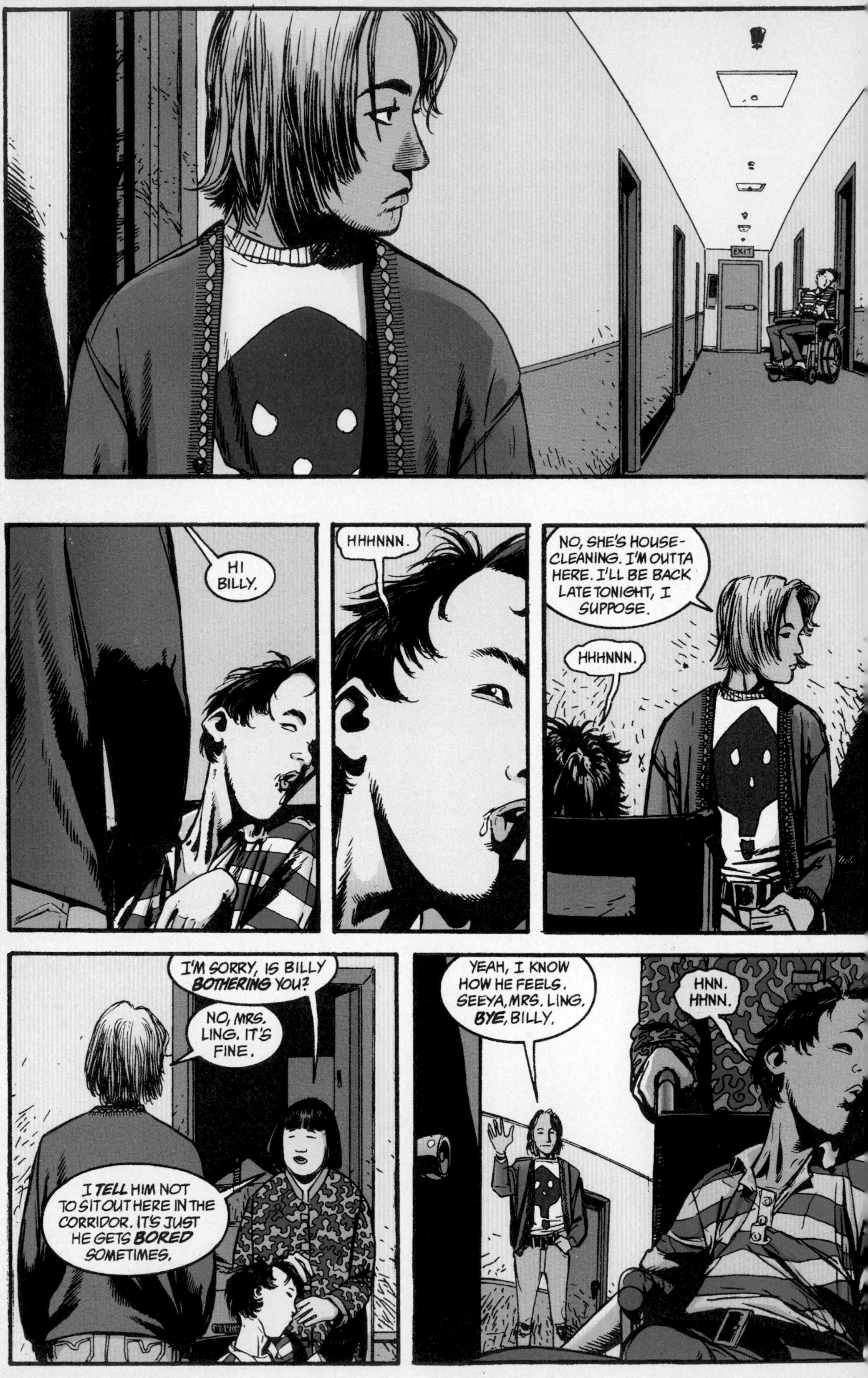
EXIT
HI BILLY.
HHHNNN.
NO, SHE'S HOUSE-CLEANING. I'M OUTTA HERE. I'LL BE BACK LATE TONIGHT, I SUPPOSE.
HHHNNN.
I'M SORRY, IS BILLY BOTHERING YOU?
NO, MRS. LING. IT'S FINE.
I TELL HIM NOT TO SIT OUT HERE IN THE CORRIDOR. IT'S JUST HE GETS BORED SOMETIMES.
YEAH, I KNOW HOW HE FEELS. SEEYA, MRS. LING. BYE, BILLY.
HNN. HHNN.

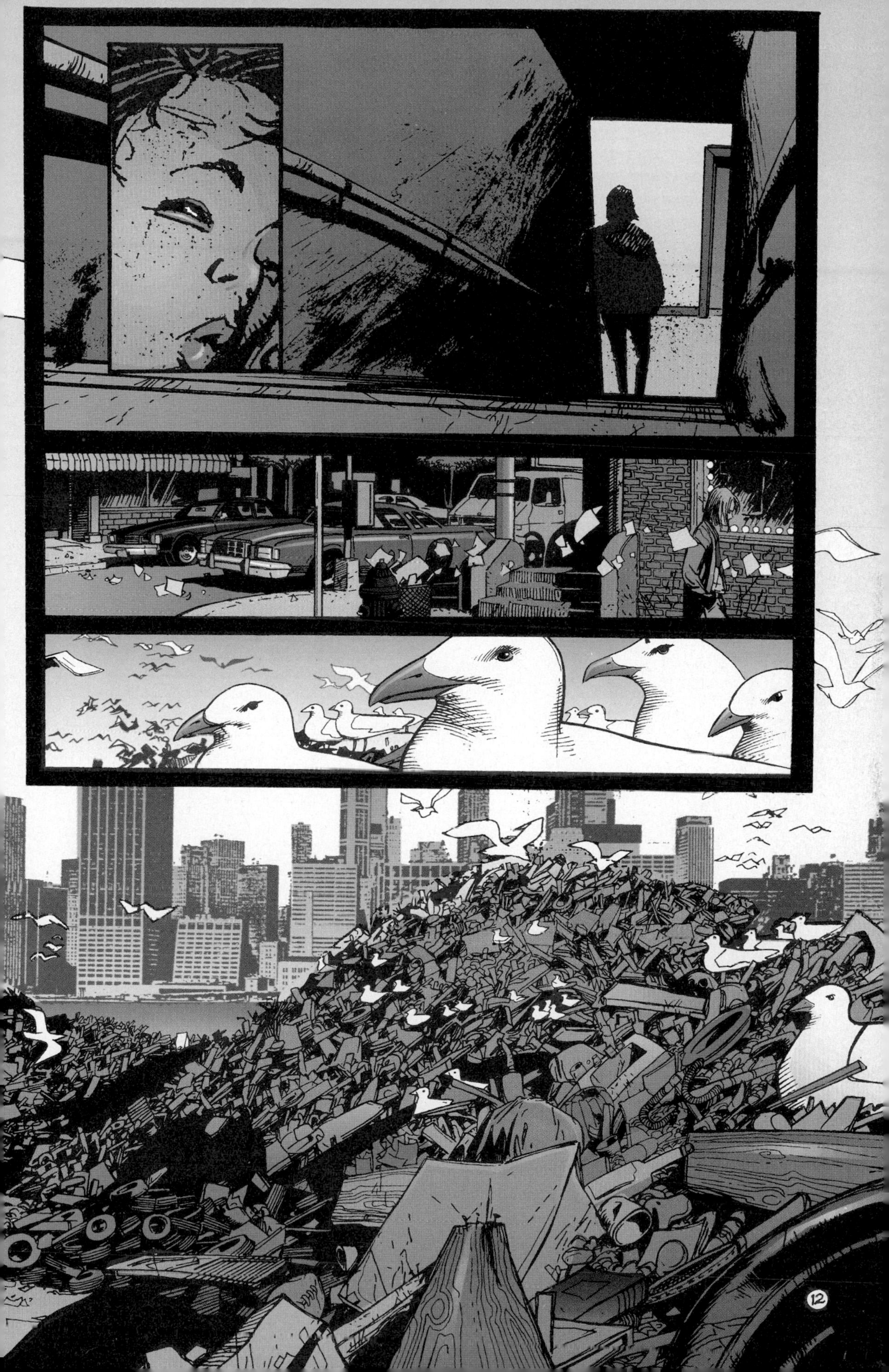

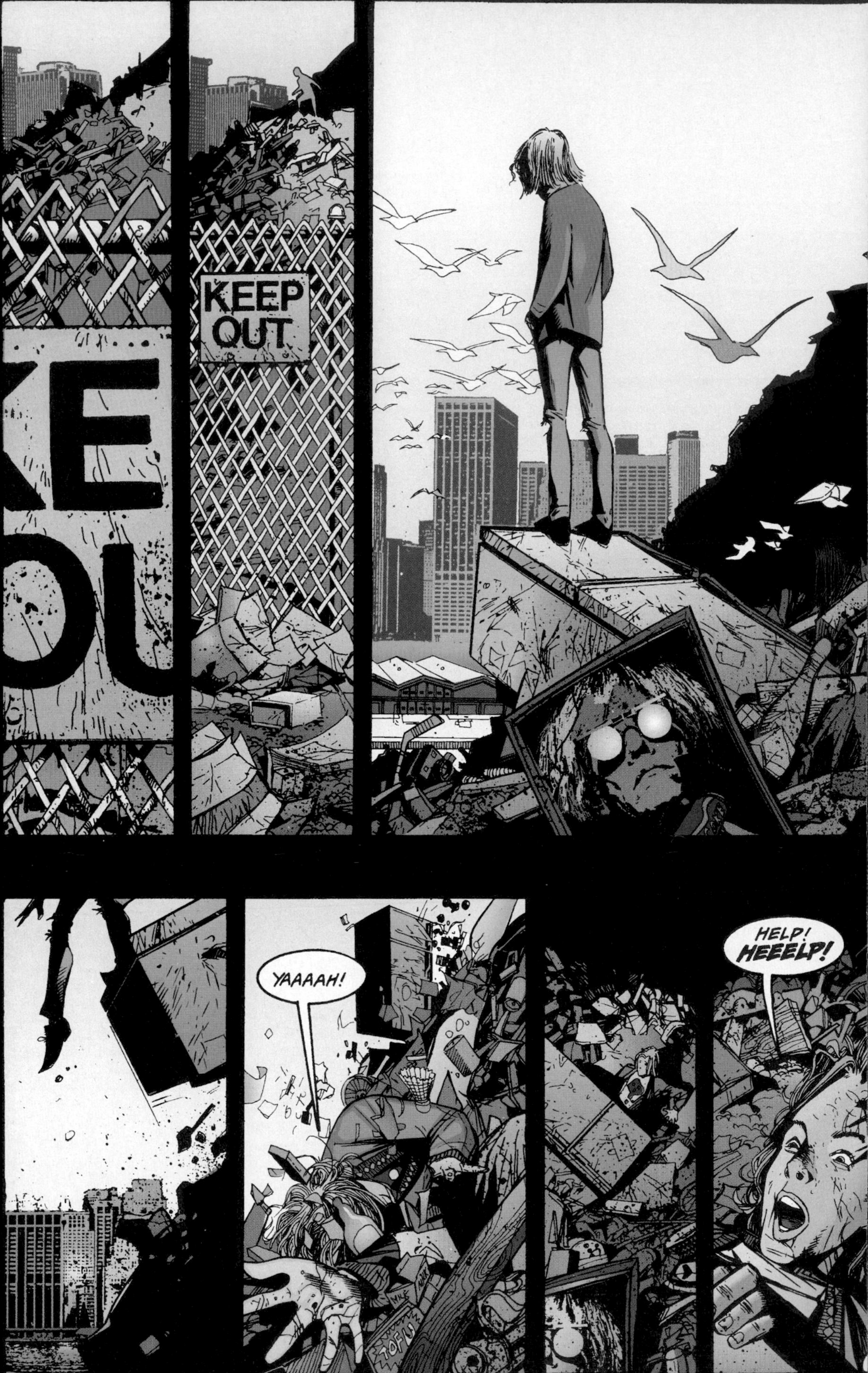
KEEP OUT
YAAAAH!
HELP! HEEELP!

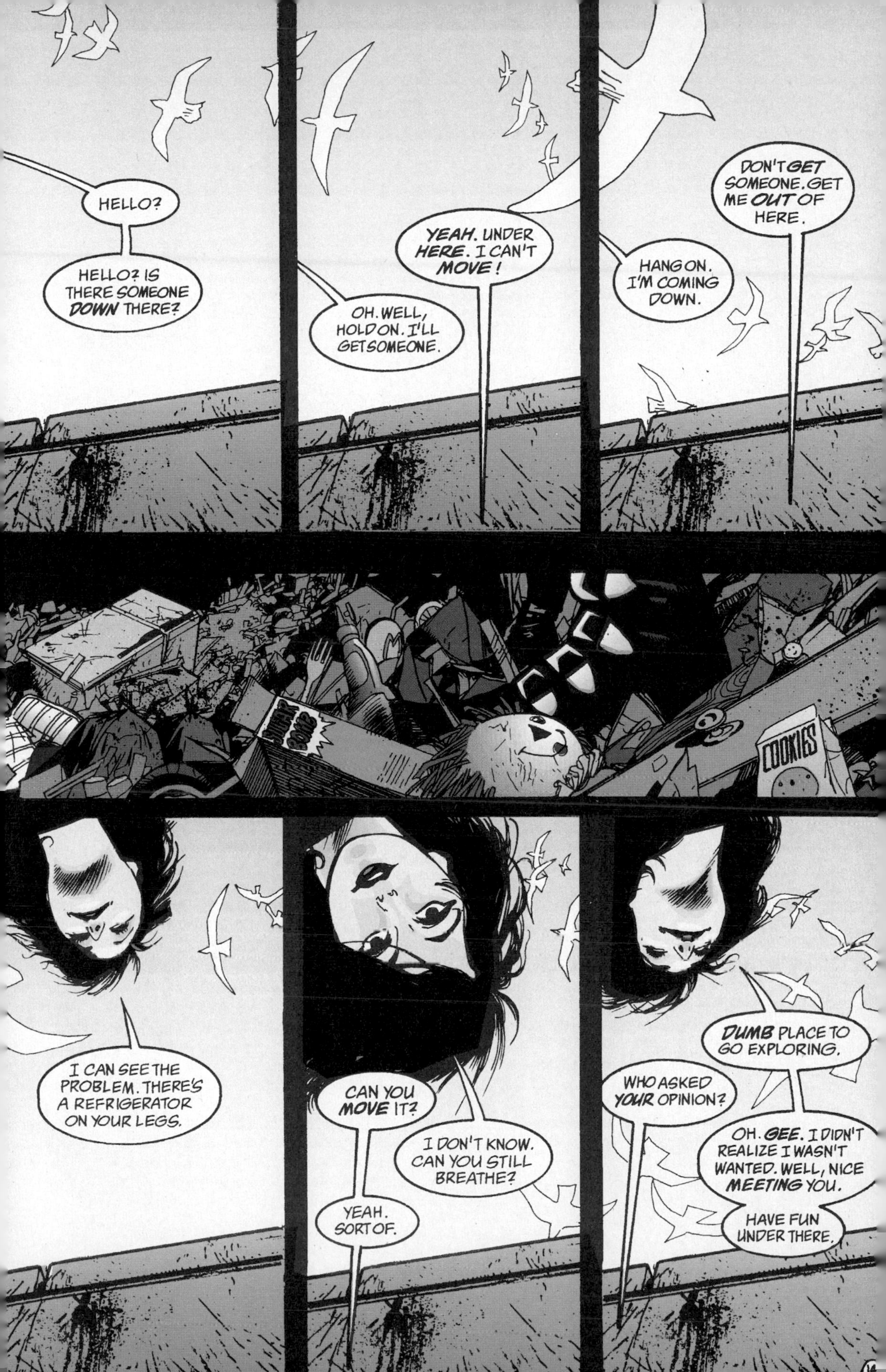
HELLO?
HELLO? IS THERE SOMEONE DOWN THERE?
YEAH. UNDER HERE. I CAN'T MOVE!
OH. WELL, HOLD ON. I'LL GET SOMEONE.
DON'T GET SOMEONE. GET ME OUT OF HERE.
HANG ON. I'M COMING DOWN.
COOKIES
I CAN SEE THE PROBLEM. THERE'S A REFRIGERATOR ON YOUR LEGS.
CAN YOU MOVE IT?
I DON'T KNOW. CAN YOU STILL BREATHE?
YEAH. SORT OF.
DUMB PLACE TO GO EXPLORING.
WHO ASKED YOUR OPINION?
OH. GEE. I DIDN'T REALIZE I WASN'T WANTED. WELL, NICE MEETING YOU.
HAVE FUN UNDER THERE.

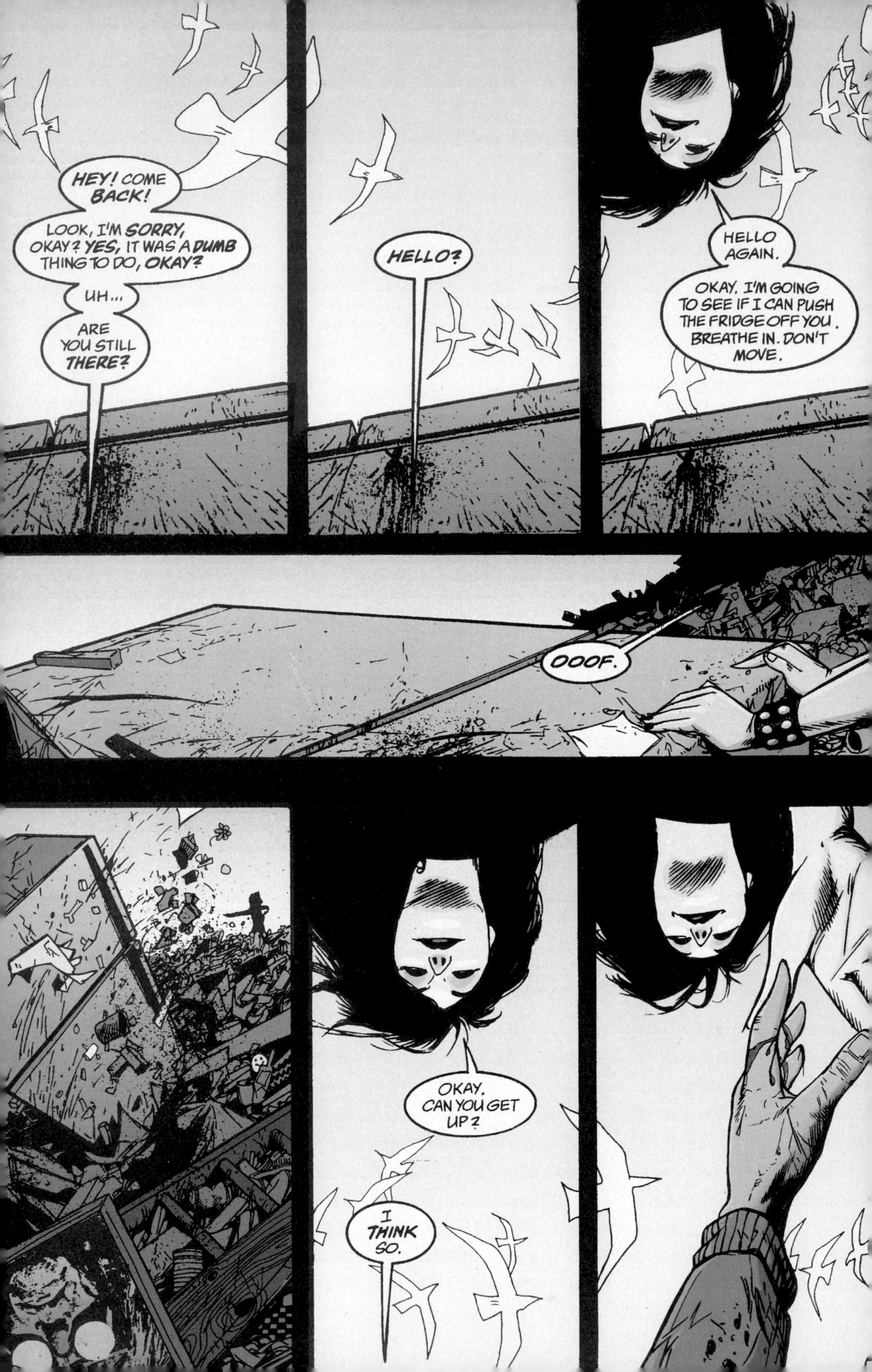
HEY! COME BACK!
LOOK, I'M SORRY, OKAY? YES, IT WAS A DUMB THING TO DO, OKAY?
UH...
ARE YOU STILL THERE?
HELLO?
HELLO AGAIN.
OKAY. I'M GOING TO SEE IF I CAN PUSH THE FRIDGE OFF YOU. BREATHE IN. DON'T MOVE.
OOOF.
OKAY. CAN YOU GET UP?
I THINK SO.

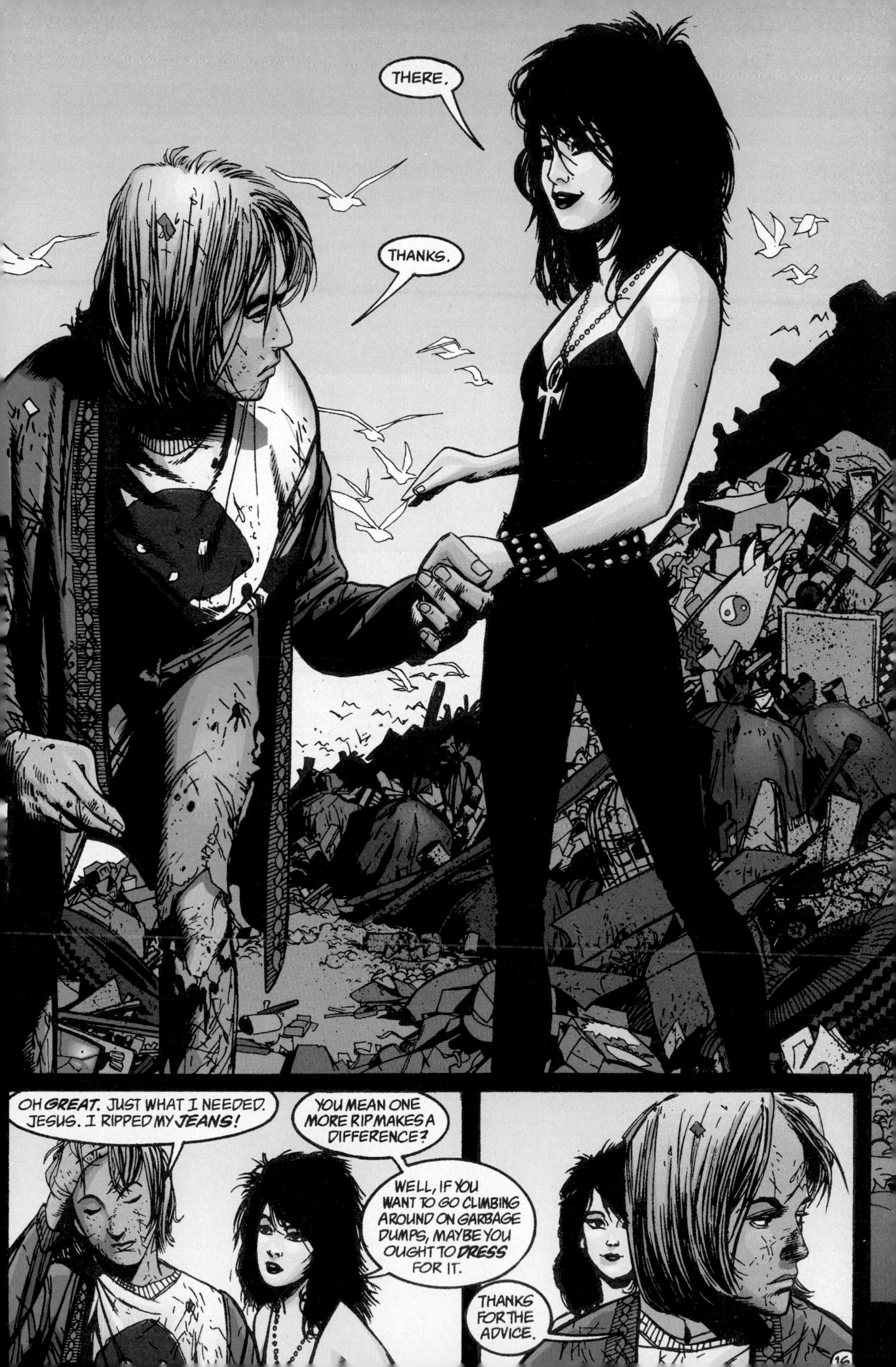
THERE.
THANKS.
OH GREAT. JUST WHAT I NEEDED. JESUS. I RIPPED MY JEANS!
YOU MEAN ONE MORE RIP MAKES A DIFFERENCE?
WELL, IF YOU WANT TO GO CLIMBING AROUND ON GARBAGE DUMPS, MAYBE YOU OUGHT TO DRESS FOR IT.
THANKS FOR THE ADVICE.

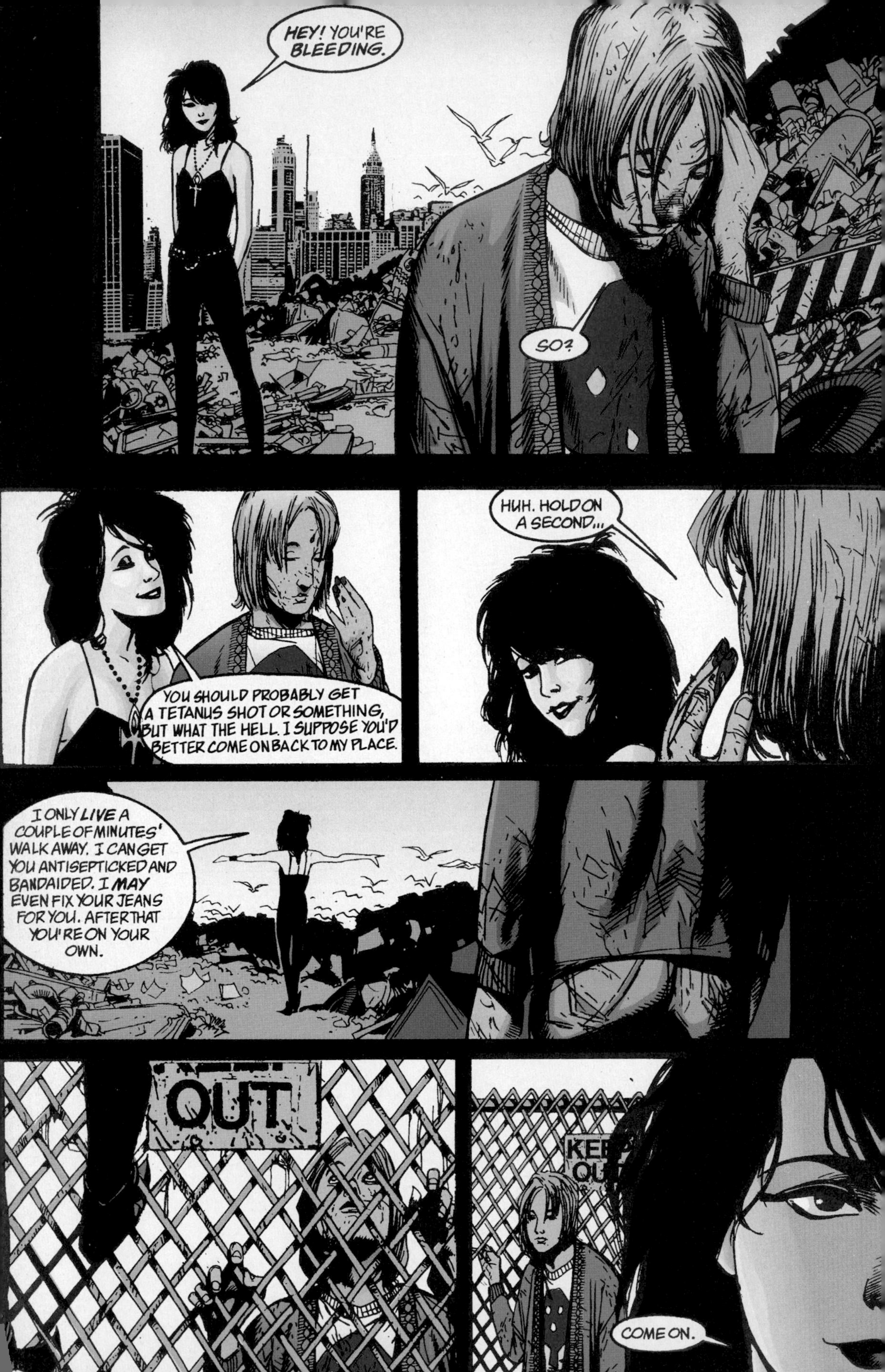
HEY! YOU'RE BLEEDING.
SO?
YOU SHOULD PROBABLY GET A TETANUS SHOT OR SOMETHING, BUT WHAT THE HELL. I SUPPOSE YOU'D BETTER COME ON BACK TO MY PLACE.
HUH. HOLD ON A SECOND...
I ONLY LIVE A COUPLE OF MINUTES' WALK AWAY. I CAN GET YOU ANTISEPTICKED AND BANDAIDED. I MAY EVEN FIX YOUR JEANS FOR YOU. AFTER THAT YOU'RE ON YOUR OWN.
OUT
COME ON.

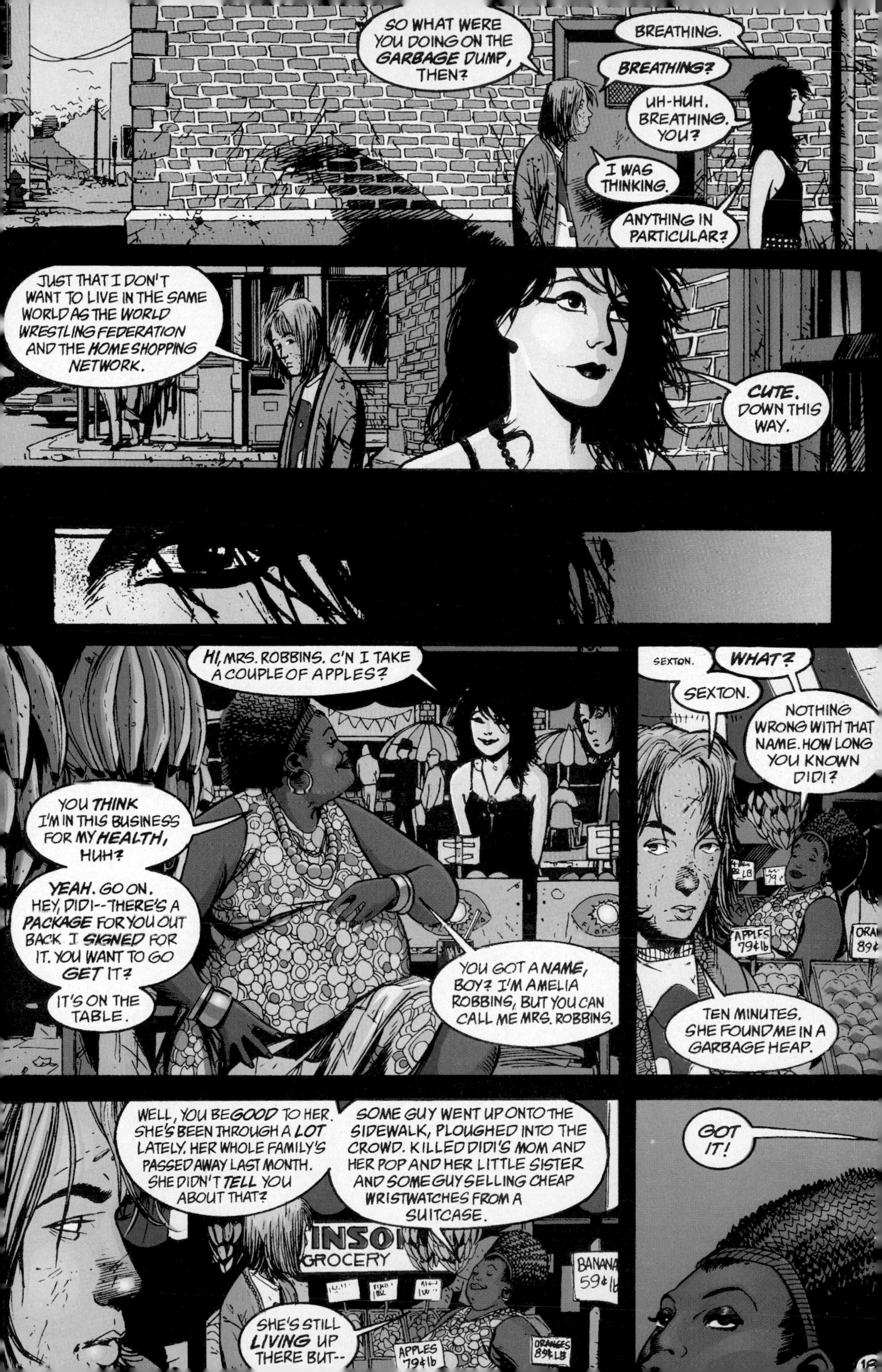
SO WHAT WERE YOU DOING ON THE GARBAGE DUMP, THEN?
BREATHING.
BREATHING?
UH-HUH. BREATHING. YOU?
I WAS THINKING.
ANYTHING IN PARTICULAR?
JUST THAT I DON'T WANT TO LIVE IN THE SAME WORLD AS THE WORLD WRESTLING FEDERATION AND THE HOME SHOPPING NETWORK.
CUTE. DOWN THIS WAY.
HI, MRS. ROBBINS. C'N I TAKE A COUPLE OF APPLES?
YOU THINK I'M IN THIS BUSINESS FOR MY HEALTH, HUH?
YEAH. GO ON. HEY, DIDI--THERE'S A PACKAGE FOR YOU OUT BACK. I SIGNED FOR IT. YOU WANT TO GO GET IT?
IT'S ON THE TABLE.
YOU GOT A NAME, BOY? I'M AMELIA ROBBINS, BUT YOU CAN CALL ME MRS. ROBBINS.
SEXTON.
WHAT?
SEXTON.
NOTHING WRONG WITH THAT NAME. HOW LONG YOU KNOWN DIDI?
APPLES 79¢ lb
TEN MINUTES. SHE FOUND ME IN A GARBAGE HEAP.
WELL, YOU BE GOOD TO HER. SHE'S BEEN THROUGH A LOT LATELY. HER WHOLE FAMILY'S PASSED AWAY LAST MONTH. SHE DIDN'T TELL YOU ABOUT THAT?
SOME GUY WENT UP ONTO THE SIDEWALK, PLOUGHED INTO THE CROWD. KILLED DIDI'S MOM AND HER POP AND HER LITTLE SISTER AND SOME GUY SELLING CHEAP WRISTWATCHES FROM A SUITCASE.
GROCERY
SHE'S STILL LIVING UP THERE BUT--
APPLES 79¢ lb
ORANGES 89¢ LB
GOT IT!

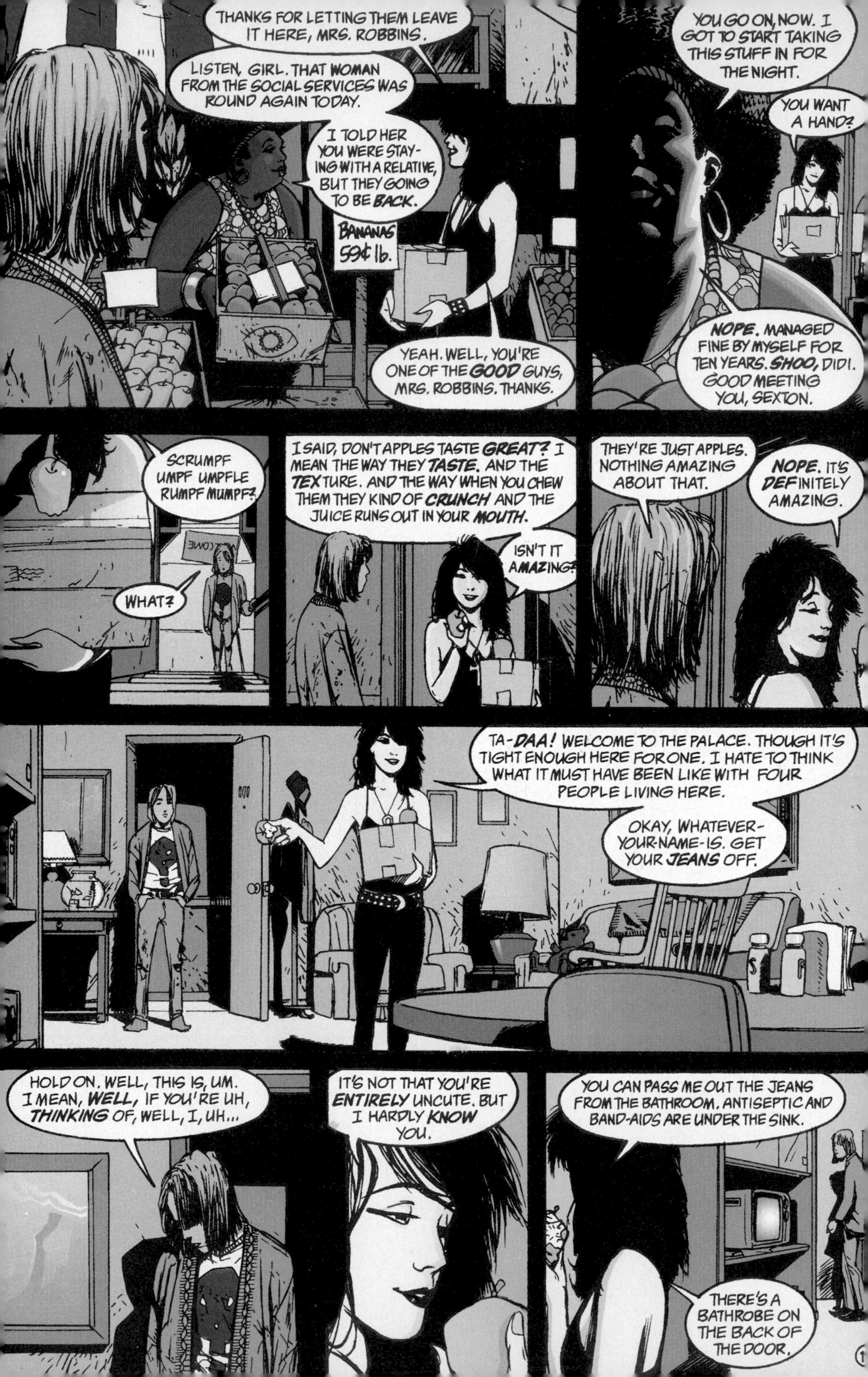
THANKS FOR LETTING THEM LEAVE IT HERE, MRS. ROBBINS.
LISTEN, GIRL. THAT WOMAN FROM THE SOCIAL SERVICES WAS ROUND AGAIN TODAY.
I TOLD HER YOU WERE STAYING WITH A RELATIVE, BUT THEY GOING TO BE BACK.
BANANAS 59¢ lb.
YEAH. WELL, YOU'RE ONE OF THE GOOD GUYS, MRS. ROBBINS. THANKS.
YOU GO ON, NOW. I GOT TO START TAKING THIS STUFF IN FOR THE NIGHT.
YOU WANT A HAND?
NOPE. MANAGED FINE BY MYSELF FOR TEN YEARS. SHOO, DIDI. GOOD MEETING YOU, SEXTON.
SCRUMPF UMPF UMPFLE RUMPF MUMPF?
WHAT?
I SAID, DON'T APPLES TASTE GREAT? I MEAN THE WAY THEY TASTE. AND THE TEXTURE. AND THE WAY WHEN YOU CHEW THEM THEY KIND OF CRUNCH AND THE JUICE RUNS OUT IN YOUR MOUTH.
ISN'T IT AMAZING?
THEY'RE JUST APPLES. NOTHING AMAZING ABOUT THAT.
NOPE. IT'S DEFINITELY AMAZING.
TA-DAA! WELCOME TO THE PALACE. THOUGH IT'S TIGHT ENOUGH HERE FOR ONE. I HATE TO THINK WHAT IT MUST HAVE BEEN LIKE WITH FOUR PEOPLE LIVING HERE.
OKAY, WHATEVER-YOUR-NAME-IS. GET YOUR JEANS OFF.
HOLD ON. WELL, THIS IS, UM. I MEAN, WELL, IF YOU'RE UH, THINKING OF, WELL, I, UH...
IT'S NOT THAT YOU'RE ENTIRELY UNCUTE. BUT I HARDLY KNOW YOU.
YOU CAN PASS ME OUT THE JEANS FROM THE BATHROOM. ANTISEPTIC AND BAND-AIDS ARE UNDER THE SINK.
THERE'S A BATHROBE ON THE BACK OF THE DOOR.

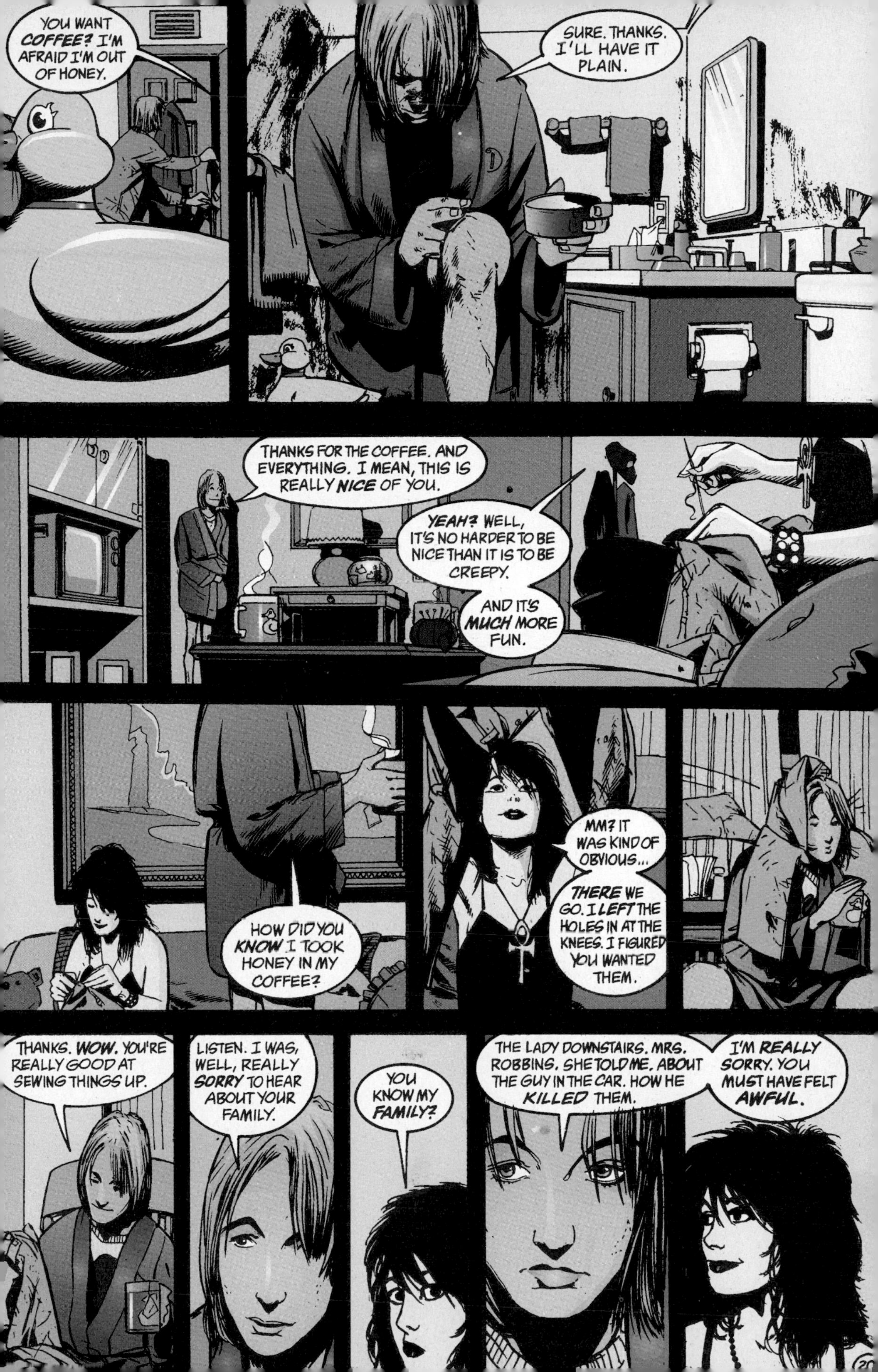
YOU WANT COFFEE? I'M AFRAID I'M OUT OF HONEY.
SURE. THANKS. I'LL HAVE IT PLAIN.
THANKS FOR THE COFFEE. AND EVERYTHING. I MEAN, THIS IS REALLY NICE OF YOU.
YEAH? WELL, IT'S NO HARDER TO BE NICE THAN IT IS TO BE CREEPY.
AND IT'S MUCH MORE FUN.
HOW DID YOU KNOW I TOOK HONEY IN MY COFFEE?
MM? IT WAS KIND OF OBVIOUS...
THERE WE GO. I LEFT THE HOLES IN AT THE KNEES. I FIGURED YOU WANTED THEM.
THANKS. WOW. YOU'RE REALLY GOOD AT SEWING THINGS UP.
LISTEN. I WAS, WELL, REALLY SORRY TO HEAR ABOUT YOUR FAMILY.
YOU KNOW MY FAMILY?
THE LADY DOWNSTAIRS. MRS. ROBBINS. SHE TOLD ME. ABOUT THE GUY IN THE CAR. HOW HE KILLED THEM.
I'M REALLY SORRY. YOU MUST HAVE FELT AWFUL.

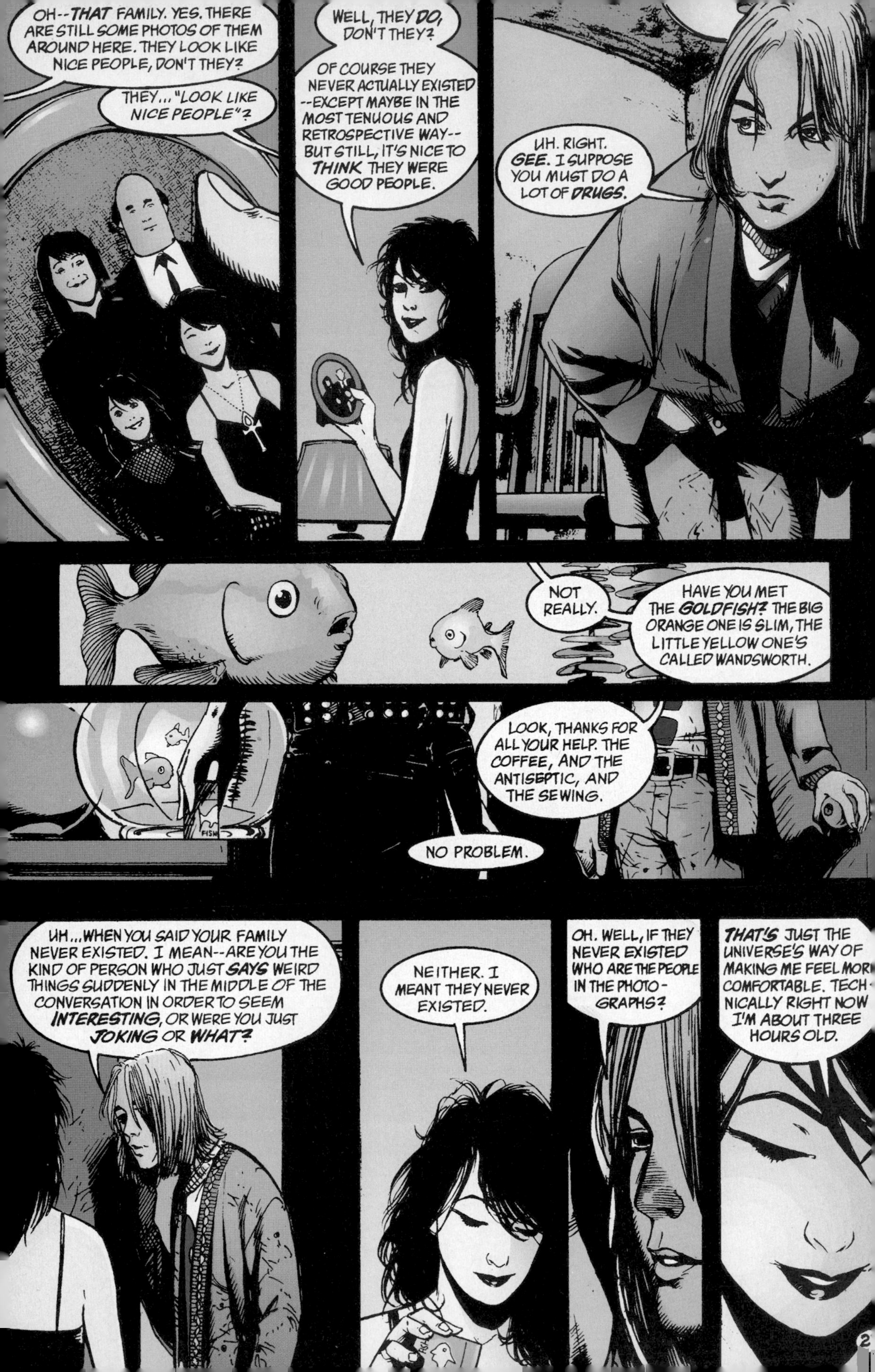
OH--THAT FAMILY. YES. THERE ARE STILL SOME PHOTOS OF THEM AROUND HERE. THEY LOOK LIKE NICE PEOPLE, DON'T THEY?
THEY... "LOOK LIKE NICE PEOPLE"?
WELL, THEY DO, DON'T THEY?
OF COURSE THEY NEVER ACTUALLY EXISTED --EXCEPT MAYBE IN THE MOST TENUOUS AND RETROSPECTIVE WAY-- BUT STILL, IT'S NICE TO THINK THEY WERE GOOD PEOPLE.
UH. RIGHT. GEE. I SUPPOSE YOU MUST DO A LOT OF DRUGS.
NOT REALLY.
HAVE YOU MET THE GOLDFISH? THE BIG ORANGE ONE IS SLIM, THE LITTLE YELLOW ONE'S CALLED WANDSWORTH.
LOOK, THANKS FOR ALL YOUR HELP. THE COFFEE, AND THE ANTISEPTIC, AND THE SEWING.
NO PROBLEM.
UH... WHEN YOU SAID YOUR FAMILY NEVER EXISTED. I MEAN--ARE YOU THE KIND OF PERSON WHO JUST SAYS WEIRD THINGS SUDDENLY IN THE MIDDLE OF THE CONVERSATION IN ORDER TO SEEM INTERESTING, OR WERE YOU JUST JOKING OR WHAT?
NEITHER. I MEANT THEY NEVER EXISTED.
OH. WELL, IF THEY NEVER EXISTED WHO ARE THE PEOPLE IN THE PHOTO-GRAPHS?
THAT'S JUST THE UNIVERSE'S WAY OF MAKING ME FEEL MORE COMFORTABLE. TECH-NICALLY RIGHT NOW I'M ABOUT THREE HOURS OLD.

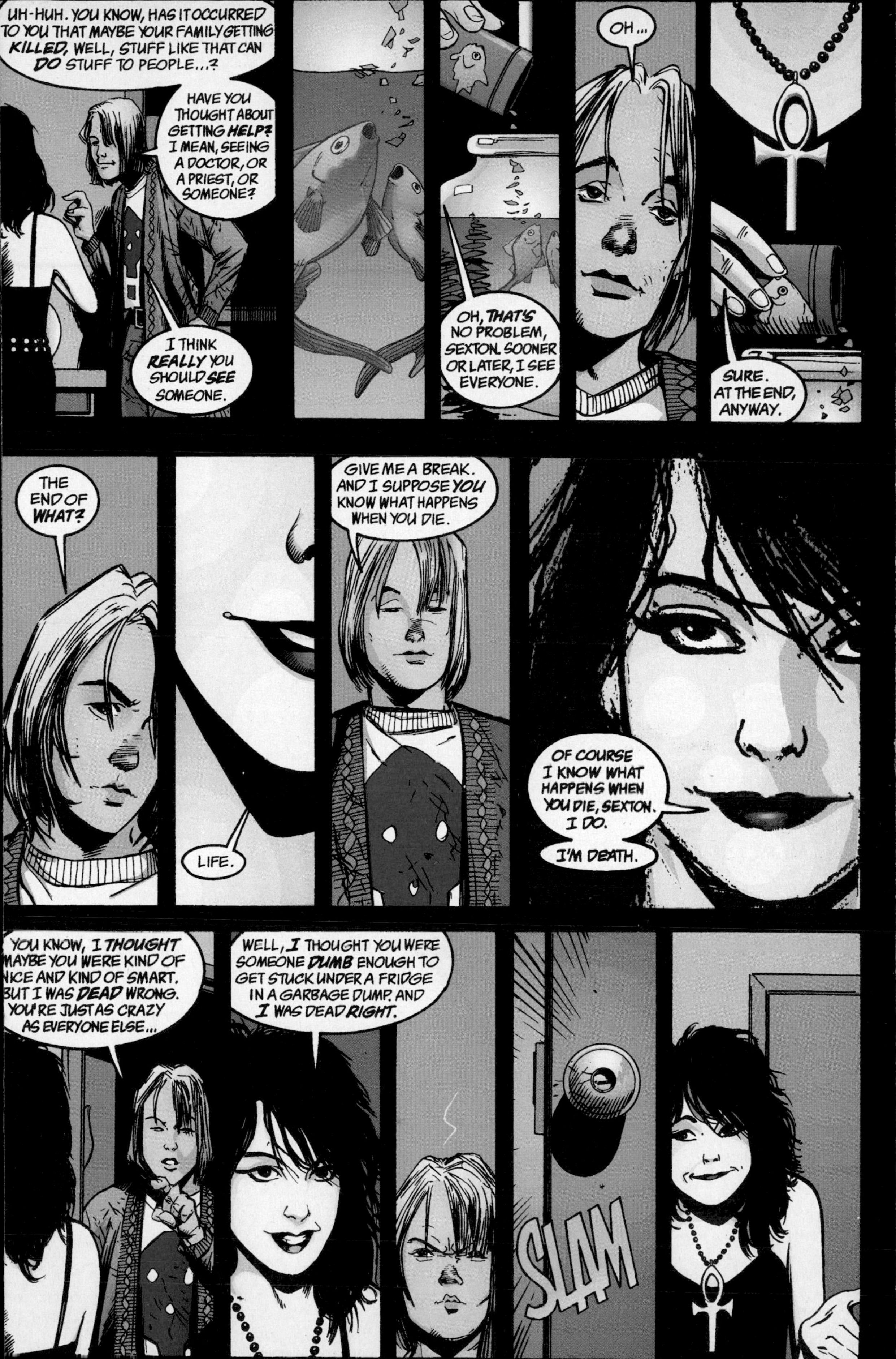
UH-HUH. YOU KNOW, HAS IT OCCURRED TO YOU THAT MAYBE YOUR FAMILY GETTING KILLED, WELL, STUFF LIKE THAT CAN DO STUFF TO PEOPLE...?
HAVE YOU THOUGHT ABOUT GETTING HELP? I MEAN, SEEING A DOCTOR, OR A PRIEST, OR SOMEONE?
I THINK REALLY YOU SHOULD SEE SOMEONE.
OH, THAT'S NO PROBLEM, SEXTON. SOONER OR LATER, I SEE EVERYONE.
OH...
SURE. AT THE END, ANYWAY.
THE END OF WHAT?
LIFE.
GIVE ME A BREAK. AND I SUPPOSE YOU KNOW WHAT HAPPENS WHEN YOU DIE.
OF COURSE I KNOW WHAT HAPPENS WHEN YOU DIE, SEXTON. I DO.
I'M DEATH.
YOU KNOW, I THOUGHT MAYBE YOU WERE KIND OF NICE AND KIND OF SMART. BUT I WAS DEAD WRONG. YOU'RE JUST AS CRAZY AS EVERYONE ELSE...
WELL, I THOUGHT YOU WERE SOMEONE DUMB ENOUGH TO GET STUCK UNDER A FRIDGE IN A GARBAGE DUMP. AND I WAS DEAD RIGHT.
SLAM

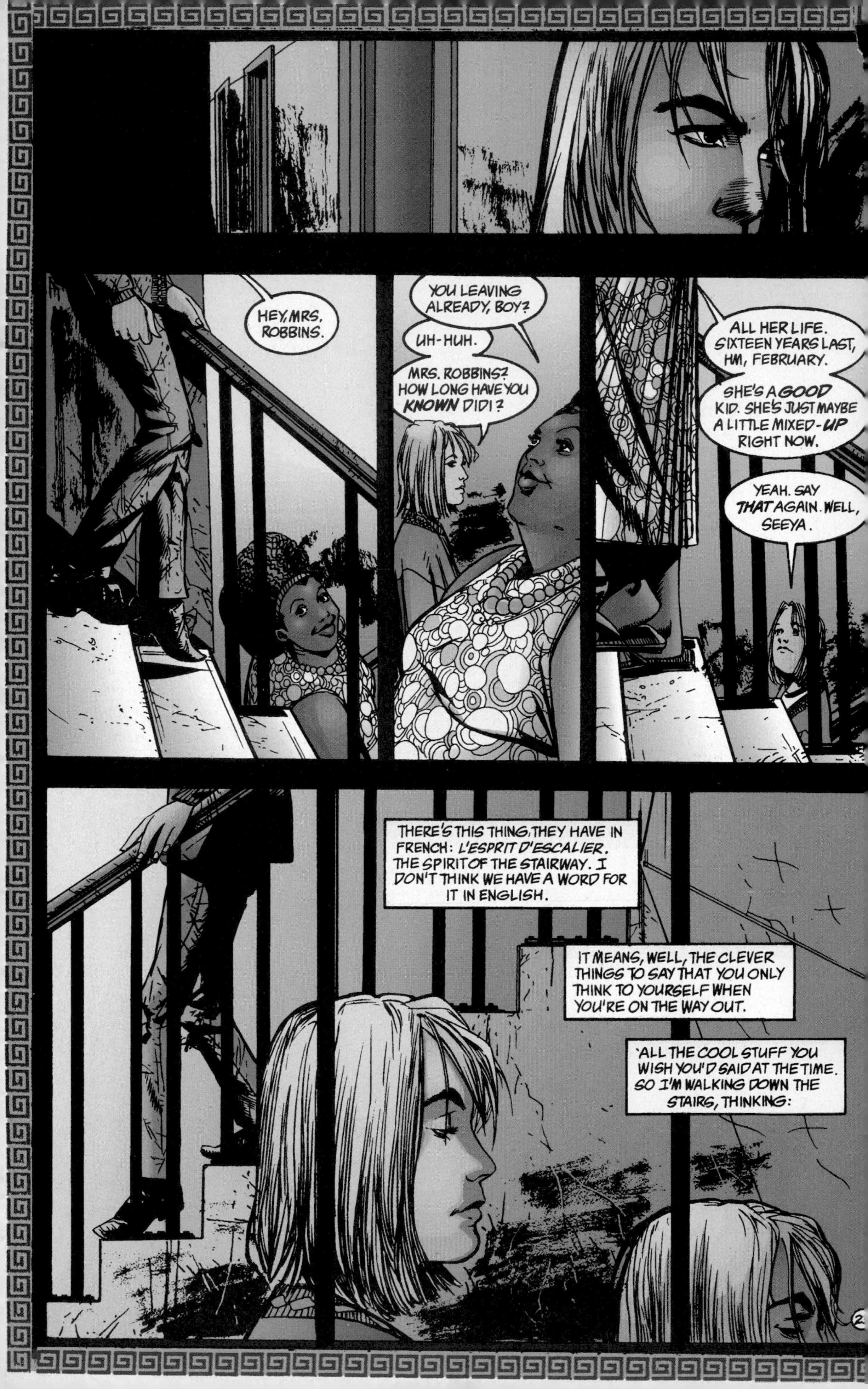
HEY, MRS. ROBBINS.
YOU LEAVING ALREADY, BOY?
UH-HUH.
MRS. ROBBINS? HOW LONG HAVE YOU KNOWN DIDI?
ALL HER LIFE. SIXTEEN YEARS LAST, HM, FEBRUARY.
SHE'S A GOOD KID. SHE'S JUST MAYBE A LITTLE MIXED-UP RIGHT NOW.
YEAH. SAY THAT AGAIN. WELL, SEEYA.
THERE'S THIS THING, THEY HAVE IN FRENCH: L'ESPRIT D'ESCALIER. THE SPIRIT OF THE STAIRWAY. I DON'T THINK WE HAVE A WORD FOR IT IN ENGLISH.
IT MEANS, WELL, THE CLEVER THINGS TO SAY THAT YOU ONLY THINK TO YOURSELF WHEN YOU'RE ON THE WAY OUT.
'ALL THE COOL STUFF YOU WISH YOU'D SAID AT THE TIME. SO I'M WALKING DOWN THE STAIRS, THINKING:

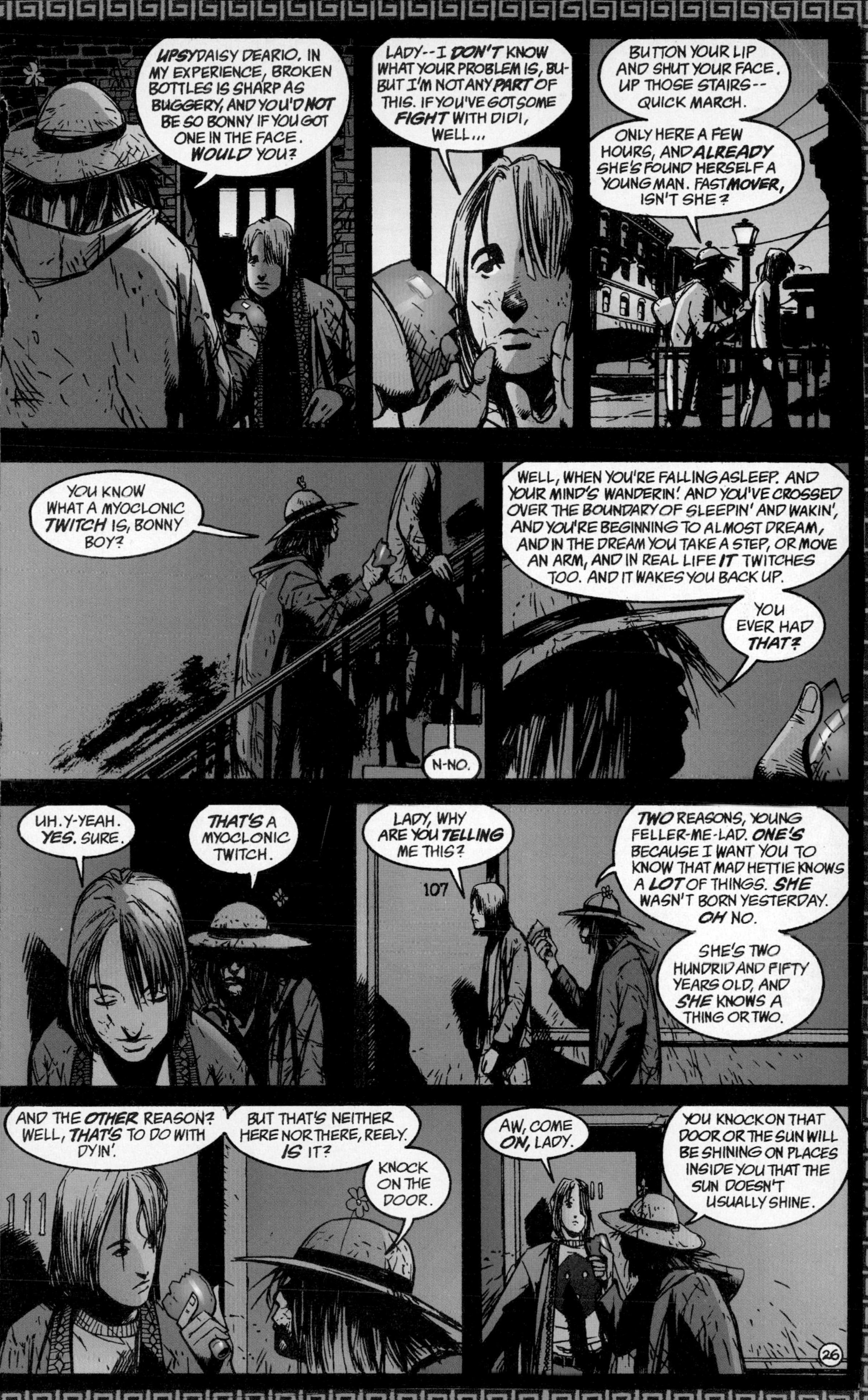
UPSYDAISY DEARIO. IN MY EXPERIENCE, BROKEN BOTTLES IS SHARP AS BUGGERY, AND YOU'D NOT BE SO BONNY IF YOU GOT ONE IN THE FACE. WOULD YOU?
LADY--I DON'T KNOW WHAT YOUR PROBLEM IS, BU-BUT I'M NOT ANY PART OF THIS. IF YOU'VE GOT SOME FIGHT WITH DIDI, WELL...
BUTTON YOUR LIP AND SHUT YOUR FACE. UP THOSE STAIRS--QUICK MARCH.
ONLY HERE A FEW HOURS, AND ALREADY SHE'S FOUND HERSELF A YOUNG MAN. FAST MOVER, ISN'T SHE?
YOU KNOW WHAT A MYOCLONIC TWITCH IS, BONNY BOY?
WELL, WHEN YOU'RE FALLING ASLEEP. AND YOUR MIND'S WANDERIN'. AND YOU'VE CROSSED OVER THE BOUNDARY OF SLEEPIN' AND WAKIN', AND YOU'RE BEGINNING TO ALMOST DREAM, AND IN THE DREAM YOU TAKE A STEP, OR MOVE AN ARM, AND IN REAL LIFE IT TWITCHES TOO. AND IT WAKES YOU BACK UP.
YOU EVER HAD THAT?
N-NO.
UH. Y-YEAH. YES. SURE.
THAT'S A MYOCLONIC TWITCH.
LADY, WHY ARE YOU TELLING ME THIS?
107
TWO REASONS, YOUNG FELLER-ME-LAD. ONE'S BECAUSE I WANT YOU TO KNOW THAT MAD HETTIE KNOWS A LOT OF THINGS. SHE WASN'T BORN YESTERDAY. OH NO.
SHE'S TWO HUNDRID AND FIFTY YEARS OLD, AND SHE KNOWS A THING OR TWO.
AND THE OTHER REASON? WELL, THAT'S TO DO WITH DYIN'.
BUT THAT'S NEITHER HERE NOR THERE, REELY. IS IT?
KNOCK ON THE DOOR.
AW, COME ON, LADY.
YOU KNOCK ON THAT DOOR OR THE SUN WILL BE SHINING ON PLACES INSIDE YOU THAT THE SUN DOESN'T USUALLY SHINE.

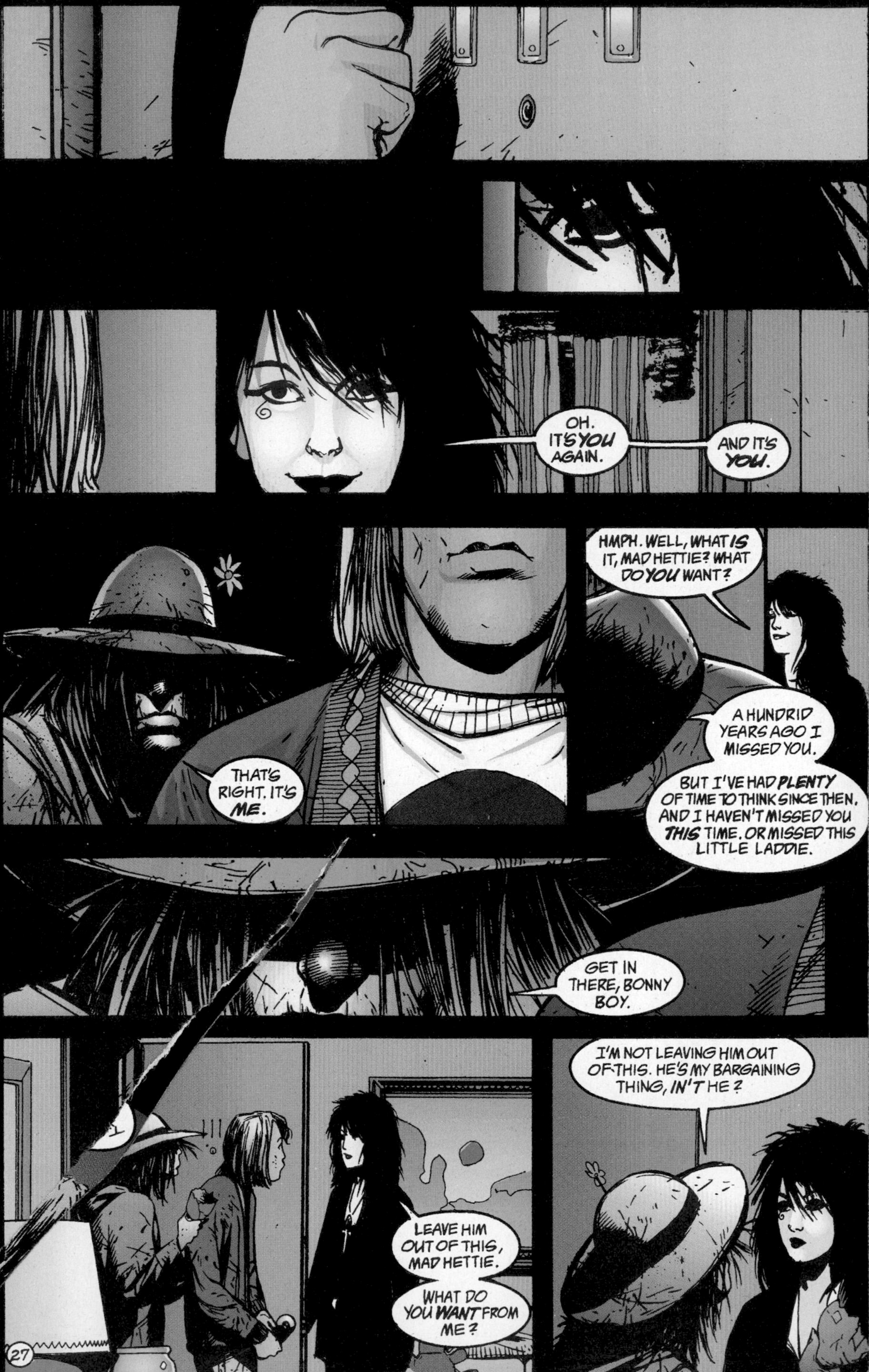
OH. IT'S YOU AGAIN.
AND IT'S YOU.
HMPH. WELL, WHAT IS IT, MAD HETTIE? WHAT DO YOU WANT?
THAT'S RIGHT. IT'S ME.
A HUNDRID YEARS AGO I MISSED YOU.
BUT I'VE HAD PLENTY OF TIME TO THINK SINCE THEN. AND I HAVEN'T MISSED YOU THIS TIME. OR MISSED THIS LITTLE LADDIE.
GET IN THERE, BONNY BOY.
LEAVE HIM OUT OF THIS, MAD HETTIE.
WHAT DO YOU WANT FROM ME?
I'M NOT LEAVING HIM OUT OF THIS. HE'S MY BARGAINING THING, IN'T HE?

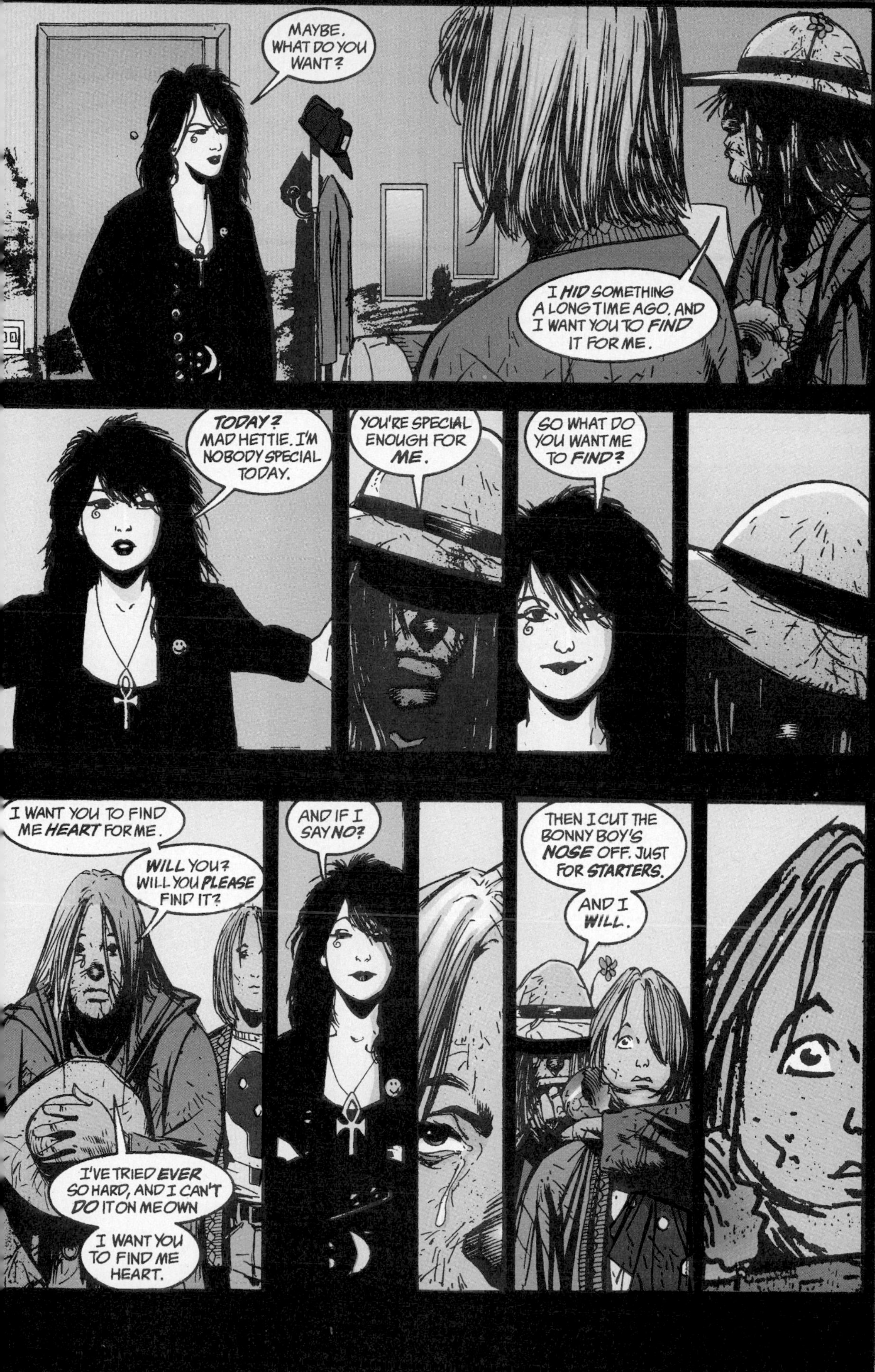
MAYBE. WHAT DO YOU WANT?
I HID SOMETHING A LONG TIME AGO, AND I WANT YOU TO FIND IT FOR ME.
TODAY? MAD HETTIE. I'M NOBODY SPECIAL TODAY.
YOU'RE SPECIAL ENOUGH FOR ME.
SO WHAT DO YOU WANT ME TO FIND?
I WANT YOU TO FIND ME HEART FOR ME.
WILL YOU? WILL YOU PLEASE FIND IT?
I'VE TRIED EVER SO HARD, AND I CAN'T DO IT ON ME OWN
I WANT YOU TO FIND ME HEART.
AND IF I SAY NO?
THEN I CUT THE BONNY BOY'S NOSE OFF. JUST FOR STARTERS.
AND I WILL.

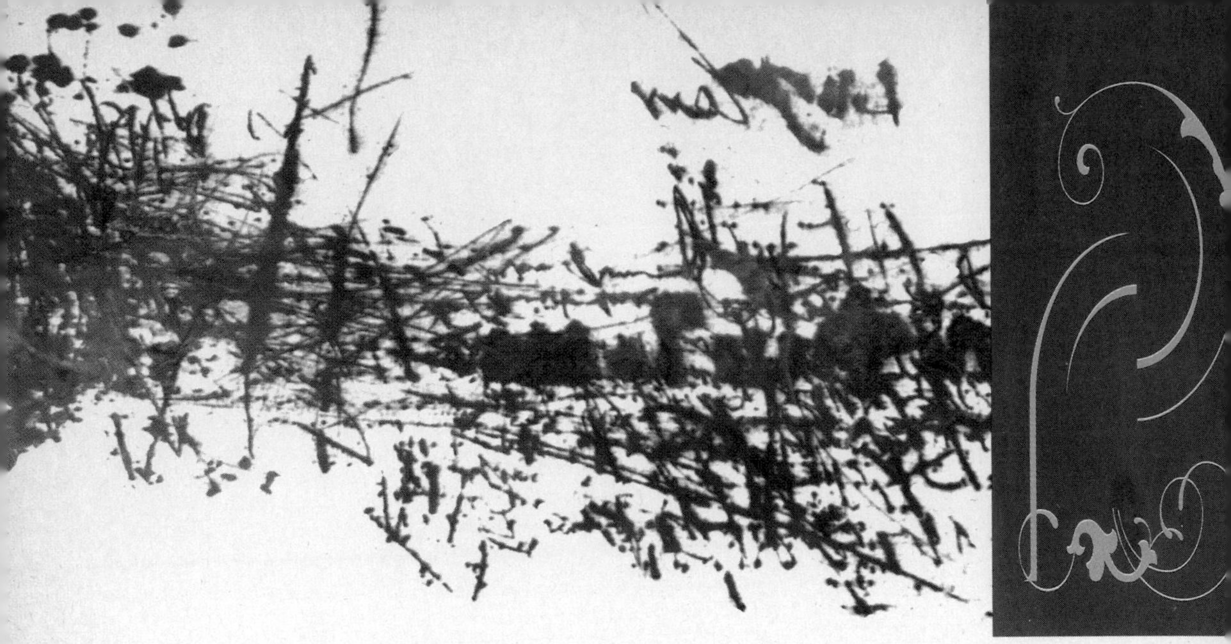

A NIGHT TO REMEMBER

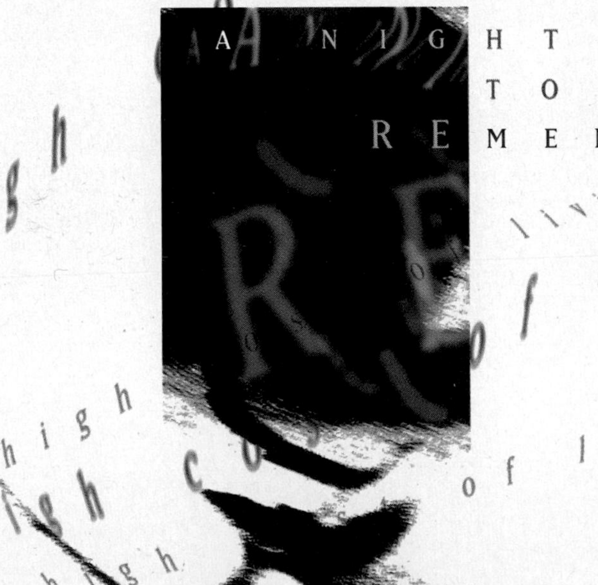

the high cost of living

the high cost of living

the high cost of living

the high cost of living

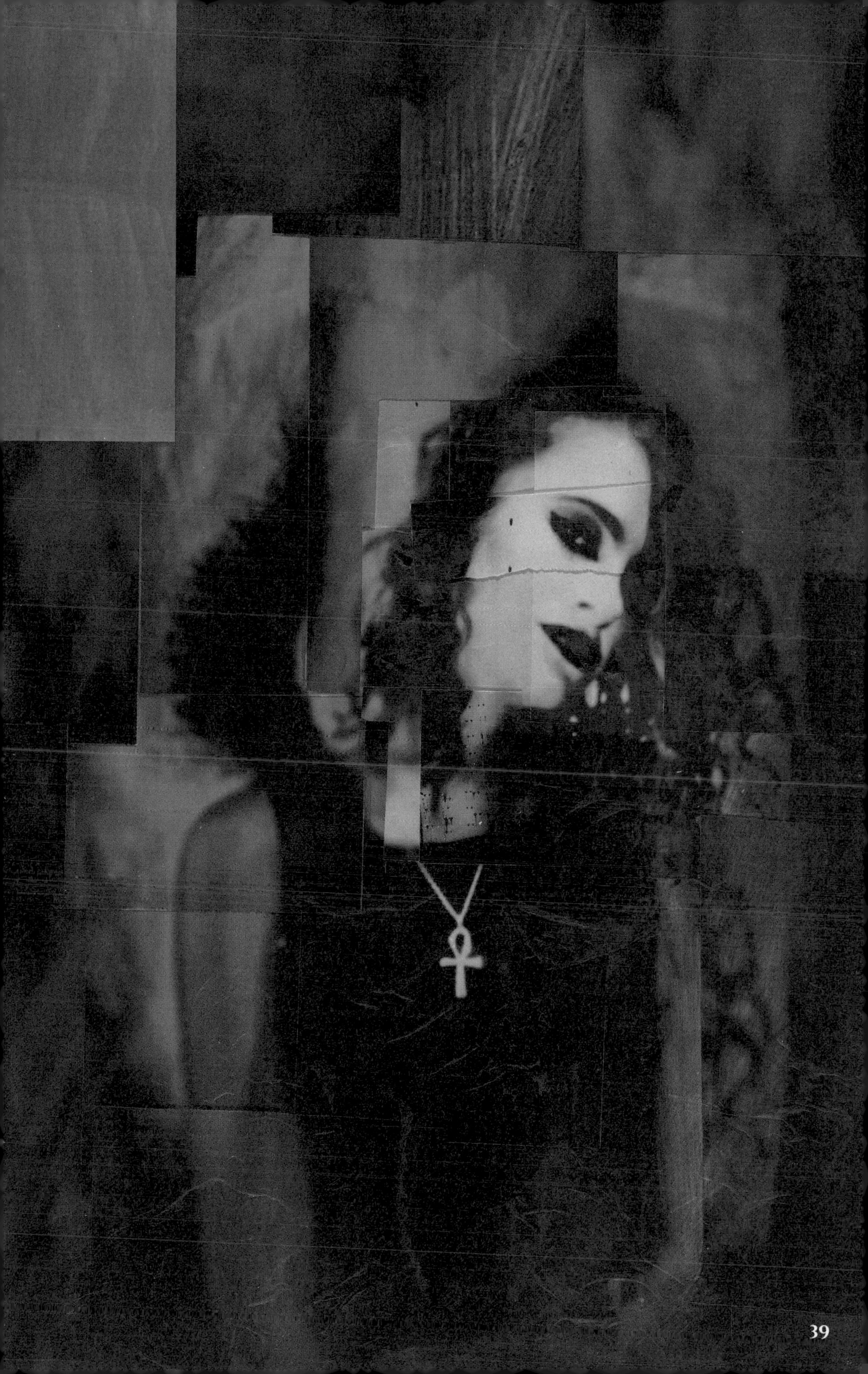

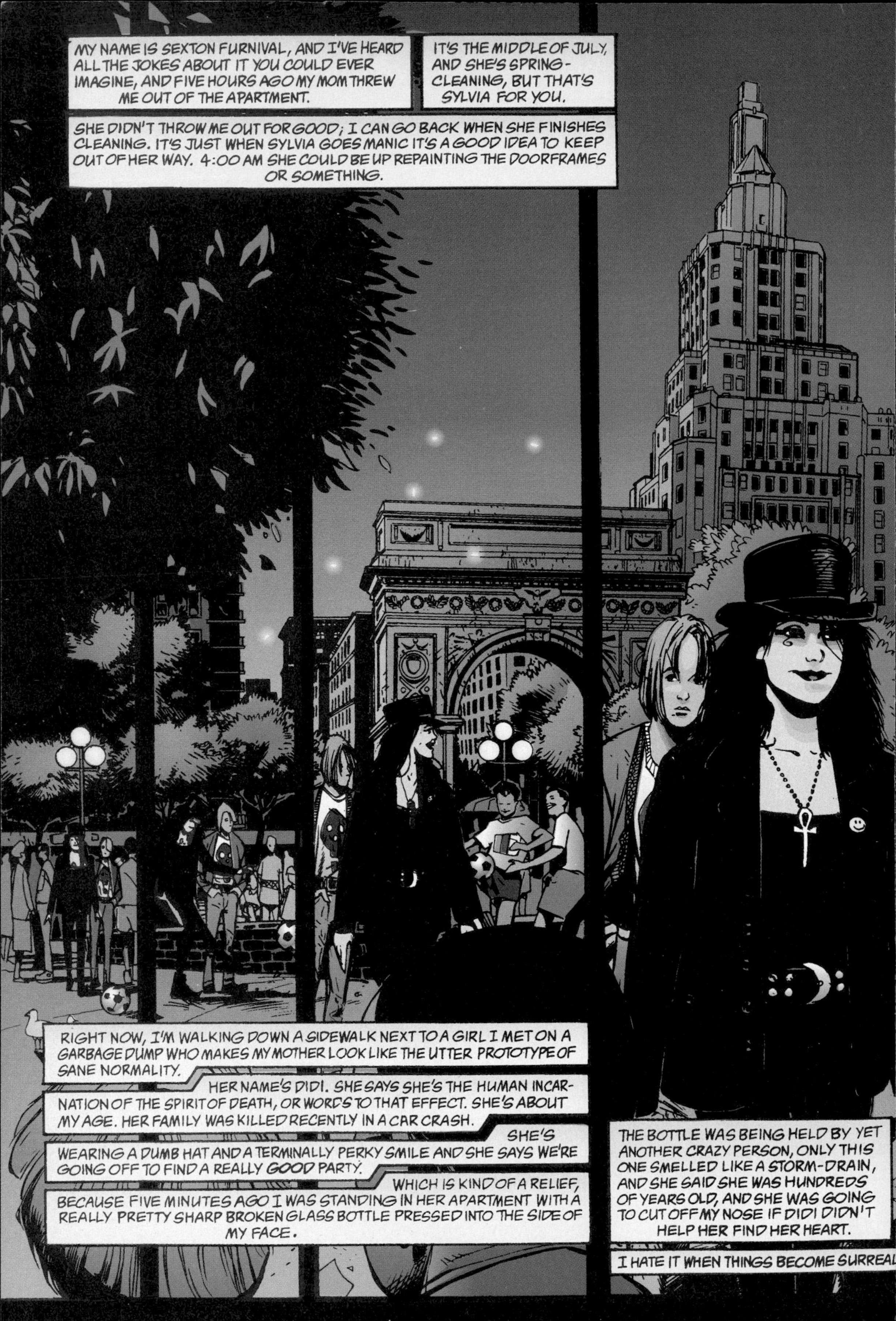

MY NAME IS SEXTON FURNIVAL, AND I'VE HEARD ALL THE JOKES ABOUT IT YOU COULD EVER IMAGINE, AND FIVE HOURS AGO MY MOM THREW ME OUT OF THE APARTMENT.
IT'S THE MIDDLE OF JULY, AND SHE'S SPRING-CLEANING, BUT THAT'S SYLVIA FOR YOU.
SHE DIDN'T THROW ME OUT FOR GOOD; I CAN GO BACK WHEN SHE FINISHES CLEANING. IT'S JUST WHEN SYLVIA GOES MANIC IT'S A GOOD IDEA TO KEEP OUT OF HER WAY. 4:00 AM SHE COULD BE UP REPAINTING THE DOORFRAMES OR SOMETHING.
RIGHT NOW, I'M WALKING DOWN A SIDEWALK NEXT TO A GIRL I MET ON A GARBAGE DUMP WHO MAKES MY MOTHER LOOK LIKE THE UTTER PROTOTYPE OF SANE NORMALITY.
HER NAME'S DIDI. SHE SAYS SHE'S THE HUMAN INCARNATION OF THE SPIRIT OF DEATH, OR WORDS TO THAT EFFECT. SHE'S ABOUT MY AGE. HER FAMILY WAS KILLED RECENTLY IN A CAR CRASH.
SHE'S WEARING A DUMB HAT AND A TERMINALLY PERKY SMILE AND SHE SAYS WE'RE GOING OFF TO FIND A REALLY *GOOD* PARTY.
WHICH IS KIND OF A RELIEF, BECAUSE FIVE MINUTES AGO I WAS STANDING IN HER APARTMENT WITH A REALLY PRETTY SHARP BROKEN GLASS BOTTLE PRESSED INTO THE SIDE OF MY FACE.
THE BOTTLE WAS BEING HELD BY YET ANOTHER CRAZY PERSON, ONLY THIS ONE SMELLED LIKE A STORM-DRAIN, AND SHE SAID SHE WAS HUNDREDS OF YEARS OLD, AND SHE WAS GOING TO CUT OFF MY NOSE IF DIDI DIDN'T HELP HER FIND HER HEART.
I HATE IT WHEN THINGS BECOME SURREAL

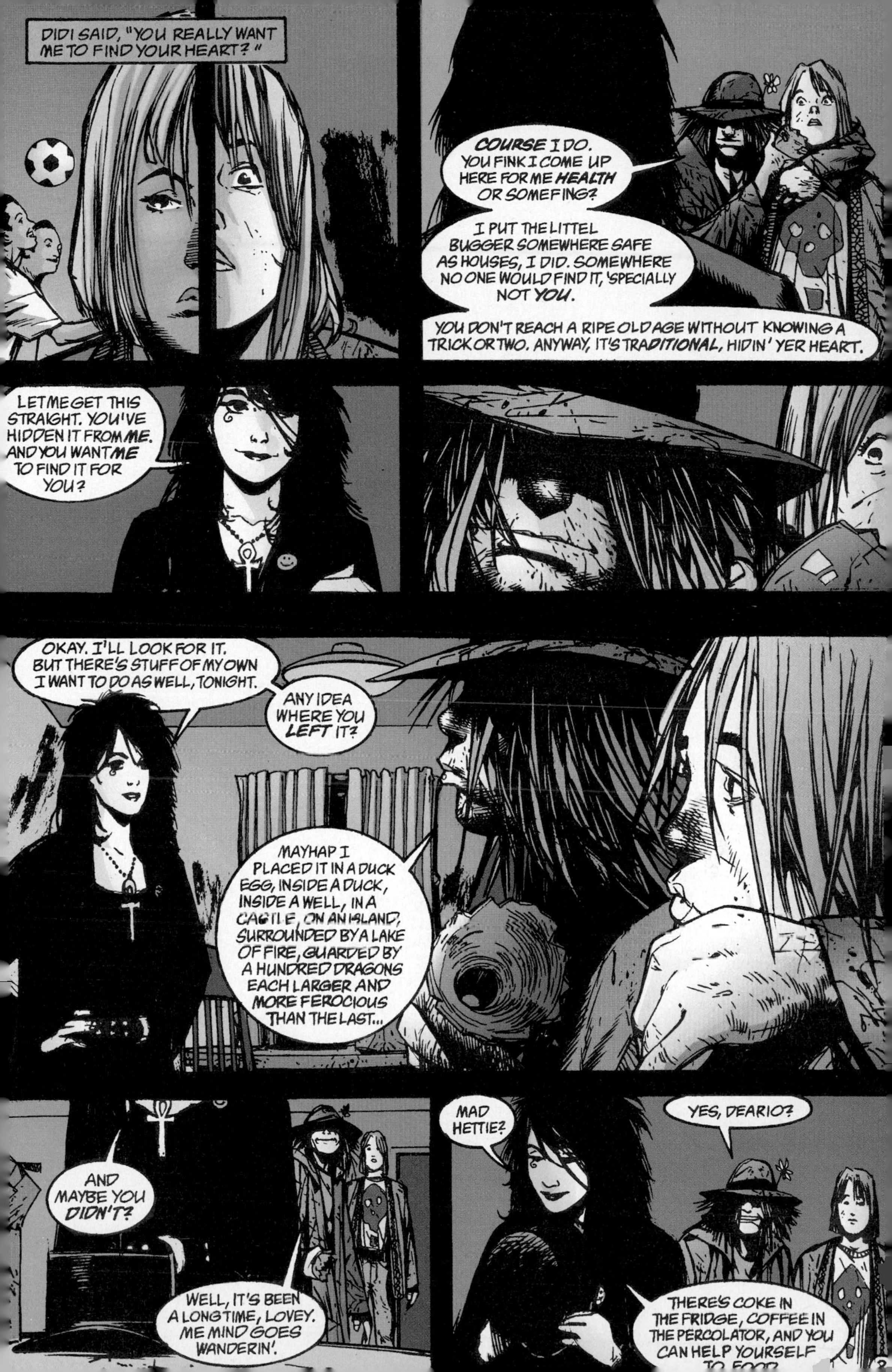
DIDI SAID, "YOU REALLY WANT ME TO FIND YOUR HEART?"
COURSE I DO. YOU FINK I COME UP HERE FOR ME HEALTH OR SOMEFING?
I PUT THE LITTEL BUGGER SOMEWHERE SAFE AS HOUSES, I DID. SOMEWHERE NO ONE WOULD FIND IT, 'SPECIALLY NOT YOU.
YOU DON'T REACH A RIPE OLD AGE WITHOUT KNOWING A TRICK OR TWO. ANYWAY, IT'S TRADITIONAL, HIDIN' YER HEART.
LET ME GET THIS STRAIGHT. YOU'VE HIDDEN IT FROM ME. AND YOU WANT ME TO FIND IT FOR YOU?
OKAY. I'LL LOOK FOR IT. BUT THERE'S STUFF OF MY OWN I WANT TO DO AS WELL, TONIGHT.
ANY IDEA WHERE YOU LEFT IT?
MAYHAP I PLACED IT IN A DUCK EGG, INSIDE A DUCK, INSIDE A WELL, IN A CASTLE, ON AN ISLAND, SURROUNDED BY A LAKE OF FIRE, GUARDED BY A HUNDRED DRAGONS EACH LARGER AND MORE FEROCIOUS THAN THE LAST...
AND MAYBE YOU DIDN'T?
WELL, IT'S BEEN A LONG TIME, LOVEY. ME MIND GOES WANDERIN'.
MAD HETTIE?
YES, DEARIO?
THERE'S COKE IN THE FRIDGE, COFFEE IN THE PERCOLATOR, AND YOU CAN HELP YOURSELF TO FOOD

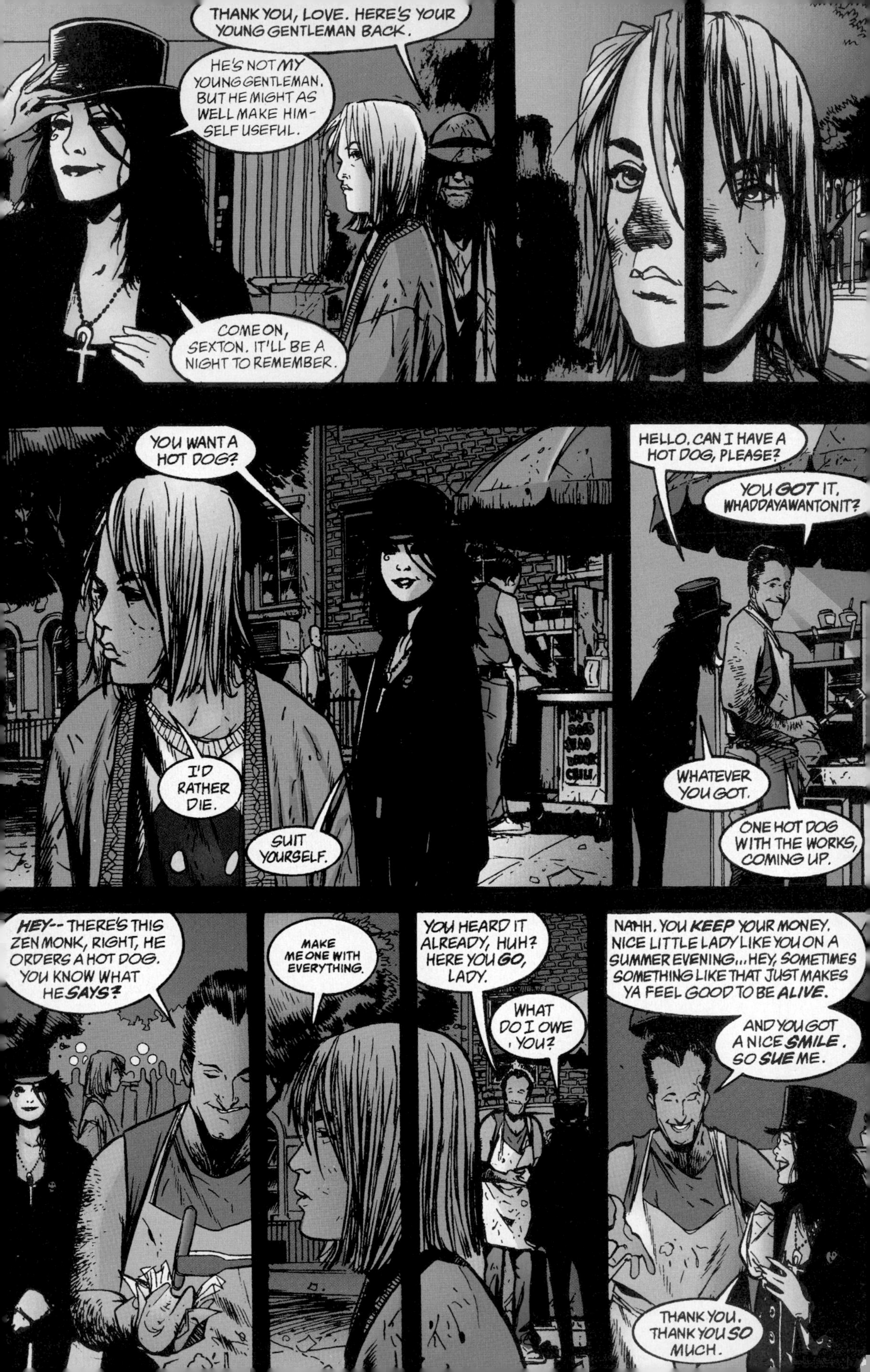
THANK YOU, LOVE. HERE'S YOUR YOUNG GENTLEMAN BACK.
HE'S NOT MY YOUNG GENTLEMAN. BUT HE MIGHT AS WELL MAKE HIM-SELF USEFUL.
COME ON, SEXTON. IT'LL BE A NIGHT TO REMEMBER.
YOU WANT A HOT DOG?
I'D RATHER DIE.
SUIT YOURSELF.
HELLO. CAN I HAVE A HOT DOG, PLEASE?
YOU GOT IT. WHADDAYAWANTONIT?
WHATEVER YOU GOT.
ONE HOT DOG WITH THE WORKS, COMING UP.
HEY-- THERE'S THIS ZEN MONK, RIGHT, HE ORDERS A HOT DOG. YOU KNOW WHAT HE SAYS?
MAKE ME ONE WITH EVERYTHING.
YOU HEARD IT ALREADY, HUH? HERE YOU GO, LADY.
WHAT DO I OWE YOU?
NAHH. YOU KEEP YOUR MONEY. NICE LITTLE LADY LIKE YOU ON A SUMMER EVENING... HEY, SOMETIMES SOMETHING LIKE THAT JUST MAKES YA FEEL GOOD TO BE ALIVE.
AND YOU GOT A NICE SMILE. SO SUE ME.
THANK YOU. THANK YOU SO MUCH.

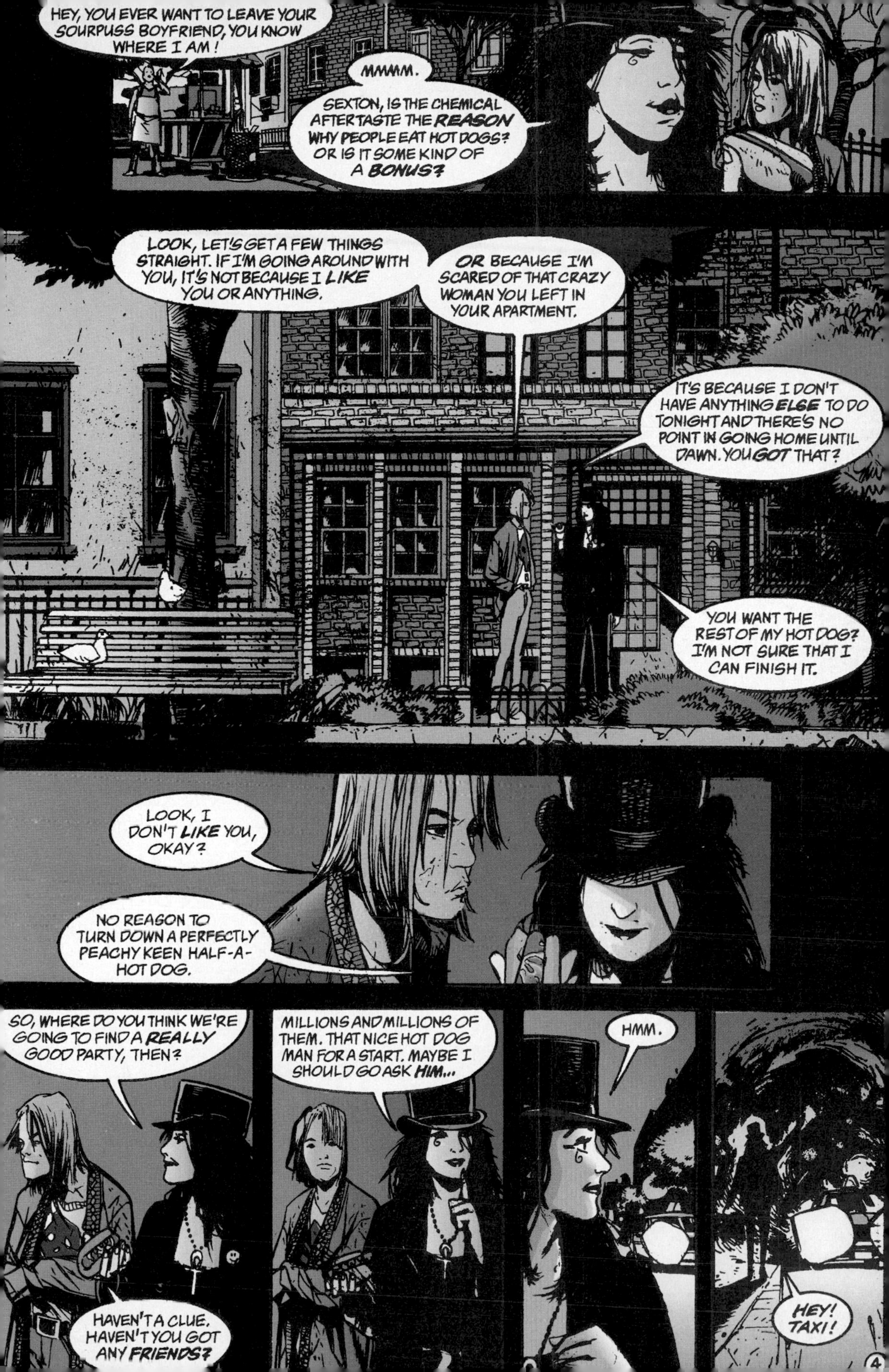
HEY, YOU EVER WANT TO LEAVE YOUR SOURPUSS BOYFRIEND, YOU KNOW WHERE I AM!
MMMM.
SEXTON, IS THE CHEMICAL AFTERTASTE THE REASON WHY PEOPLE EAT HOT DOGS? OR IS IT SOME KIND OF A BONUS?
LOOK, LET'S GET A FEW THINGS STRAIGHT. IF I'M GOING AROUND WITH YOU, IT'S NOT BECAUSE I LIKE YOU OR ANYTHING.
OR BECAUSE I'M SCARED OF THAT CRAZY WOMAN YOU LEFT IN YOUR APARTMENT.
IT'S BECAUSE I DON'T HAVE ANYTHING ELSE TO DO TONIGHT AND THERE'S NO POINT IN GOING HOME UNTIL DAWN. YOU GOT THAT?
YOU WANT THE REST OF MY HOT DOG? I'M NOT SURE THAT I CAN FINISH IT.
LOOK, I DON'T LIKE YOU, OKAY?
NO REASON TO TURN DOWN A PERFECTLY PEACHY KEEN HALF-A-HOT DOG.
SO, WHERE DO YOU THINK WE'RE GOING TO FIND A REALLY GOOD PARTY, THEN?
HAVEN'T A CLUE. HAVEN'T YOU GOT ANY FRIENDS?
MILLIONS AND MILLIONS OF THEM. THAT NICE HOT DOG MAN FOR A START. MAYBE I SHOULD GO ASK HIM...
HMM.
HEY! TAXI!
4

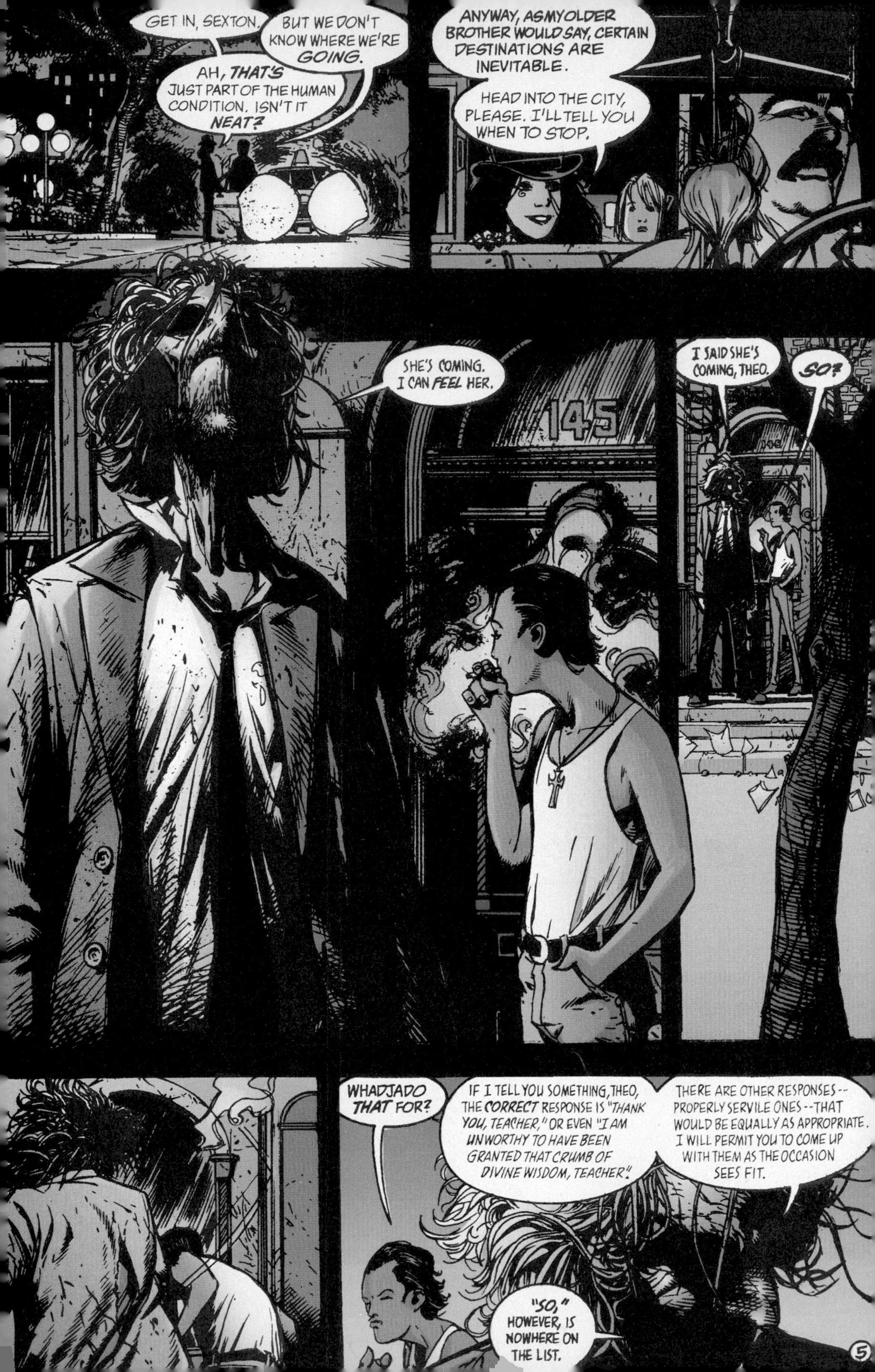
GET IN, SEXTON.
BUT WE DON'T KNOW WHERE WE'RE GOING.
AH, THAT'S JUST PART OF THE HUMAN CONDITION. ISN'T IT NEAT?
ANYWAY, AS MY OLDER BROTHER WOULD SAY, CERTAIN DESTINATIONS ARE INEVITABLE.
HEAD INTO THE CITY, PLEASE. I'LL TELL YOU WHEN TO STOP.
SHE'S COMING. I CAN FEEL HER.
145
I SAID SHE'S COMING, THEO.
SO?
WHADJADO THAT FOR?
IF I TELL YOU SOMETHING, THEO, THE CORRECT RESPONSE IS "THANK YOU, TEACHER," OR EVEN "I AM UNWORTHY TO HAVE BEEN GRANTED THAT CRUMB OF DIVINE WISDOM, TEACHER."
THERE ARE OTHER RESPONSES -- PROPERLY SERVILE ONES -- THAT WOULD BE EQUALLY AS APPROPRIATE. I WILL PERMIT YOU TO COME UP WITH THEM AS THE OCCASION SEES FIT.
"SO," HOWEVER, IS NOWHERE ON THE LIST.

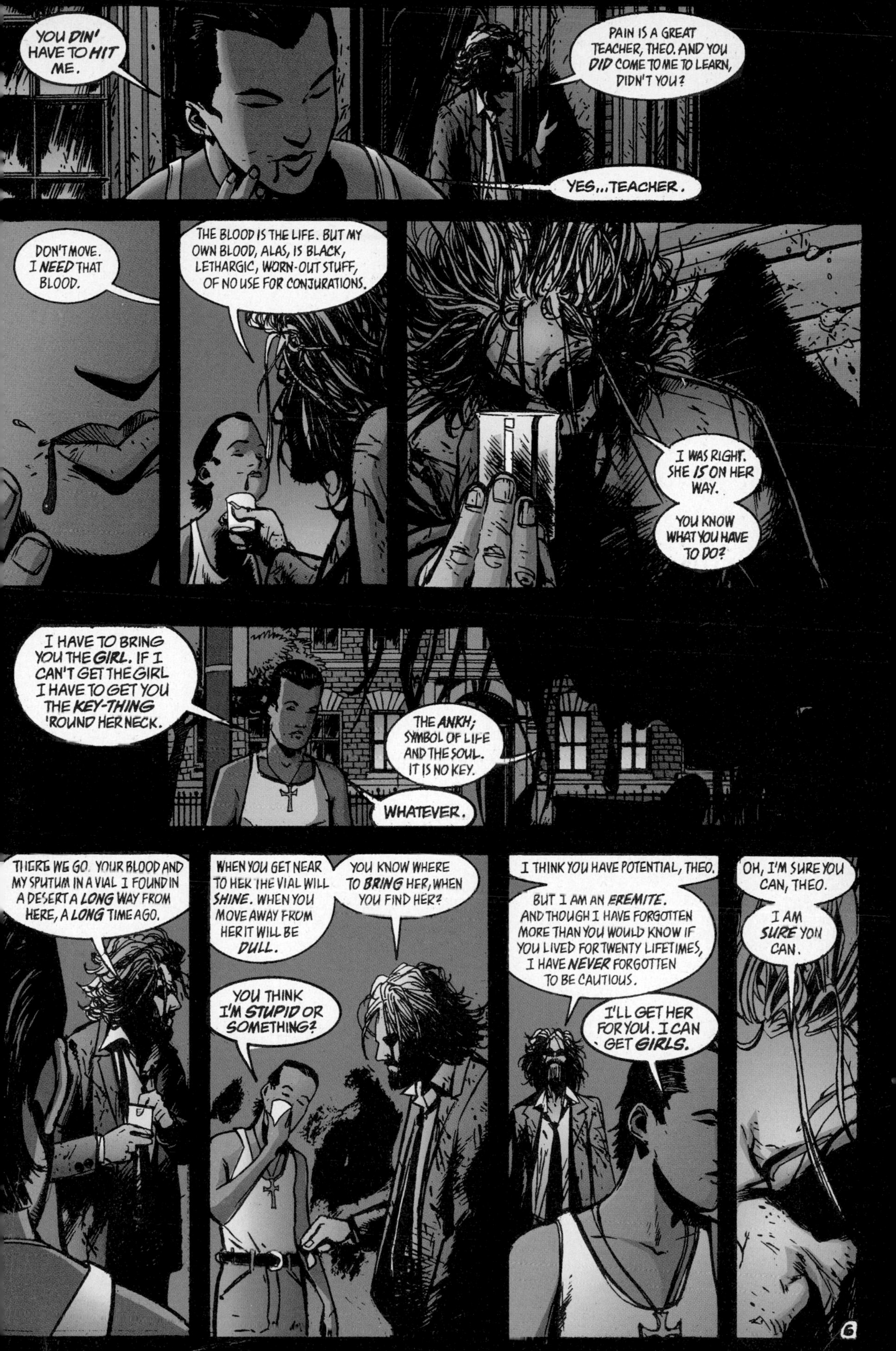
YOU DIN' HAVE TO HIT ME.
PAIN IS A GREAT TEACHER, THEO. AND YOU DID COME TO ME TO LEARN, DIDN'T YOU?
YES... TEACHER.
DON'T MOVE. I NEED THAT BLOOD.
THE BLOOD IS THE LIFE. BUT MY OWN BLOOD, ALAS, IS BLACK, LETHARGIC, WORN-OUT STUFF, OF NO USE FOR CONJURATIONS.
I WAS RIGHT. SHE IS ON HER WAY.
YOU KNOW WHAT YOU HAVE TO DO?
I HAVE TO BRING YOU THE GIRL. IF I CAN'T GET THE GIRL I HAVE TO GET YOU THE KEY-THING 'ROUND HER NECK.
THE ANKH; SYMBOL OF LIFE AND THE SOUL. IT IS NO KEY.
WHATEVER.
THERE WE GO. YOUR BLOOD AND MY SPUTUM IN A VIAL I FOUND IN A DESERT A LONG WAY FROM HERE, A LONG TIME AGO.
WHEN YOU GET NEAR TO HER THE VIAL WILL SHINE. WHEN YOU MOVE AWAY FROM HER IT WILL BE DULL.
YOU KNOW WHERE TO BRING HER, WHEN YOU FIND HER?
YOU THINK I'M STUPID OR SOMETHING?
I THINK YOU HAVE POTENTIAL, THEO.
BUT I AM AN EREMITE. AND THOUGH I HAVE FORGOTTEN MORE THAN YOU WOULD KNOW IF YOU LIVED FOR TWENTY LIFETIMES, I HAVE NEVER FORGOTTEN TO BE CAUTIOUS.
I'LL GET HER FOR YOU. I CAN GET GIRLS.
OH, I'M SURE YOU CAN, THEO.
I AM SURE YOU CAN.
6

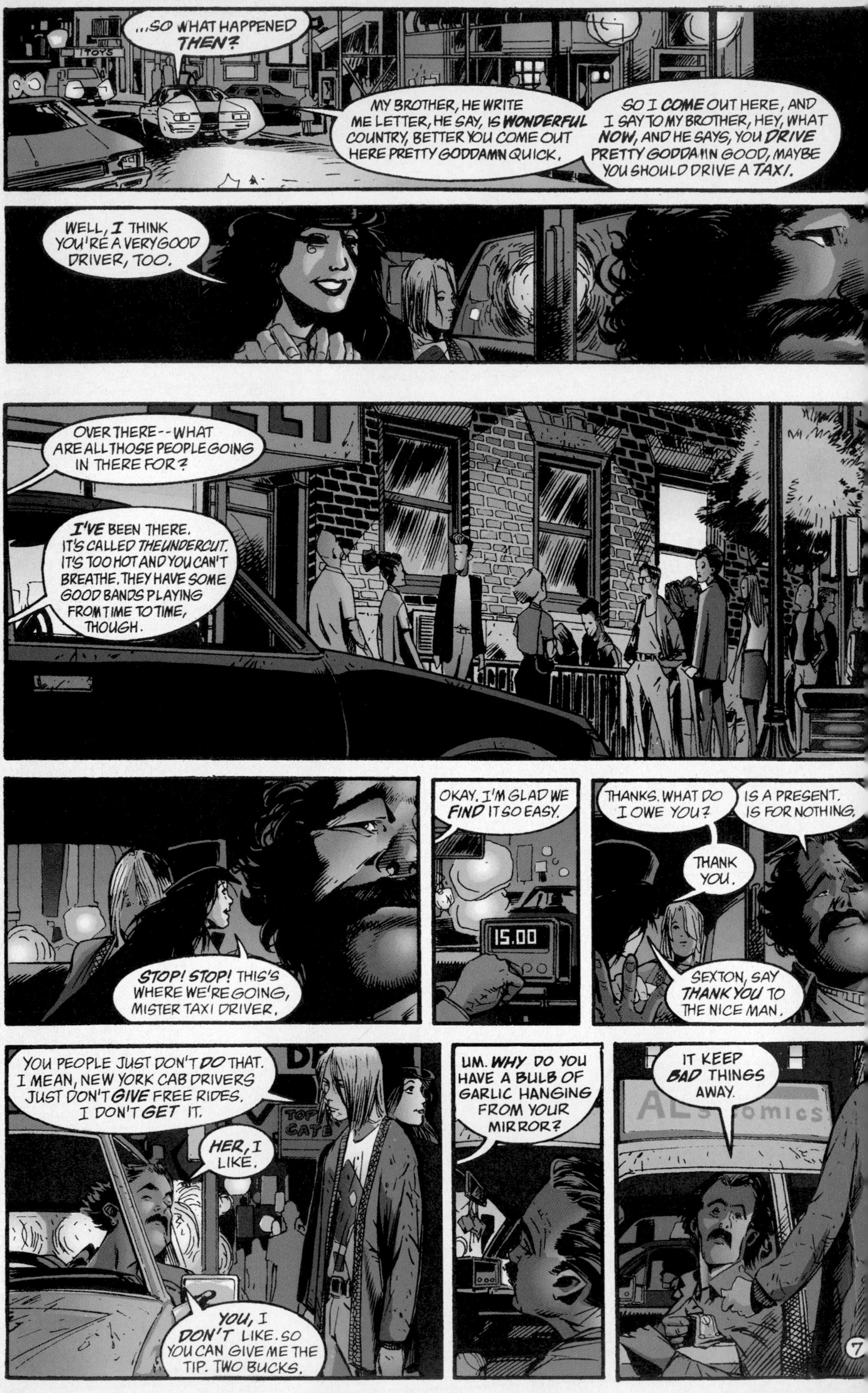
...SO WHAT HAPPENED THEN?
MY BROTHER, HE WRITE ME LETTER, HE SAY, IS WONDERFUL COUNTRY, BETTER YOU COME OUT HERE PRETTY GODDAMN QUICK.
SO I COME OUT HERE, AND I SAY TO MY BROTHER, HEY, WHAT NOW, AND HE SAYS, YOU DRIVE PRETTY GODDAMN GOOD, MAYBE YOU SHOULD DRIVE A TAXI.
WELL, I THINK YOU'RE A VERY GOOD DRIVER, TOO.
OVER THERE--WHAT ARE ALL THOSE PEOPLE GOING IN THERE FOR?
I'VE BEEN THERE. IT'S CALLED THE UNDERCUT. IT'S TOO HOT AND YOU CAN'T BREATHE. THEY HAVE SOME GOOD BANDS PLAYING FROM TIME TO TIME, THOUGH.
STOP! STOP! THIS'S WHERE WE'RE GOING, MISTER TAXI DRIVER.
OKAY. I'M GLAD WE FIND IT SO EASY.
15.00
THANKS. WHAT DO I OWE YOU?
IS A PRESENT. IS FOR NOTHING.
THANK YOU.
SEXTON, SAY THANK YOU TO THE NICE MAN.
YOU PEOPLE JUST DON'T DO THAT. I MEAN, NEW YORK CAB DRIVERS JUST DON'T GIVE FREE RIDES. I DON'T GET IT.
HER, I LIKE.
YOU, I DON'T LIKE. SO YOU CAN GIVE ME THE TIP. TWO BUCKS.
UM. WHY DO YOU HAVE A BULB OF GARLIC HANGING FROM YOUR MIRROR?
IT KEEP BAD THINGS AWAY.

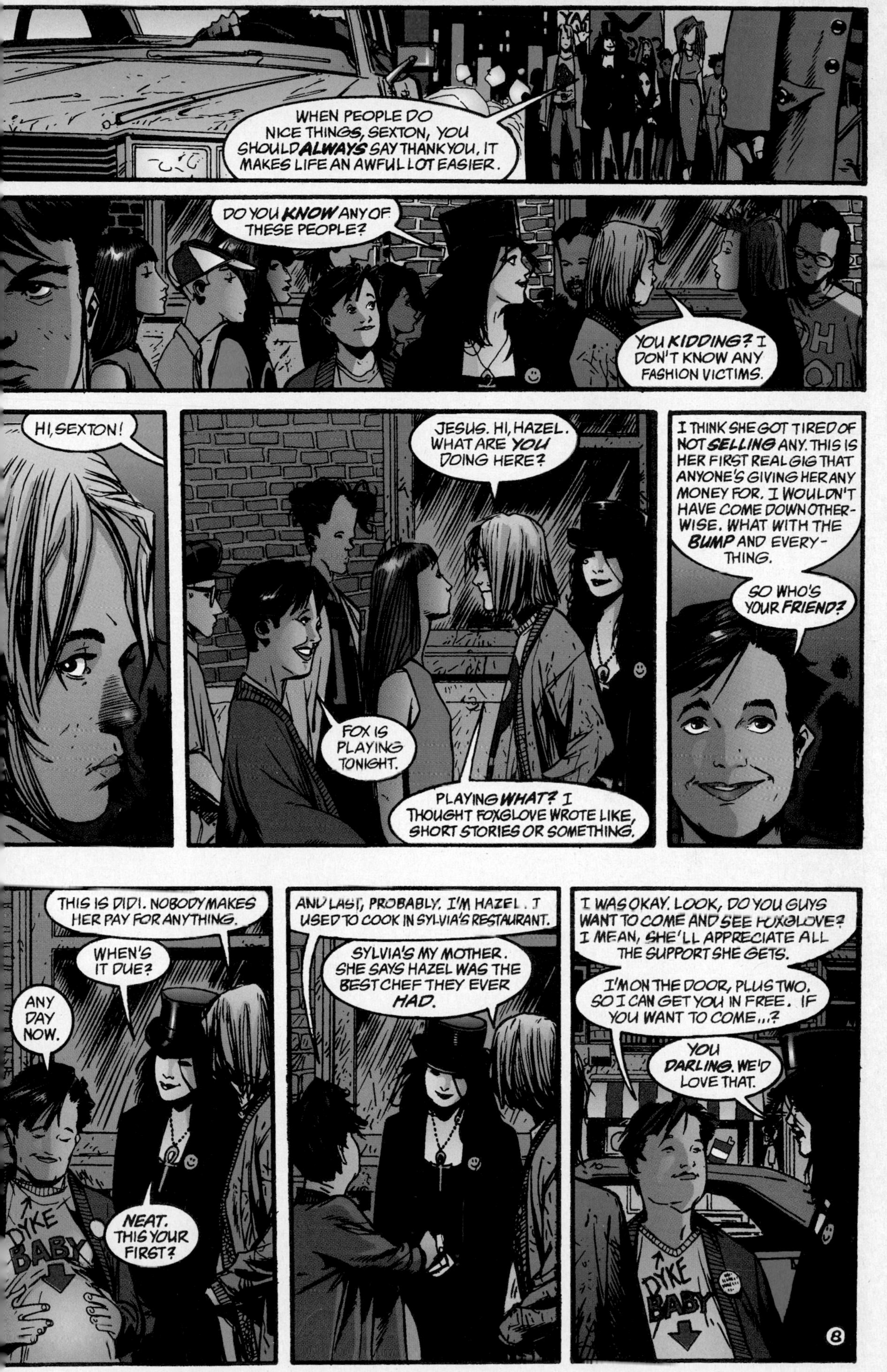
WHEN PEOPLE DO NICE THINGS, SEXTON, YOU SHOULD ALWAYS SAY THANK YOU. IT MAKES LIFE AN AWFUL LOT EASIER.
DO YOU KNOW ANY OF THESE PEOPLE?
YOU KIDDING? I DON'T KNOW ANY FASHION VICTIMS.
HI, SEXTON!
JESUS. HI, HAZEL. WHAT ARE YOU DOING HERE?
FOX IS PLAYING TONIGHT.
PLAYING WHAT? I THOUGHT FOXGLOVE WROTE LIKE, SHORT STORIES OR SOMETHING.
I THINK SHE GOT TIRED OF NOT SELLING ANY. THIS IS HER FIRST REAL GIG THAT ANYONE'S GIVING HER ANY MONEY FOR. I WOULDN'T HAVE COME DOWN OTHERWISE. WHAT WITH THE BUMP AND EVERYTHING.
SO WHO'S YOUR FRIEND?
THIS IS DIDI. NOBODY MAKES HER PAY FOR ANYTHING.
WHEN'S IT DUE?
ANY DAY NOW.
NEAT. THIS YOUR FIRST?
DYKE BABY
AND LAST, PROBABLY. I'M HAZEL. I USED TO COOK IN SYLVIA'S RESTAURANT.
SYLVIA'S MY MOTHER. SHE SAYS HAZEL WAS THE BEST CHEF THEY EVER HAD.
I WAS OKAY. LOOK, DO YOU GUYS WANT TO COME AND SEE FOXGLOVE? I MEAN, SHE'LL APPRECIATE ALL THE SUPPORT SHE GETS.
I'M ON THE DOOR, PLUS TWO, SO I CAN GET YOU IN FREE. IF YOU WANT TO COME...?
YOU DARLING. WE'D LOVE THAT.
DYKE BABY
8

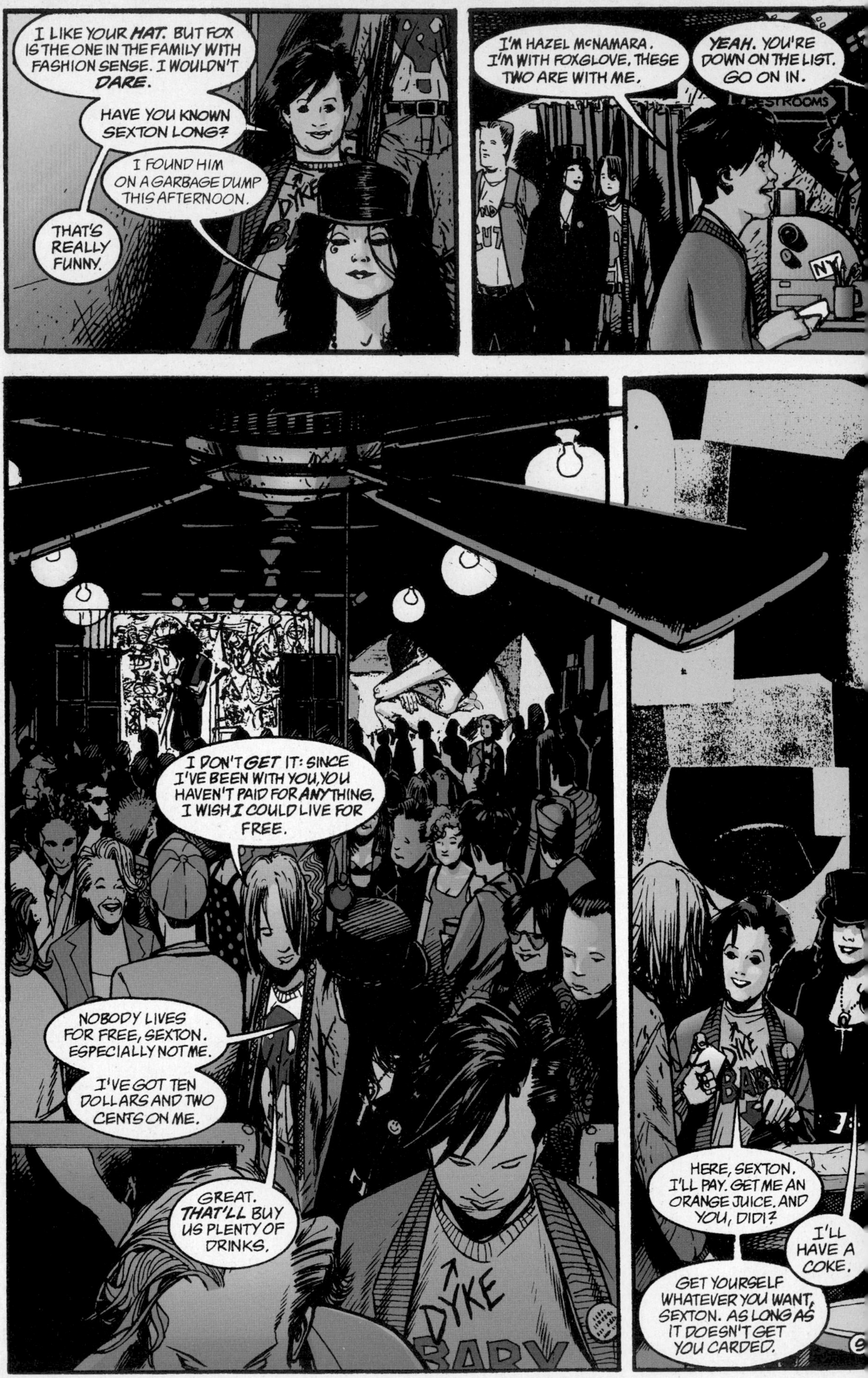

I LIKE YOUR HAT. BUT FOX IS THE ONE IN THE FAMILY WITH FASHION SENSE. I WOULDN'T DARE.
HAVE YOU KNOWN SEXTON LONG?
I FOUND HIM ON A GARBAGE DUMP THIS AFTERNOON.
THAT'S REALLY FUNNY.
I'M HAZEL McNAMARA. I'M WITH FOXGLOVE. THESE TWO ARE WITH ME.
YEAH. YOU'RE DOWN ON THE LIST. GO ON IN.
RESTROOMS
NY
I DON'T GET IT: SINCE I'VE BEEN WITH YOU, YOU HAVEN'T PAID FOR ANYTHING. I WISH I COULD LIVE FOR FREE.
NOBODY LIVES FOR FREE, SEXTON. ESPECIALLY NOT ME.
I'VE GOT TEN DOLLARS AND TWO CENTS ON ME.
GREAT. THAT'LL BUY US PLENTY OF DRINKS.
HERE, SEXTON. I'LL PAY. GET ME AN ORANGE JUICE. AND YOU, DIDI?
I'LL HAVE A COKE.
GET YOURSELF WHATEVER YOU WANT, SEXTON. AS LONG AS IT DOESN'T GET YOU CARDED.

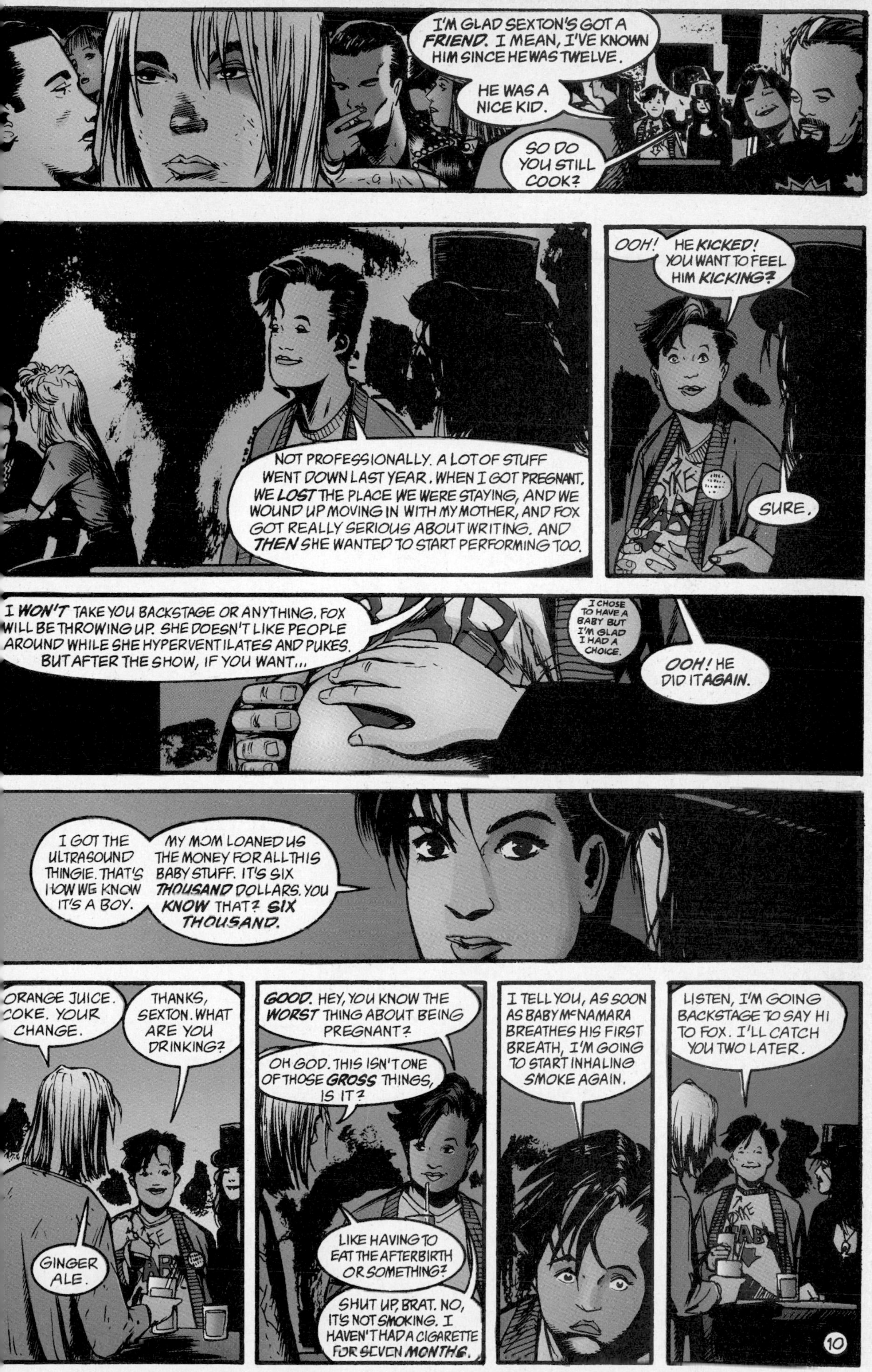
I'M GLAD SEXTON'S GOT A FRIEND. I MEAN, I'VE KNOWN HIM SINCE HE WAS TWELVE.
HE WAS A NICE KID.
SO DO YOU STILL COOK?
NOT PROFESSIONALLY. A LOT OF STUFF WENT DOWN LAST YEAR. WHEN I GOT PREGNANT, WE LOST THE PLACE WE WERE STAYING, AND WE WOUND UP MOVING IN WITH MY MOTHER, AND FOX GOT REALLY SERIOUS ABOUT WRITING. AND THEN SHE WANTED TO START PERFORMING TOO.
OOH!
HE KICKED! YOU WANT TO FEEL HIM KICKING?
SURE.
I WON'T TAKE YOU BACKSTAGE OR ANYTHING. FOX WILL BE THROWING UP. SHE DOESN'T LIKE PEOPLE AROUND WHILE SHE HYPERVENTILATES AND PUKES. BUT AFTER THE SHOW, IF YOU WANT...
I CHOSE TO HAVE A BABY BUT I'M GLAD I HAD A CHOICE.
OOH! HE DID IT AGAIN.
I GOT THE ULTRASOUND THINGIE. THAT'S HOW WE KNOW IT'S A BOY.
MY MOM LOANED US THE MONEY FOR ALL THIS BABY STUFF. IT'S SIX THOUSAND DOLLARS. YOU KNOW THAT? SIX THOUSAND.
ORANGE JUICE. COKE. YOUR CHANGE.
THANKS, SEXTON. WHAT ARE YOU DRINKING?
GINGER ALE.
GOOD. HEY, YOU KNOW THE WORST THING ABOUT BEING PREGNANT?
OH GOD. THIS ISN'T ONE OF THOSE GROSS THINGS, IS IT?
LIKE HAVING TO EAT THE AFTERBIRTH OR SOMETHING?
SHUT UP, BRAT. NO, IT'S NOT SMOKING. I HAVEN'T HAD A CIGARETTE FOR SEVEN MONTHS.
I TELL YOU, AS SOON AS BABY McNAMARA BREATHES HIS FIRST BREATH, I'M GOING TO START INHALING SMOKE AGAIN.
LISTEN, I'M GOING BACKSTAGE TO SAY HI TO FOX. I'LL CATCH YOU TWO LATER.

SHE'S OKAY. SYLVIA GOT PRETTY MAD AT HER WHEN SHE QUIT.

SHE'S REALLY *NICE.*

LISTEN-- THAT OLD CRAZY LADY...

MAD HETTIE?

YEAH. ARE YOU GOING TO CALL THE *POLICE,* OR ANYTHING?

OF COURSE NOT. I PROMISED HER WE'D GO AND FIND HER HEART.

I FIGURED YOU WERE, I DON'T KNOW, *HUMORING* HER. I MEAN, EVEN *YOU* SAID SHE'S MAD.

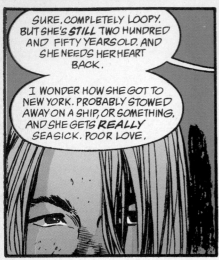

SURE, COMPLETELY LOOPY. BUT SHE'S *STILL* TWO HUNDRED AND FIFTY YEARS OLD. AND SHE NEEDS HER HEART BACK.

I WONDER HOW SHE GOT TO NEW YORK. PROBABLY STOWED AWAY ON A SHIP, OR SOMETHING, AND SHE GETS *REALLY* SEASICK. POOR LOVE.

I'M MEANT TO FEEL *SORRY* FOR A CRAZY OLD LADY WHO NEARLY CUT MY *NOSE* OFF?

IF YOU KNOW SOMEONE REALLY WELL IT'S HARD TO BE MAD AT THEM FOR VERY LONG.

AND YOU KNOW HER REALLY WELL.

I KNOW *EVERYBODY* REALLY WELL.

I...YOU *REALLY* PISS ME OFF. YOU *KNOW* THAT?

I DON'T KNOW WHY I'M HANGING OUT WITH YOU.

BECAUSE I *WANT* YOU TO. *SHUSH.* SHE'S STARTING.

HI, EVERYONE. WELCOME TO THE UNDERCUT. HER NAME'S FOXGLOVE. THIS IS HER FIRST GIG. TREAT HER KIND.

UH...GOOD EVENING, THIS SONG IS CALLED *DONNA'S DREAM.* IT'S ABOUT SOME PEOPLE I KNEW. AT LEAST ONE OF THEM IS DEAD.

11

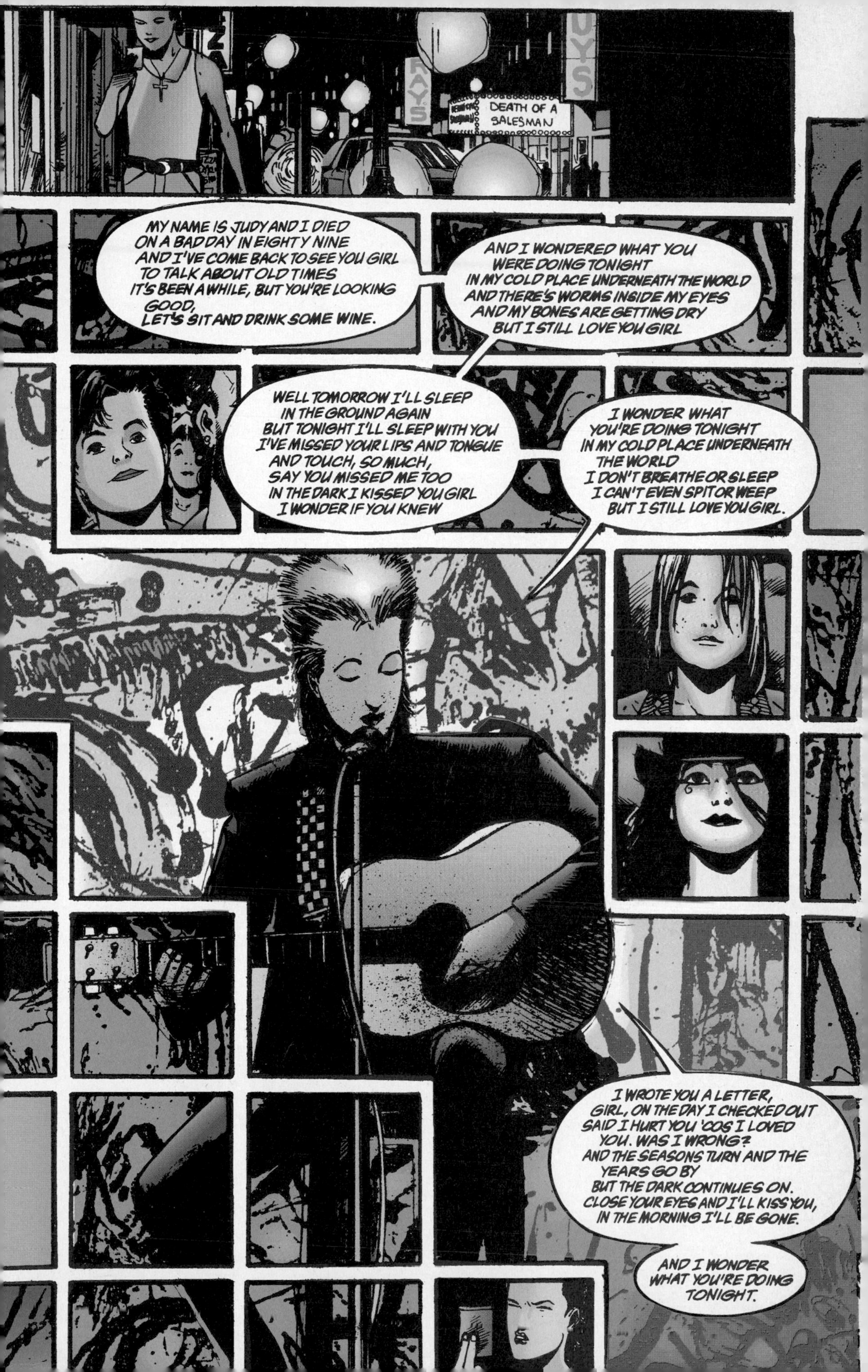

RAYS
UYS
DEATH OF A SALESMAN
MY NAME IS JUDY AND I DIED ON A BAD DAY IN EIGHTY NINE AND I'VE COME BACK TO SEE YOU GIRL TO TALK ABOUT OLD TIMES IT'S BEEN A WHILE, BUT YOU'RE LOOKING GOOD, LET'S SIT AND DRINK SOME WINE.
AND I WONDERED WHAT YOU WERE DOING TONIGHT IN MY COLD PLACE UNDERNEATH THE WORLD AND THERE'S WORMS INSIDE MY EYES AND MY BONES ARE GETTING DRY BUT I STILL LOVE YOU GIRL
WELL TOMORROW I'LL SLEEP IN THE GROUND AGAIN BUT TONIGHT I'LL SLEEP WITH YOU I'VE MISSED YOUR LIPS AND TONGUE AND TOUCH, SO MUCH, SAY YOU MISSED ME TOO IN THE DARK I KISSED YOU GIRL I WONDER IF YOU KNEW
I WONDER WHAT YOU'RE DOING TONIGHT IN MY COLD PLACE UNDERNEATH THE WORLD I DON'T BREATHE OR SLEEP I CAN'T EVEN SPIT OR WEEP BUT I STILL LOVE YOU GIRL.
I WROTE YOU A LETTER, GIRL, ON THE DAY I CHECKED OUT SAID I HURT YOU 'COS I LOVED YOU. WAS I WRONG? AND THE SEASONS TURN AND THE YEARS GO BY BUT THE DARK CONTINUES ON. CLOSE YOUR EYES AND I'LL KISS YOU, IN THE MORNING I'LL BE GONE.
AND I WONDER WHAT YOU'RE DOING TONIGHT.

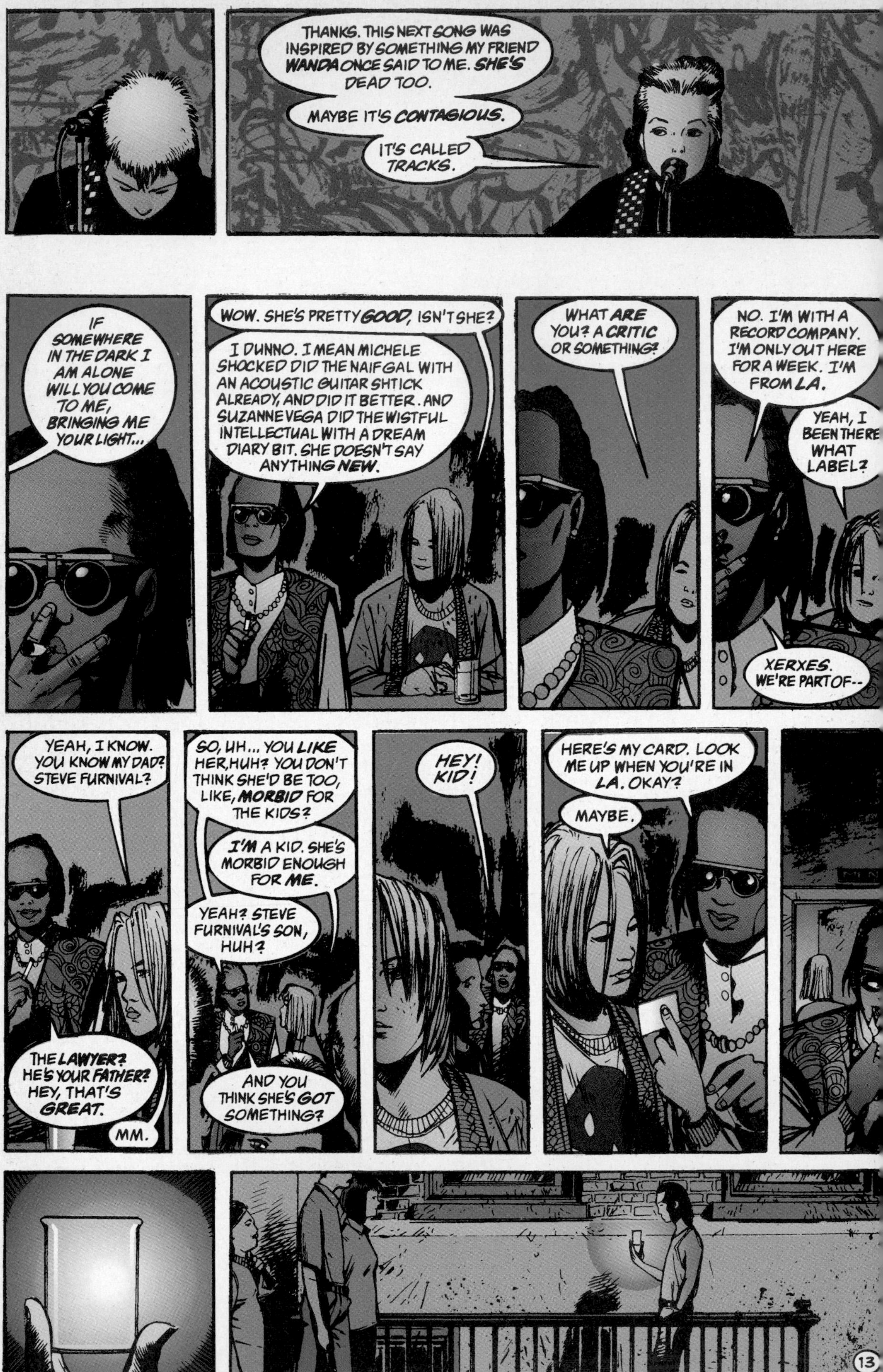
THANKS. THIS NEXT SONG WAS INSPIRED BY SOMETHING MY FRIEND WANDA ONCE SAID TO ME. SHE'S DEAD TOO.
MAYBE IT'S CONTAGIOUS.
IT'S CALLED TRACKS.
IF SOMEWHERE IN THE DARK I AM ALONE WILL YOU COME TO ME, BRINGING ME YOUR LIGHT...
WOW. SHE'S PRETTY GOOD, ISN'T SHE?
I DUNNO. I MEAN MICHELE SHOCKED DID THE NAIF GAL WITH AN ACOUSTIC GUITAR SHTICK ALREADY, AND DID IT BETTER. AND SUZANNE VEGA DID THE WISTFUL INTELLECTUAL WITH A DREAM DIARY BIT. SHE DOESN'T SAY ANYTHING NEW.
WHAT ARE YOU? A CRITIC OR SOMETHING?
NO. I'M WITH A RECORD COMPANY. I'M ONLY OUT HERE FOR A WEEK. I'M FROM LA.
YEAH, I BEEN THERE. WHAT LABEL?
XERXES. WE'RE PART OF--
YEAH, I KNOW. YOU KNOW MY DAD? STEVE FURNIVAL?
THE LAWYER? HE'S YOUR FATHER? HEY, THAT'S GREAT.
MM.
SO, UH... YOU LIKE HER, HUH? YOU DON'T THINK SHE'D BE TOO, LIKE, MORBID FOR THE KIDS?
I'M A KID. SHE'S MORBID ENOUGH FOR ME.
YEAH? STEVE FURNIVAL'S SON, HUH?
AND YOU THINK SHE'S GOT SOMETHING?
HEY! KID!
HERE'S MY CARD. LOOK ME UP WHEN YOU'RE IN LA. OKAY?
MAYBE.

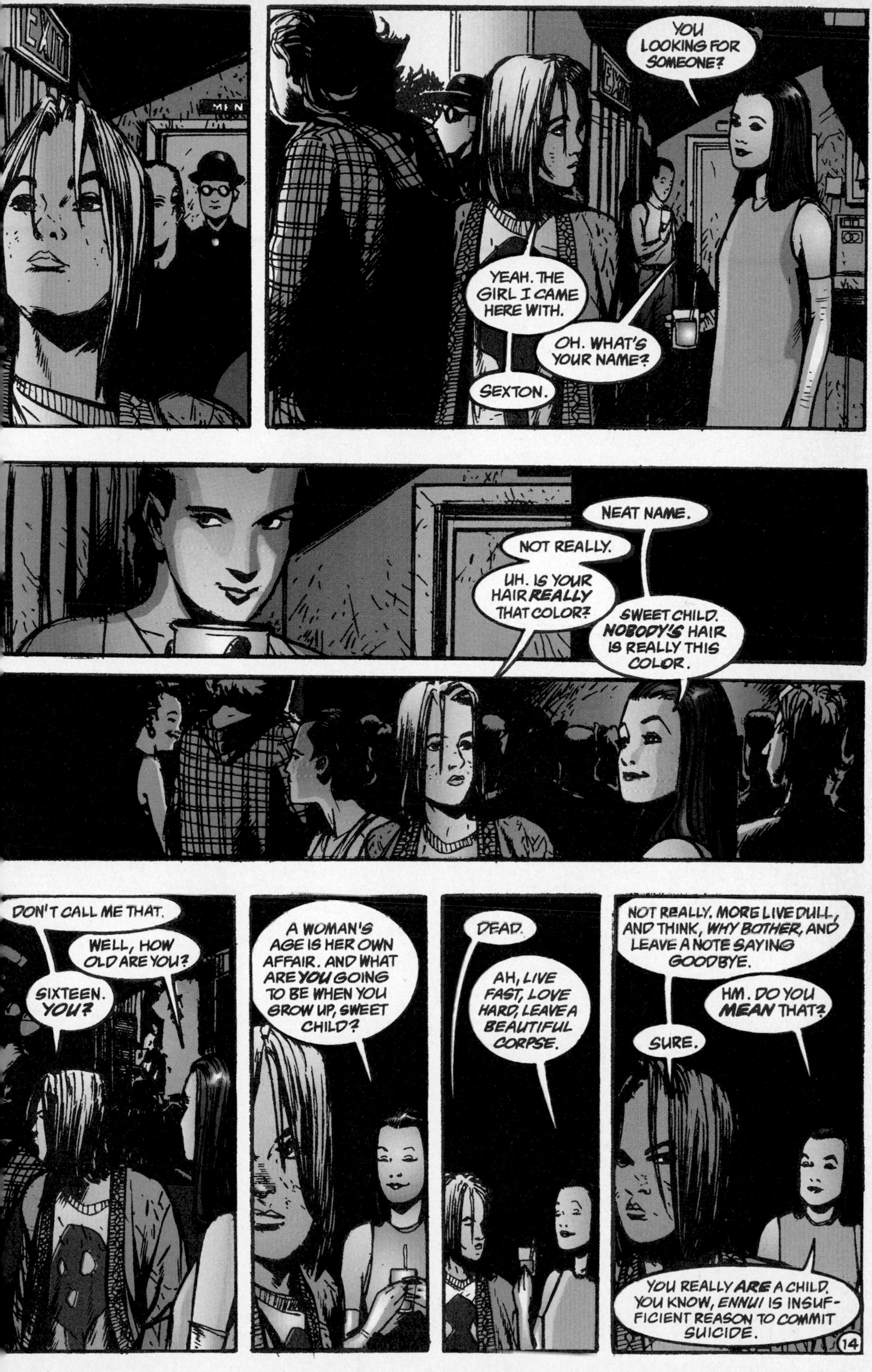

EXIT
MEN
YOU LOOKING FOR SOMEONE?
YEAH. THE GIRL I CAME HERE WITH.
OH. WHAT'S YOUR NAME?
SEXTON.
NEAT NAME.
NOT REALLY.
UH. IS YOUR HAIR REALLY THAT COLOR?
SWEET CHILD. NOBODY'S HAIR IS REALLY THIS COLOR.
DON'T CALL ME THAT.
WELL, HOW OLD ARE YOU?
SIXTEEN. YOU?
A WOMAN'S AGE IS HER OWN AFFAIR. AND WHAT ARE YOU GOING TO BE WHEN YOU GROW UP, SWEET CHILD?
DEAD.
AH, LIVE FAST, LOVE HARD, LEAVE A BEAUTIFUL CORPSE.
NOT REALLY. MORE LIVE DULL, AND THINK, WHY BOTHER, AND LEAVE A NOTE SAYING GOODBYE.
HM. DO YOU MEAN THAT?
SURE.
YOU REALLY ARE A CHILD. YOU KNOW, ENNUI IS INSUFFICIENT REASON TO COMMIT SUICIDE.

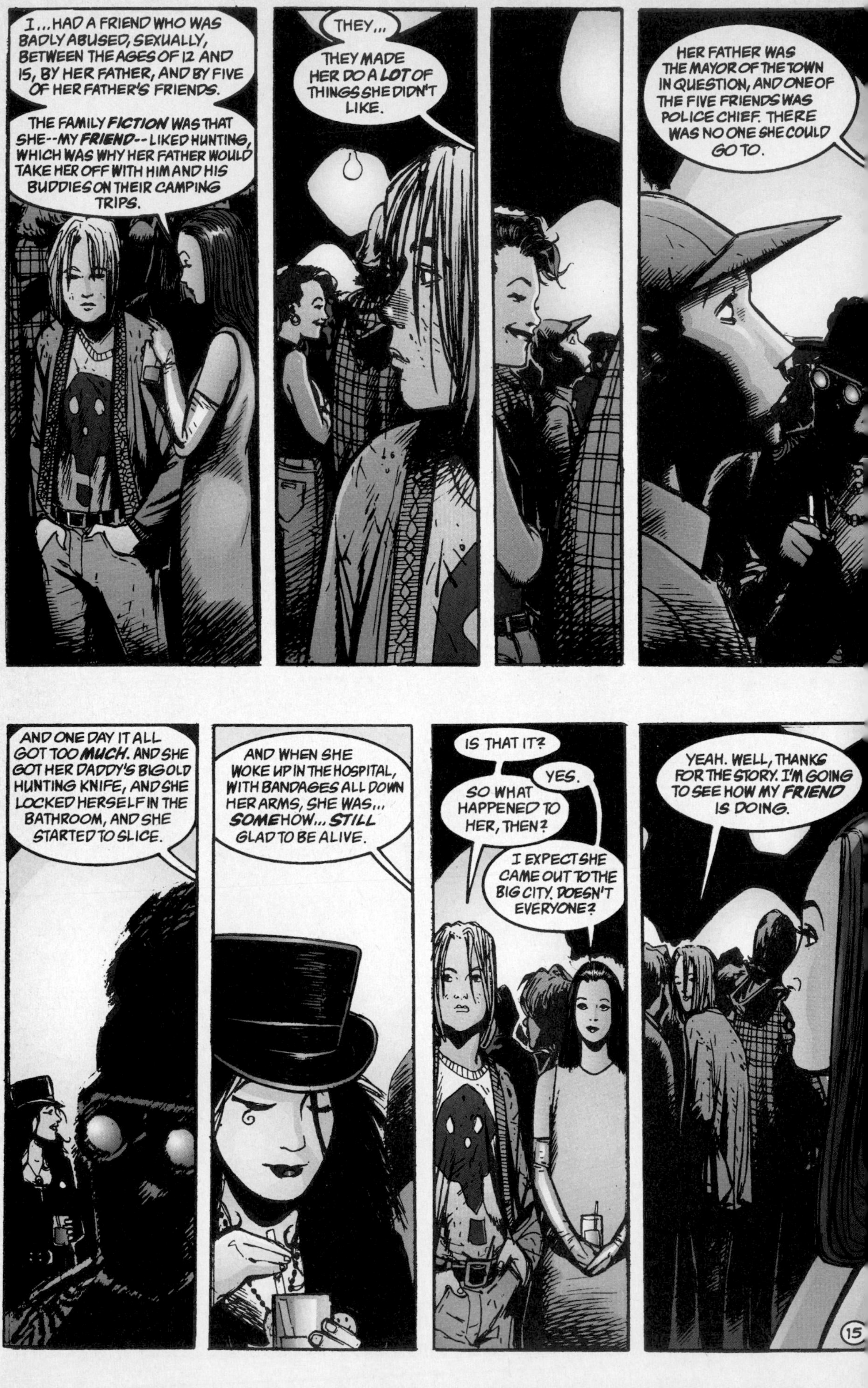
I... HAD A FRIEND WHO WAS BADLY ABUSED, SEXUALLY, BETWEEN THE AGES OF 12 AND 15, BY HER FATHER, AND BY FIVE OF HER FATHER'S FRIENDS.
THE FAMILY FICTION WAS THAT SHE--MY FRIEND--LIKED HUNTING, WHICH WAS WHY HER FATHER WOULD TAKE HER OFF WITH HIM AND HIS BUDDIES ON THEIR CAMPING TRIPS.
THEY...
THEY MADE HER DO A LOT OF THINGS SHE DIDN'T LIKE.
HER FATHER WAS THE MAYOR OF THE TOWN IN QUESTION, AND ONE OF THE FIVE FRIENDS WAS POLICE CHIEF. THERE WAS NO ONE SHE COULD GO TO.
AND ONE DAY IT ALL GOT TOO MUCH. AND SHE GOT HER DADDY'S BIG OLD HUNTING KNIFE, AND SHE LOCKED HERSELF IN THE BATHROOM, AND SHE STARTED TO SLICE.
AND WHEN SHE WOKE UP IN THE HOSPITAL, WITH BANDAGES ALL DOWN HER ARMS, SHE WAS... SOMEHOW... STILL GLAD TO BE ALIVE.
IS THAT IT?
YES.
SO WHAT HAPPENED TO HER, THEN?
I EXPECT SHE CAME OUT TO THE BIG CITY. DOESN'T EVERYONE?
YEAH. WELL, THANKS FOR THE STORY. I'M GOING TO SEE HOW MY FRIEND IS DOING.

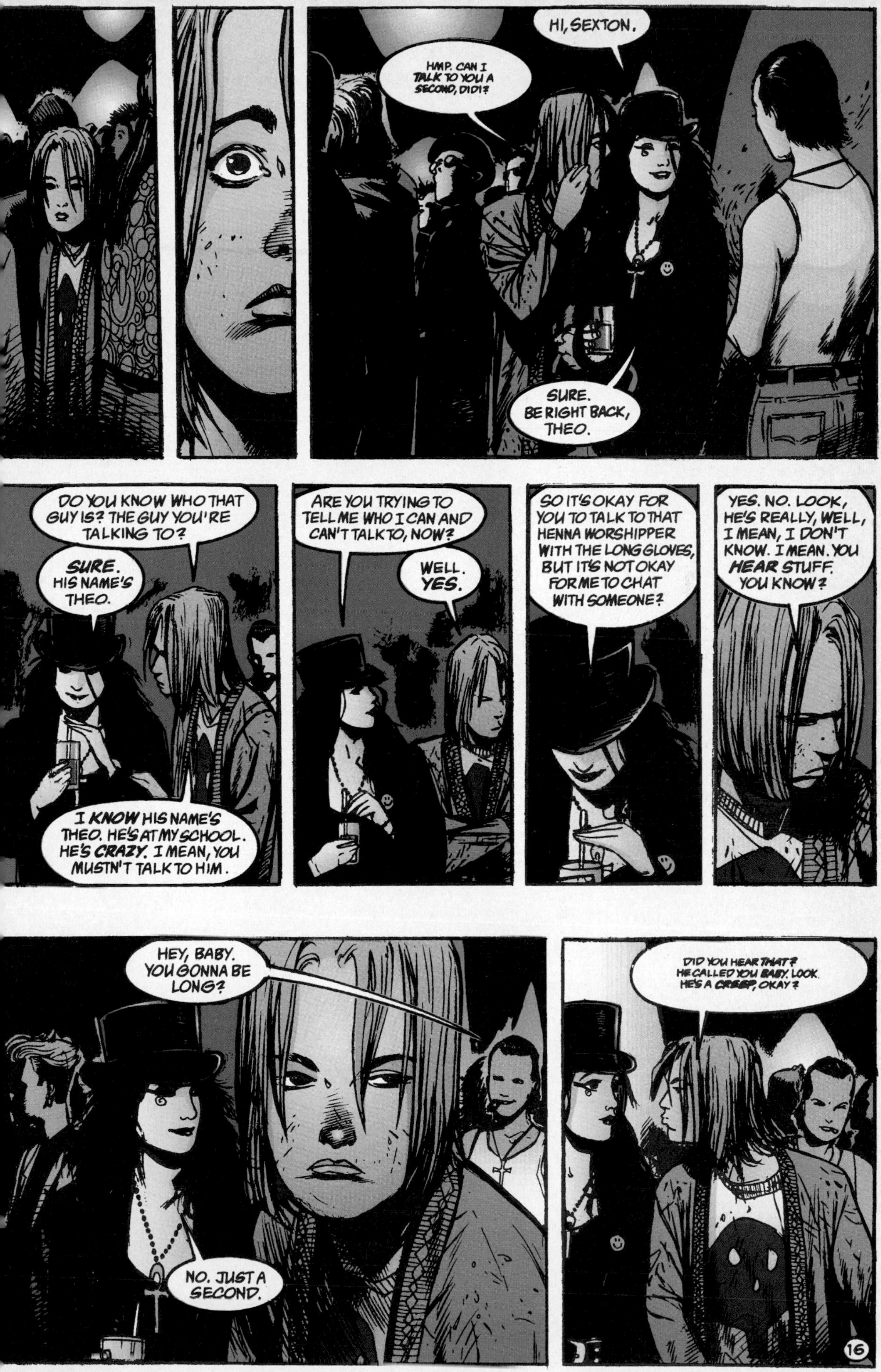
HI, SEXTON.
HMP. CAN I TALK TO YOU A SECOND, DIDI?
SURE. BE RIGHT BACK, THEO.
DO YOU KNOW WHO THAT GUY IS? THE GUY YOU'RE TALKING TO?
SURE. HIS NAME'S THEO.
I KNOW HIS NAME'S THEO. HE'S AT MY SCHOOL. HE'S CRAZY. I MEAN, YOU MUSTN'T TALK TO HIM.
ARE YOU TRYING TO TELL ME WHO I CAN AND CAN'T TALK TO, NOW?
WELL. YES.
SO IT'S OKAY FOR YOU TO TALK TO THAT HENNA WORSHIPPER WITH THE LONG GLOVES, BUT IT'S NOT OKAY FOR ME TO CHAT WITH SOMEONE?
YES. NO. LOOK, HE'S REALLY, WELL, I MEAN, I DON'T KNOW. I MEAN. YOU HEAR STUFF. YOU KNOW?
HEY, BABY. YOU GONNA BE LONG?
NO. JUST A SECOND.
DID YOU HEAR THAT? HE CALLED YOU BABY. LOOK. HE'S A CREEP, OKAY?
16

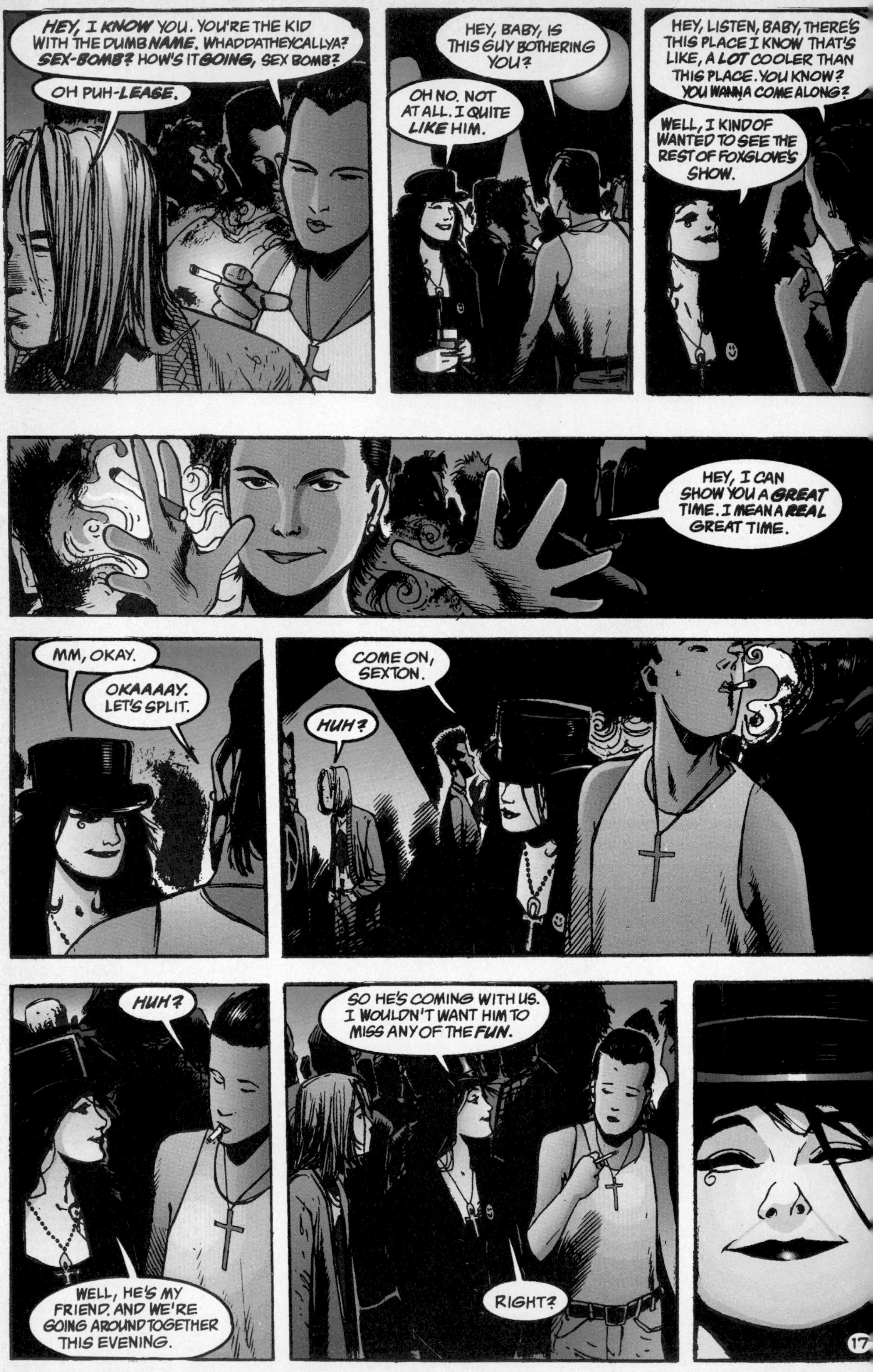
HEY, I KNOW YOU. YOU'RE THE KID WITH THE DUMB NAME. WHADDATHEYCALLYA? SEX-BOMB? HOW'S IT GOING, SEX BOMB?
OH PUH-LEASE.
HEY, BABY, IS THIS GUY BOTHERING YOU?
OH NO. NOT AT ALL. I QUITE LIKE HIM.
HEY, LISTEN, BABY, THERE'S THIS PLACE I KNOW THAT'S LIKE, A LOT COOLER THAN THIS PLACE. YOU KNOW? YOU WANNA COME ALONG?
WELL, I KIND OF WANTED TO SEE THE REST OF FOXGLOVE'S SHOW.
HEY, I CAN SHOW YOU A GREAT TIME. I MEAN A REAL GREAT TIME.
MM, OKAY.
OKAAAAY. LET'S SPLIT.
COME ON, SEXTON.
HUH?
HUH?
WELL, HE'S MY FRIEND. AND WE'RE GOING AROUND TOGETHER THIS EVENING.
SO HE'S COMING WITH US. I WOULDN'T WANT HIM TO MISS ANY OF THE FUN.
RIGHT?

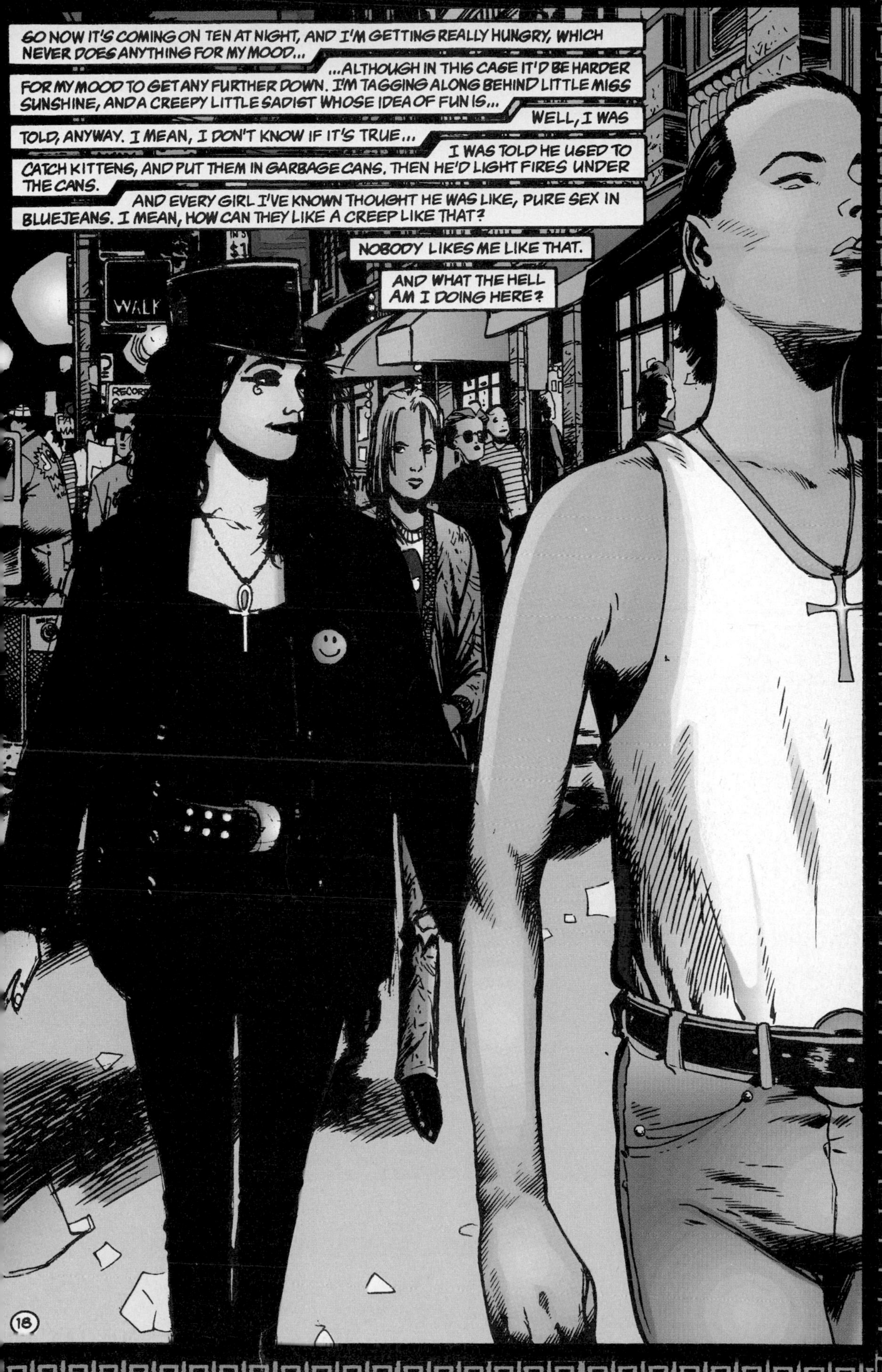

SO NOW IT'S COMING ON TEN AT NIGHT, AND I'M GETTING REALLY HUNGRY, WHICH NEVER DOES ANYTHING FOR MY MOOD...
...ALTHOUGH IN THIS CASE IT'D BE HARDER FOR MY MOOD TO GET ANY FURTHER DOWN. I'M TAGGING ALONG BEHIND LITTLE MISS SUNSHINE, AND A CREEPY LITTLE SADIST WHOSE IDEA OF FUN IS...
WELL, I WAS TOLD, ANYWAY. I MEAN, I DON'T KNOW IF IT'S TRUE...
I WAS TOLD HE USED TO CATCH KITTENS, AND PUT THEM IN GARBAGE CANS. THEN HE'D LIGHT FIRES UNDER THE CANS.
AND EVERY GIRL I'VE KNOWN THOUGHT HE WAS LIKE, PURE SEX IN BLUEJEANS. I MEAN, HOW CAN THEY LIKE A CREEP LIKE THAT?
NOBODY LIKES ME LIKE THAT.
AND WHAT THE HELL AM I DOING HERE?
WALK

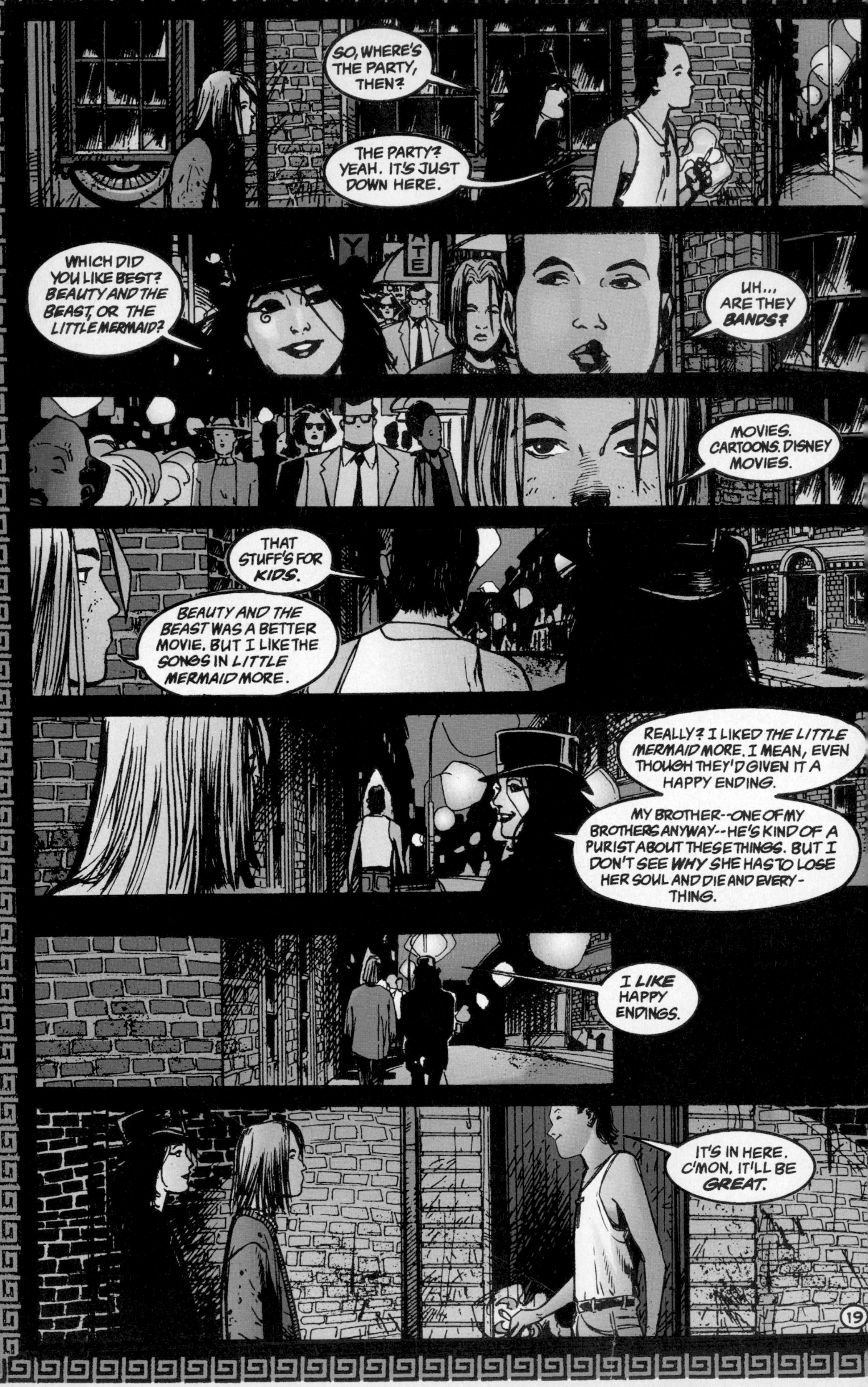
SO, WHERE'S THE PARTY, THEN?
THE PARTY? YEAH. IT'S JUST DOWN HERE.
WHICH DID YOU LIKE BEST? BEAUTY AND THE BEAST, OR THE LITTLE MERMAID?
UH... ARE THEY BANDS?
MOVIES. CARTOONS. DISNEY MOVIES.
THAT STUFF'S FOR KIDS.
BEAUTY AND THE BEAST WAS A BETTER MOVIE. BUT I LIKE THE SONGS IN LITTLE MERMAID MORE.
REALLY? I LIKED THE LITTLE MERMAID MORE. I MEAN, EVEN THOUGH THEY'D GIVEN IT A HAPPY ENDING.
MY BROTHER--ONE OF MY BROTHERS ANYWAY--HE'S KIND OF A PURIST ABOUT THESE THINGS. BUT I DON'T SEE WHY SHE HAS TO LOSE HER SOUL AND DIE AND EVERY-THING.
I LIKE HAPPY ENDINGS.
IT'S IN HERE. C'MON, IT'LL BE GREAT.
19

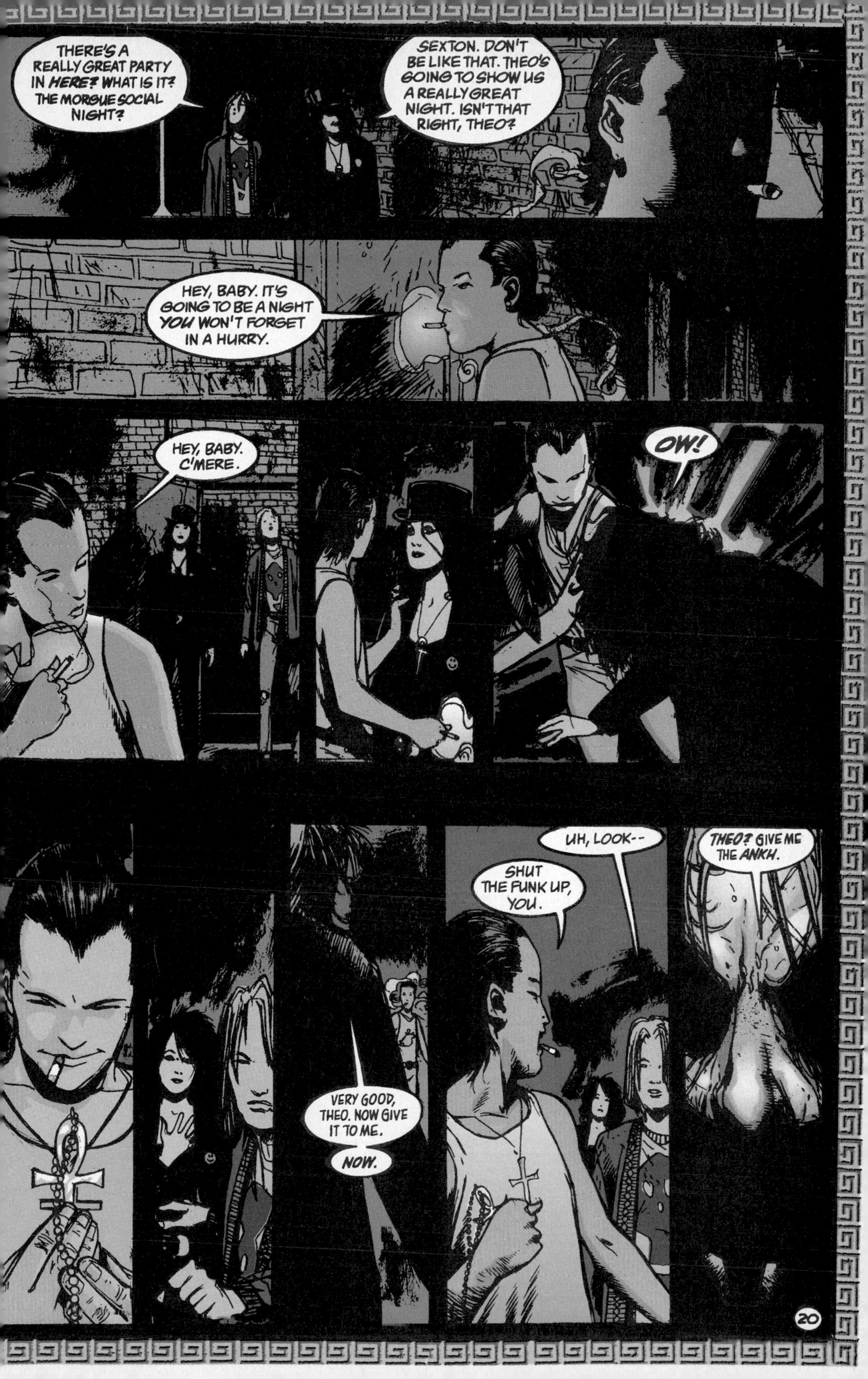
THERE'S A REALLY GREAT PARTY IN HERE? WHAT IS IT? THE MORGUE SOCIAL NIGHT?
SEXTON. DON'T BE LIKE THAT. THEO'S GOING TO SHOW US A REALLY GREAT NIGHT. ISN'T THAT RIGHT, THEO?
HEY, BABY. IT'S GOING TO BE A NIGHT YOU WON'T FORGET IN A HURRY.
HEY, BABY. C'MERE.
OW!
VERY GOOD, THEO. NOW GIVE IT TO ME.
NOW.
UH, LOOK--
SHUT THE FUNK UP, YOU.
THEO? GIVE ME THE ANKH.
20

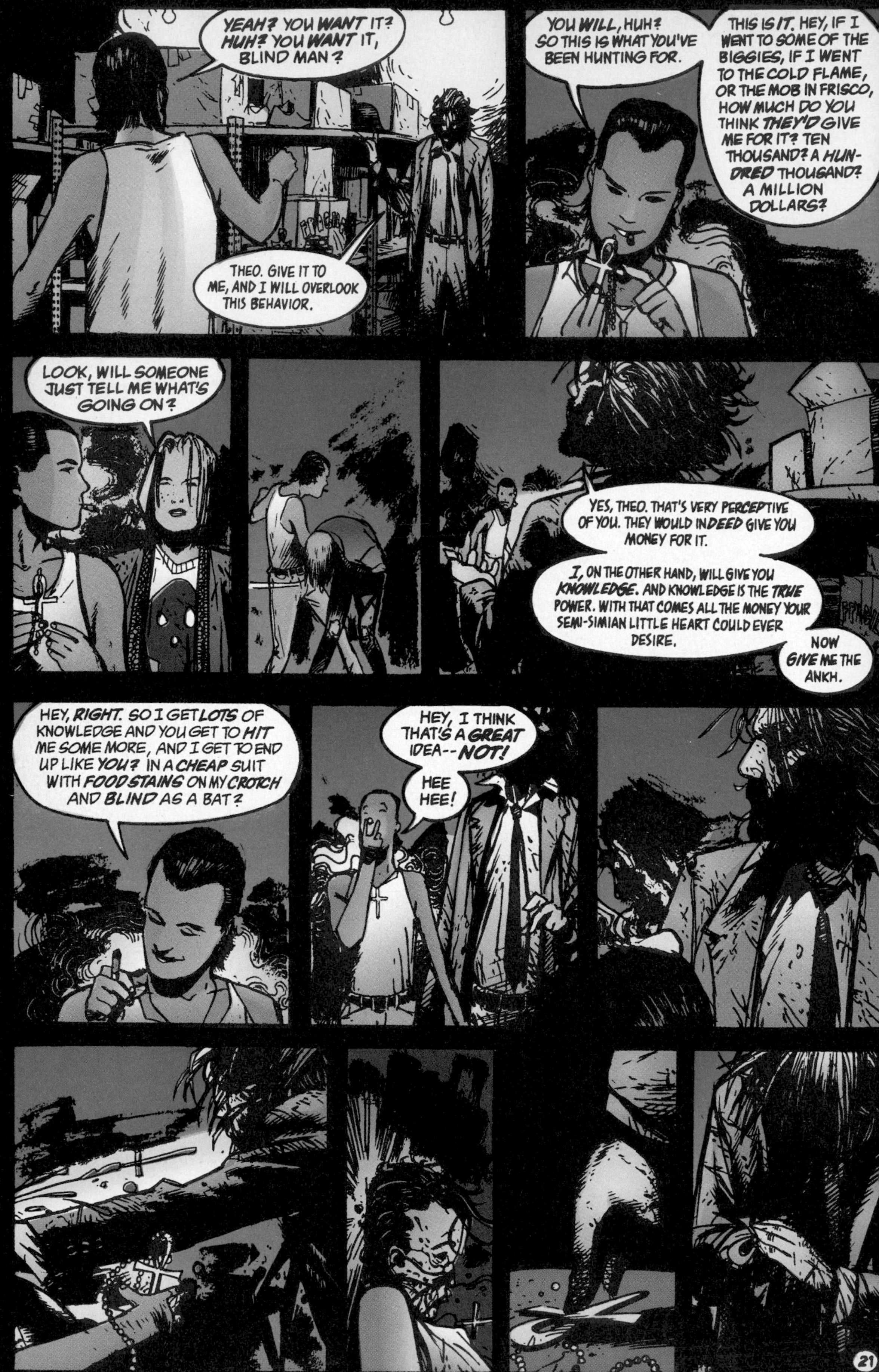
YEAH? YOU WANT IT? HUH? YOU WANT IT, BLIND MAN?
THEO. GIVE IT TO ME, AND I WILL OVERLOOK THIS BEHAVIOR.
YOU WILL, HUH? SO THIS IS WHAT YOU'VE BEEN HUNTING FOR.
THIS IS IT. HEY, IF I WENT TO SOME OF THE BIGGIES, IF I WENT TO THE COLD FLAME, OR THE MOB IN FRISCO, HOW MUCH DO YOU THINK THEY'D GIVE ME FOR IT? TEN THOUSAND? A HUNDRED THOUSAND? A MILLION DOLLARS?
LOOK, WILL SOMEONE JUST TELL ME WHAT'S GOING ON?
YES, THEO. THAT'S VERY PERCEPTIVE OF YOU. THEY WOULD INDEED GIVE YOU MONEY FOR IT.
I, ON THE OTHER HAND, WILL GIVE YOU KNOWLEDGE. AND KNOWLEDGE IS THE TRUE POWER. WITH THAT COMES ALL THE MONEY YOUR SEMI-SIMIAN LITTLE HEART COULD EVER DESIRE.
NOW GIVE ME THE ANKH.
HEY, RIGHT. SO I GET LOTS OF KNOWLEDGE AND YOU GET TO HIT ME SOME MORE, AND I GET TO END UP LIKE YOU? IN A CHEAP SUIT WITH FOOD STAINS ON MY CROTCH AND BLIND AS A BAT?
HEY, I THINK THAT'S A GREAT IDEA--NOT!
HEE HEE!

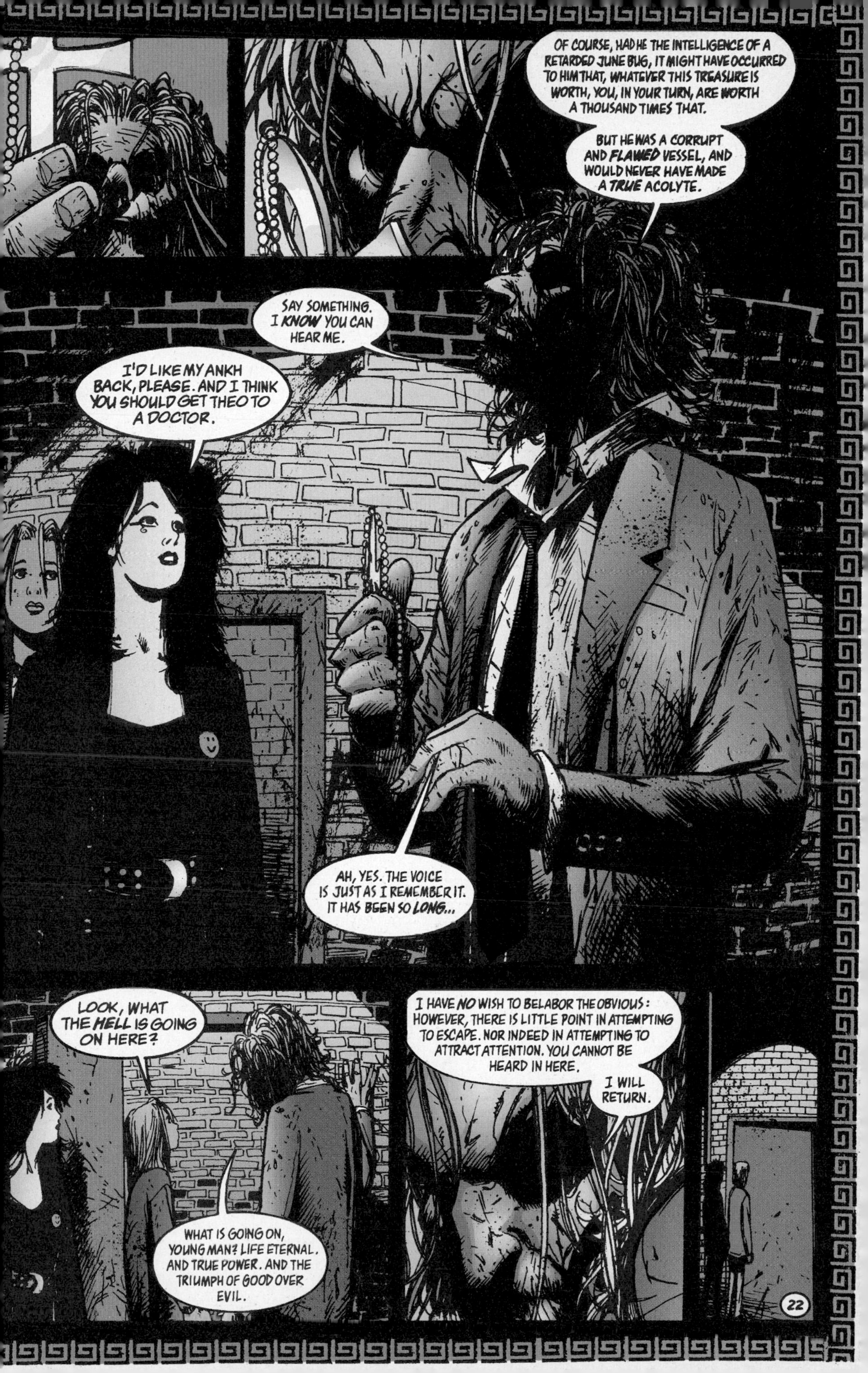

OF COURSE, HAD HE THE INTELLIGENCE OF A RETARDED JUNE BUG, IT MIGHT HAVE OCCURRED TO HIM THAT, WHATEVER THIS TREASURE IS WORTH, YOU, IN YOUR TURN, ARE WORTH A THOUSAND TIMES THAT.
BUT HE WAS A CORRUPT AND *FLAWED* VESSEL, AND WOULD NEVER HAVE MADE A *TRUE* ACOLYTE.
SAY SOMETHING. I *KNOW* YOU CAN HEAR ME.
I'D LIKE MY ANKH BACK, PLEASE. AND I THINK *YOU* SHOULD GET THEO TO A DOCTOR.
AH, YES. THE VOICE IS JUST AS I REMEMBER IT. IT HAS BEEN SO *LONG*...
LOOK, WHAT THE *HELL* IS GOING ON HERE?
WHAT IS GOING ON, YOUNG MAN? LIFE ETERNAL. AND TRUE POWER. AND THE TRIUMPH OF GOOD OVER EVIL.
I HAVE *NO* WISH TO BELABOR THE OBVIOUS: HOWEVER, THERE IS LITTLE POINT IN ATTEMPTING TO ESCAPE. NOR INDEED IN ATTEMPTING TO ATTRACT ATTENTION. YOU CANNOT BE HEARD IN HERE.
I WILL RETURN.

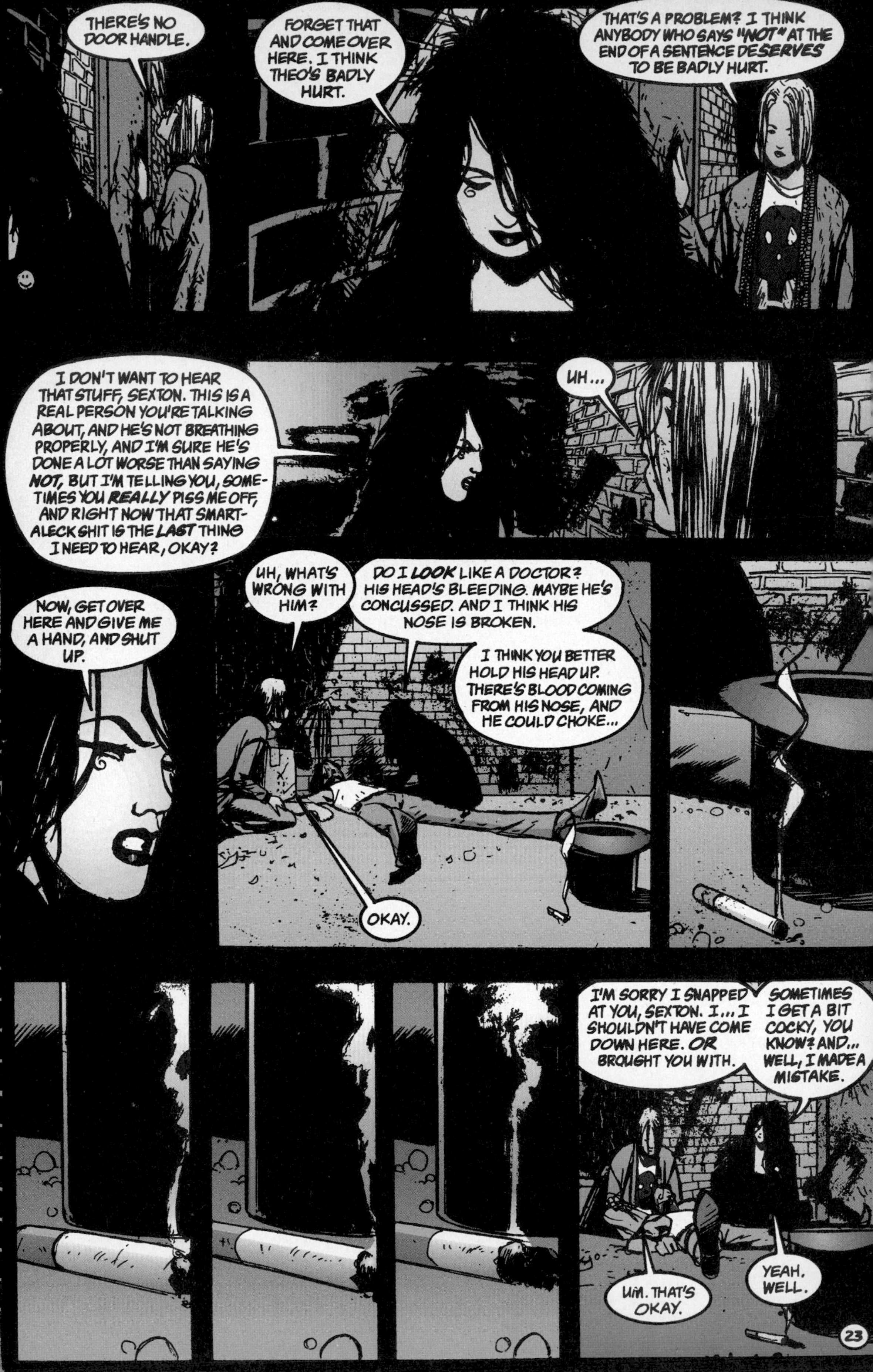
THERE'S NO DOOR HANDLE.
FORGET THAT AND COME OVER HERE. I THINK THEO'S BADLY HURT.
THAT'S A PROBLEM? I THINK ANYBODY WHO SAYS "NOT" AT THE END OF A SENTENCE DESERVES TO BE BADLY HURT.
I DON'T WANT TO HEAR THAT STUFF, SEXTON. THIS IS A REAL PERSON YOU'RE TALKING ABOUT, AND HE'S NOT BREATHING PROPERLY, AND I'M SURE HE'S DONE A LOT WORSE THAN SAYING NOT, BUT I'M TELLING YOU, SOMETIMES YOU REALLY PISS ME OFF, AND RIGHT NOW THAT SMART-ALECK SHIT IS THE LAST THING I NEED TO HEAR, OKAY?
UH...
NOW, GET OVER HERE AND GIVE ME A HAND, AND SHUT UP.
UH, WHAT'S WRONG WITH HIM?
DO I LOOK LIKE A DOCTOR? HIS HEAD'S BLEEDING. MAYBE HE'S CONCUSSED. AND I THINK HIS NOSE IS BROKEN.
I THINK YOU BETTER HOLD HIS HEAD UP. THERE'S BLOOD COMING FROM HIS NOSE, AND HE COULD CHOKE...
OKAY.
I'M SORRY I SNAPPED AT YOU, SEXTON. I... I SHOULDN'T HAVE COME DOWN HERE. OR BROUGHT YOU WITH.
SOMETIMES I GET A BIT COCKY, YOU KNOW? AND... WELL, I MADE A MISTAKE.
UM. THAT'S OKAY.
YEAH. WELL.

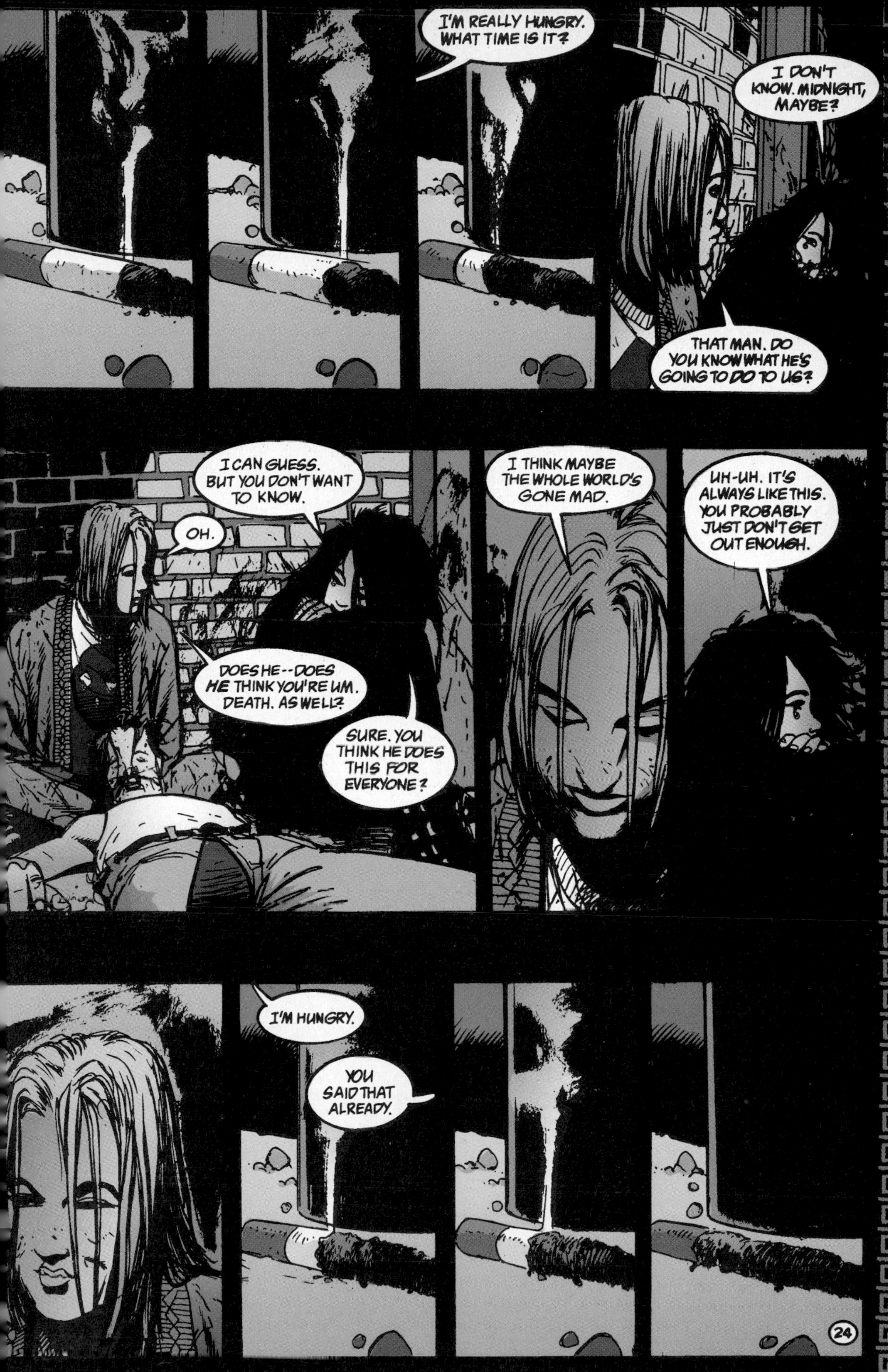
I'M REALLY HUNGRY. WHAT TIME IS IT?
I DON'T KNOW. MIDNIGHT, MAYBE?
THAT MAN. DO YOU KNOW WHAT HE'S GOING TO DO TO US?
I CAN GUESS. BUT YOU DON'T WANT TO KNOW.
OH.
DOES HE--DOES HE THINK YOU'RE UM. DEATH. AS WELL?
SURE. YOU THINK HE DOES THIS FOR EVERYONE?
I THINK MAYBE THE WHOLE WORLD'S GONE MAD.
UH-UH. IT'S ALWAYS LIKE THIS. YOU PROBABLY JUST DON'T GET OUT ENOUGH.
I'M HUNGRY.
YOU SAID THAT ALREADY.
24

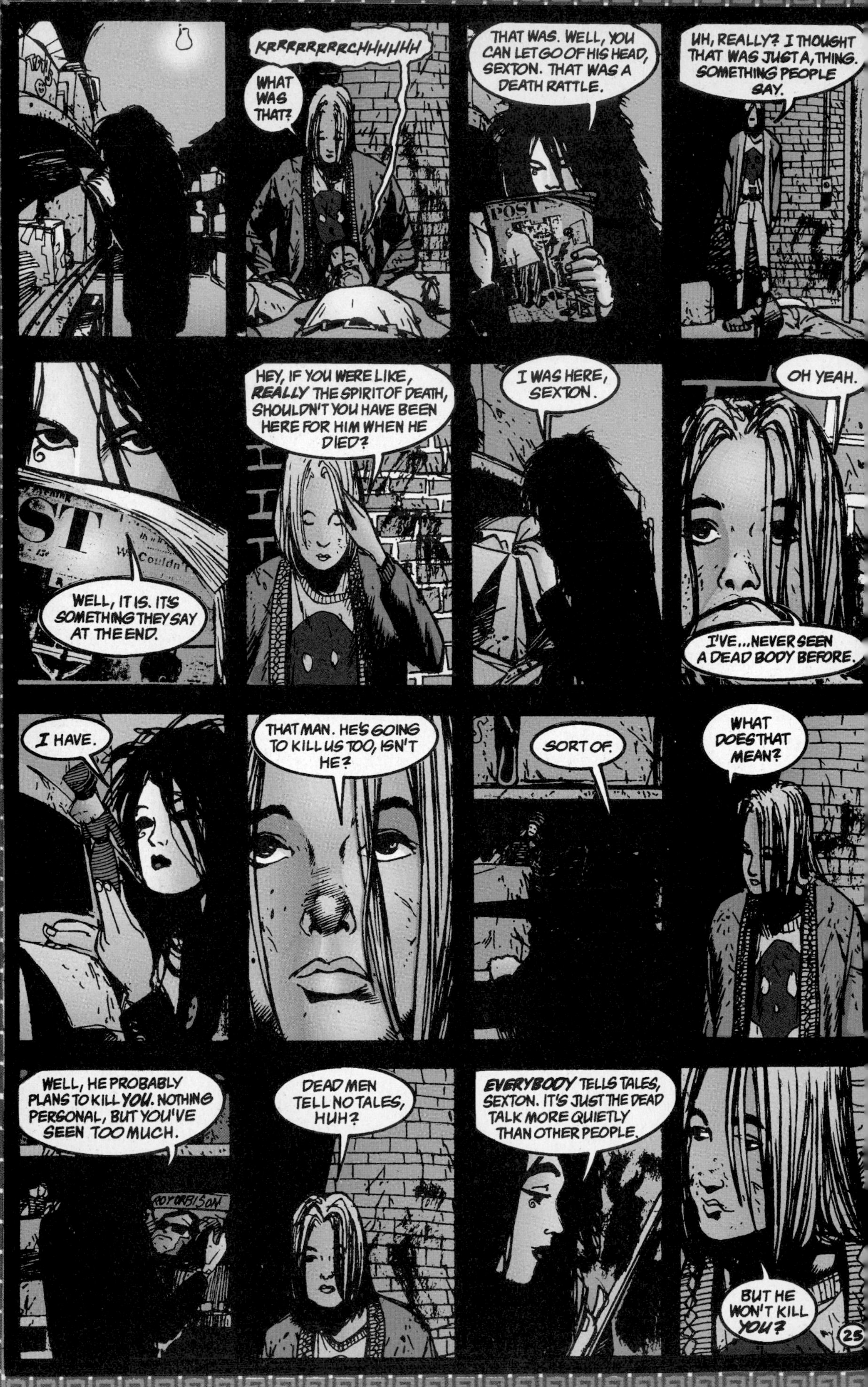

KRRRRRRRRCHHHHHH
WHAT WAS THAT?
THAT WAS. WELL, YOU CAN LET GO OF HIS HEAD, SEXTON. THAT WAS A DEATH RATTLE.
UH, REALLY? I THOUGHT THAT WAS JUST A, THING. SOMETHING PEOPLE SAY.
POST
WELL, IT IS. IT'S SOMETHING THEY SAY AT THE END.
HEY, IF YOU WERE LIKE, REALLY THE SPIRIT OF DEATH, SHOULDN'T YOU HAVE BEEN HERE FOR HIM WHEN HE DIED?
I WAS HERE, SEXTON.
OH YEAH.
I'VE...NEVER SEEN A DEAD BODY BEFORE.
I HAVE.
THAT MAN. HE'S GOING TO KILL US TOO, ISN'T HE?
SORT OF.
WHAT DOES THAT MEAN?
WELL, HE PROBABLY PLANS TO KILL YOU. NOTHING PERSONAL, BUT YOU'VE SEEN TOO MUCH.
ROY ORBISON
DEAD MEN TELL NO TALES, HUH?
EVERYBODY TELLS TALES, SEXTON. IT'S JUST THE DEAD TALK MORE QUIETLY THAN OTHER PEOPLE.
BUT HE WON'T KILL YOU?

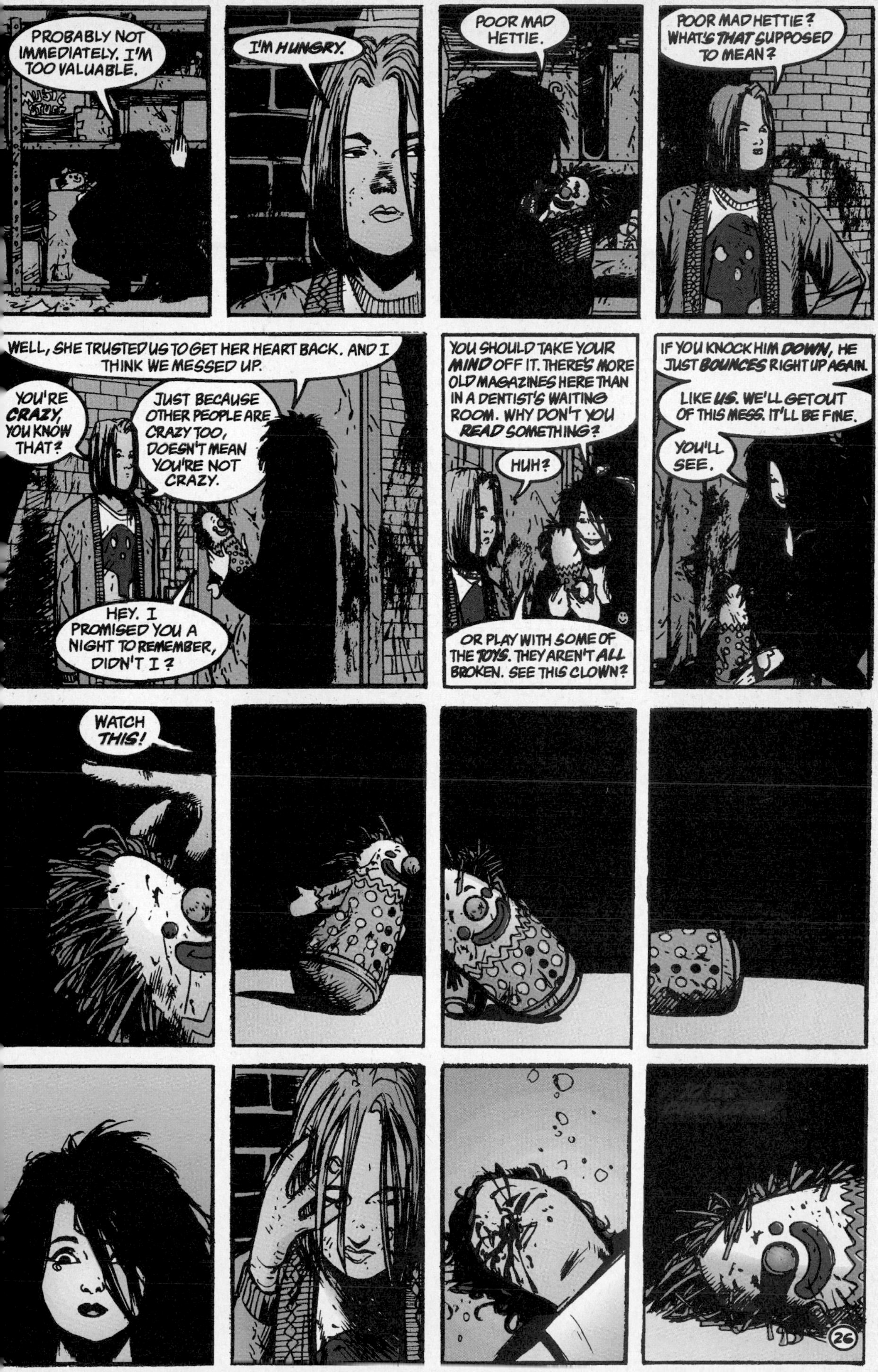
PROBABLY NOT IMMEDIATELY. I'M TOO VALUABLE.
I'M HUNGRY.
POOR MAD HETTIE.
POOR MAD HETTIE? WHAT'S THAT SUPPOSED TO MEAN?
WELL, SHE TRUSTED US TO GET HER HEART BACK. AND I THINK WE MESSED UP.
YOU'RE CRAZY, YOU KNOW THAT?
JUST BECAUSE OTHER PEOPLE ARE CRAZY TOO, DOESN'T MEAN YOU'RE NOT CRAZY.
HEY. I PROMISED YOU A NIGHT TO REMEMBER, DIDN'T I?
YOU SHOULD TAKE YOUR MIND OFF IT. THERE'S MORE OLD MAGAZINES HERE THAN IN A DENTIST'S WAITING ROOM. WHY DON'T YOU READ SOMETHING?
HUH?
OR PLAY WITH SOME OF THE TOYS. THEY AREN'T ALL BROKEN. SEE THIS CLOWN?
IF YOU KNOCK HIM DOWN, HE JUST BOUNCES RIGHT UP AGAIN.
LIKE US. WE'LL GET OUT OF THIS MESS. IT'LL BE FINE.
YOU'LL SEE.
WATCH THIS!

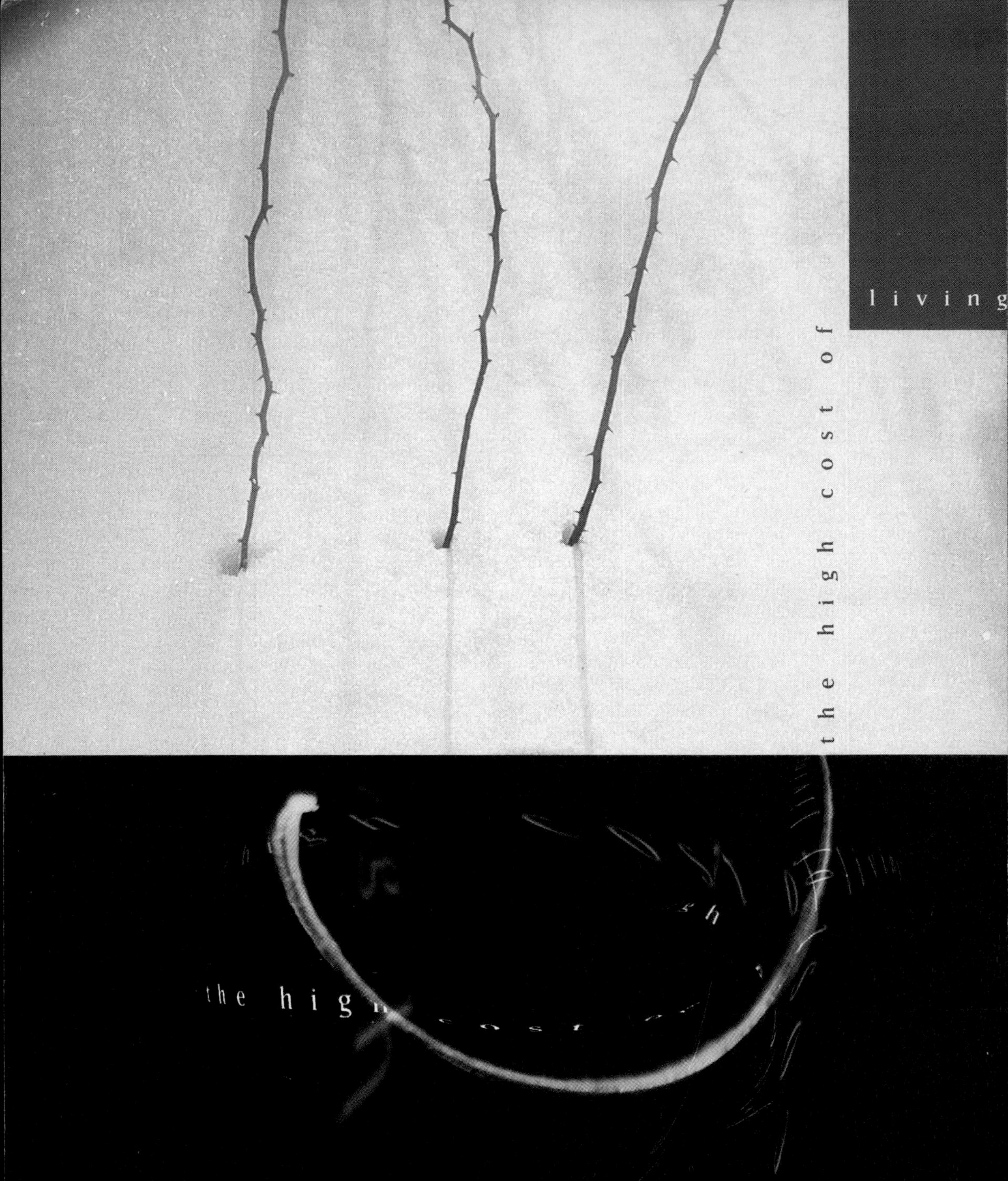

living

the high cost of

the high cost of

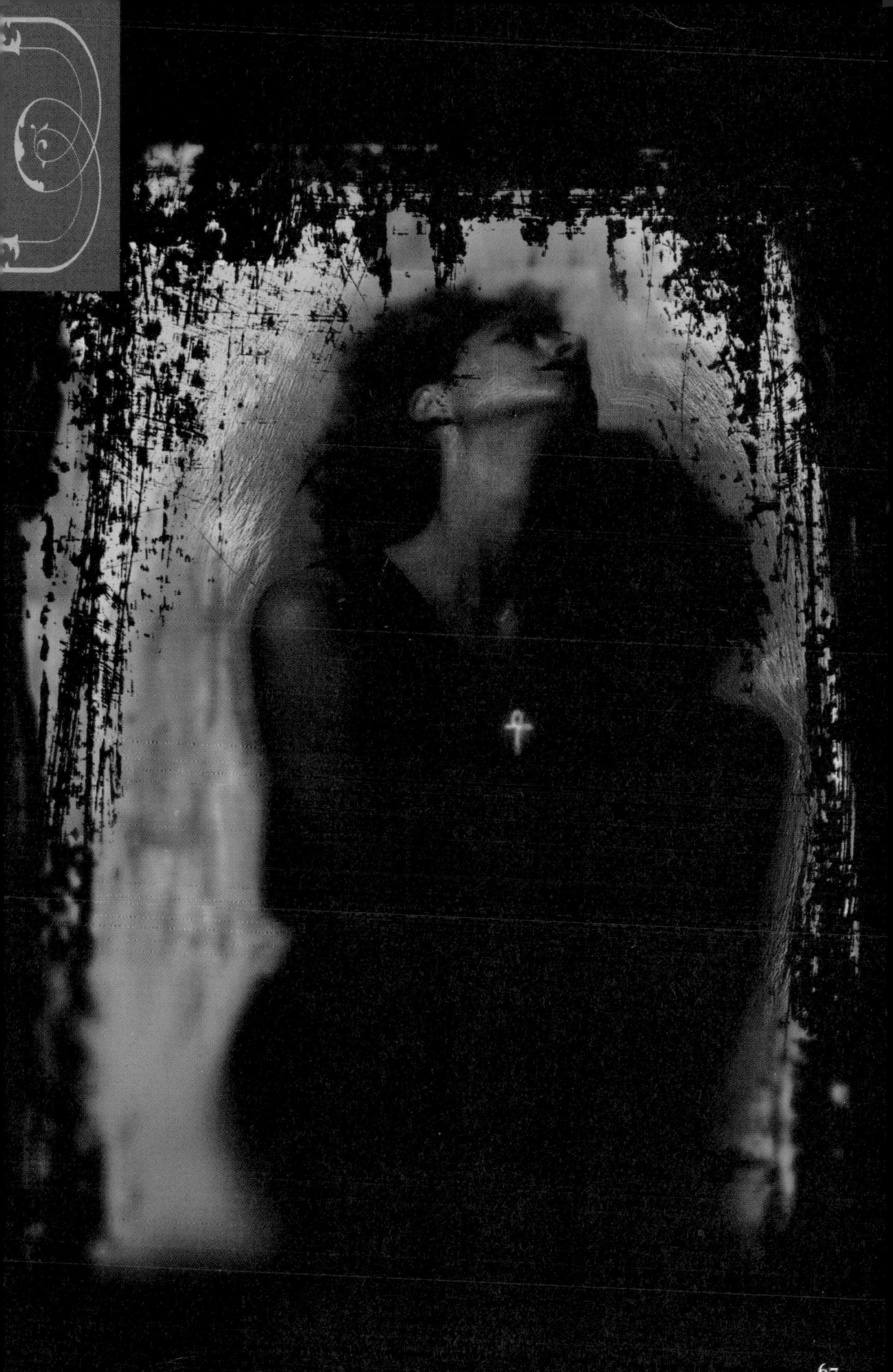

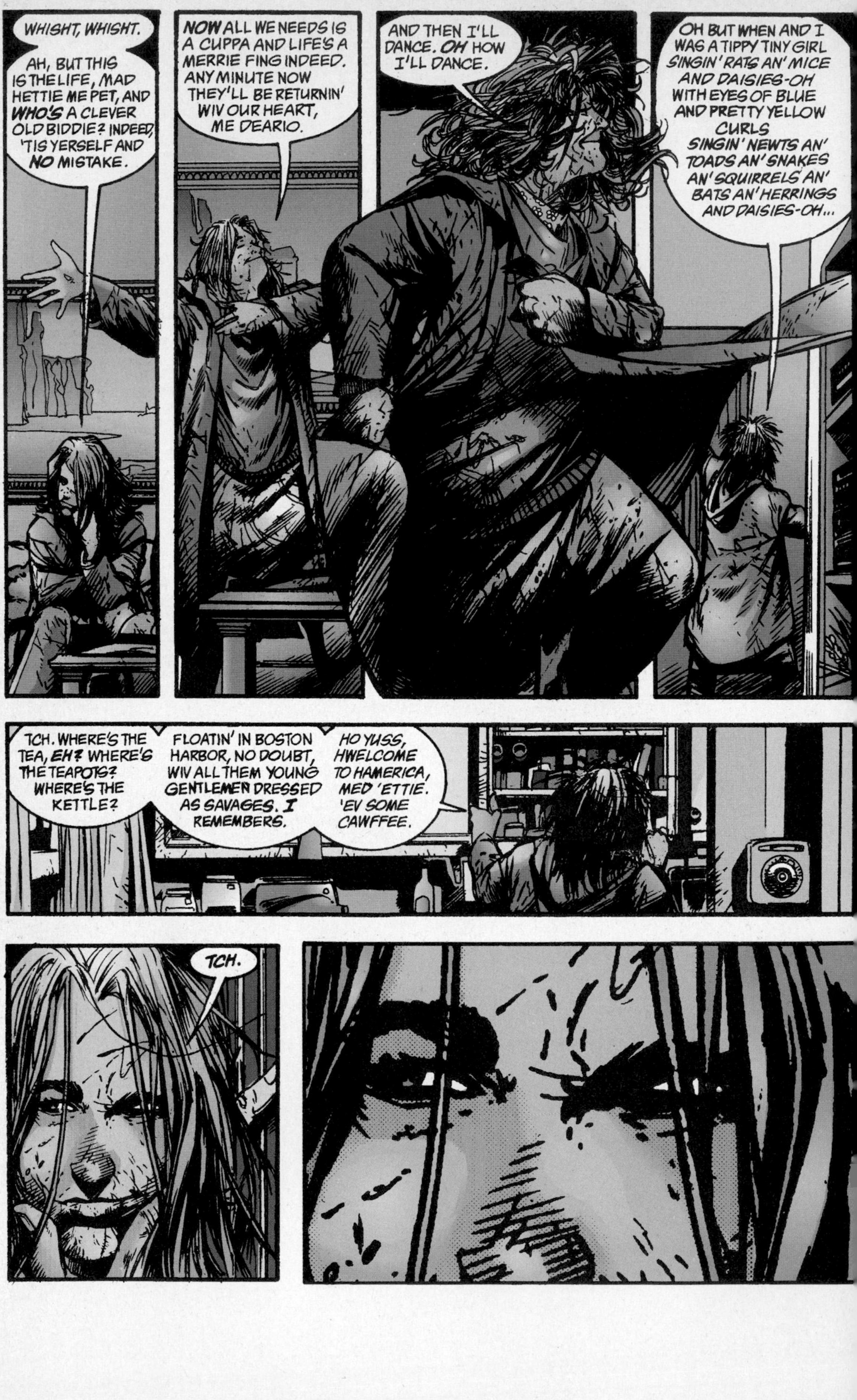
WHISHT, WHISHT.
AH, BUT THIS IS THE LIFE, MAD HETTIE ME PET, AND WHO'S A CLEVER OLD BIDDIE? INDEED, 'TIS YERSELF AND NO MISTAKE.
NOW ALL WE NEEDS IS A CUPPA AND LIFE'S A MERRIE FING INDEED. ANY MINUTE NOW THEY'LL BE RETURNIN' WIV OUR HEART, ME DEARIO.
AND THEN I'LL DANCE. OH HOW I'LL DANCE.
OH BUT WHEN AND I WAS A TIPPY TINY GIRL SINGIN' RATS AN' MICE AND DAISIES-OH WITH EYES OF BLUE AND PRETTY YELLOW CURLS SINGIN' NEWTS AN' TOADS AN' SNAKES AN' SQUIRRELS AN' BATS AN' HERRINGS AND DAISIES-OH...
TCH. WHERE'S THE TEA, EH? WHERE'S THE TEAPOTS? WHERE'S THE KETTLE?
FLOATIN' IN BOSTON HARBOR, NO DOUBT, WIV ALL THEM YOUNG GENTLEMEN DRESSED AS SAVAGES. I REMEMBERS.
HO YUSS, HWELCOME TO HAMERICA, MED 'ETTIE. 'EV SOME CAWFFEE.
TCH.

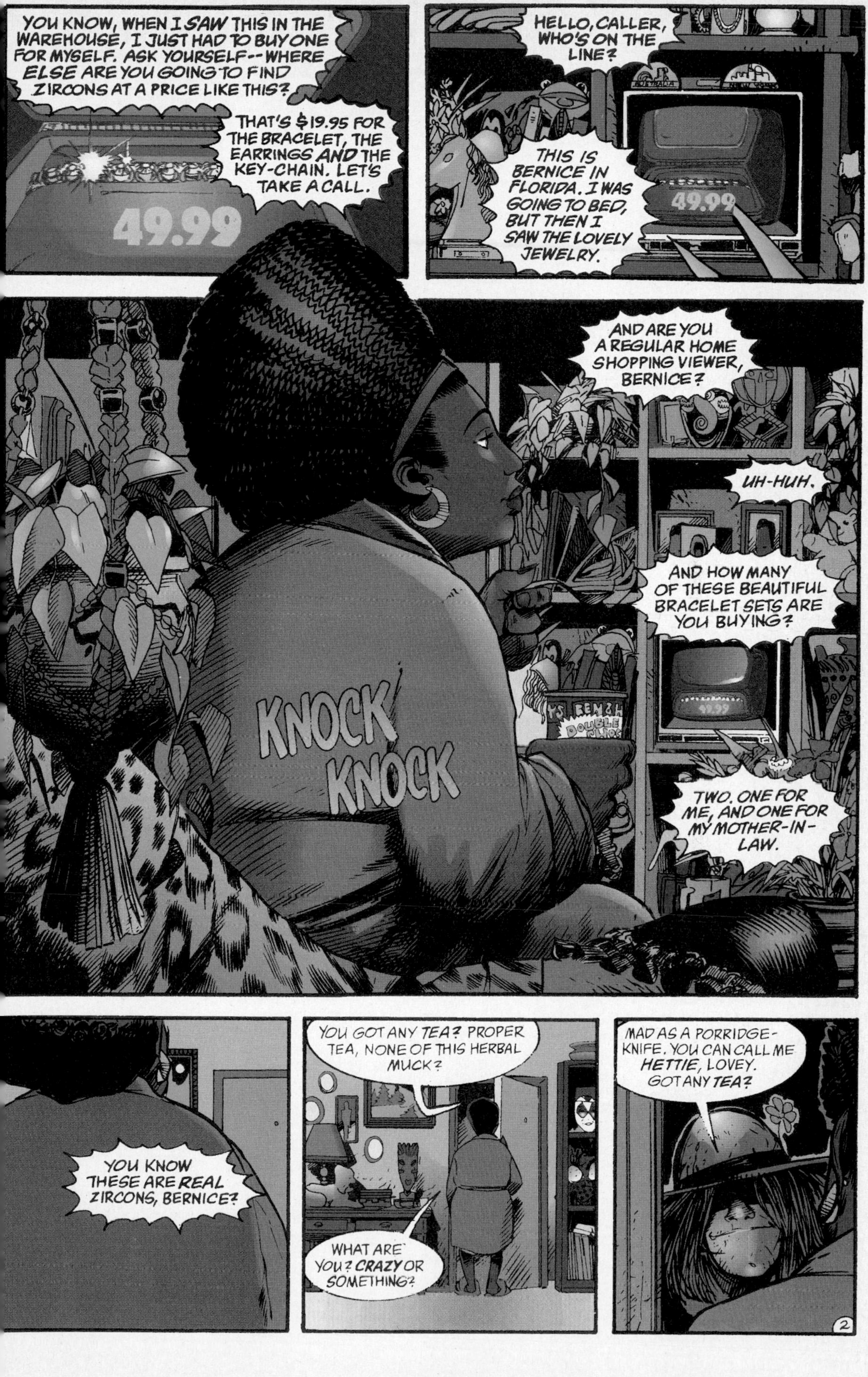
YOU KNOW, WHEN I SAW THIS IN THE WAREHOUSE, I JUST HAD TO BUY ONE FOR MYSELF. ASK YOURSELF--WHERE ELSE ARE YOU GOING TO FIND ZIRCONS AT A PRICE LIKE THIS?
THAT'S $19.95 FOR THE BRACELET, THE EARRINGS AND THE KEY-CHAIN. LET'S TAKE A CALL.
49.99
HELLO, CALLER, WHO'S ON THE LINE?
THIS IS BERNICE IN FLORIDA. I WAS GOING TO BED, BUT THEN I SAW THE LOVELY JEWELRY.
49.99
AND ARE YOU A REGULAR HOME SHOPPING VIEWER, BERNICE?
UH-HUH.
AND HOW MANY OF THESE BEAUTIFUL BRACELET SETS ARE YOU BUYING?
KNOCK KNOCK
TWO. ONE FOR ME, AND ONE FOR MY MOTHER-IN-LAW.
YOU KNOW THESE ARE REAL ZIRCONS, BERNICE?
YOU GOT ANY TEA? PROPER TEA, NONE OF THIS HERBAL MUCK?
WHAT ARE YOU? CRAZY OR SOMETHING?
MAD AS A PORRIDGE-KNIFE. YOU CAN CALL ME HETTIE, LOVEY. GOT ANY TEA?

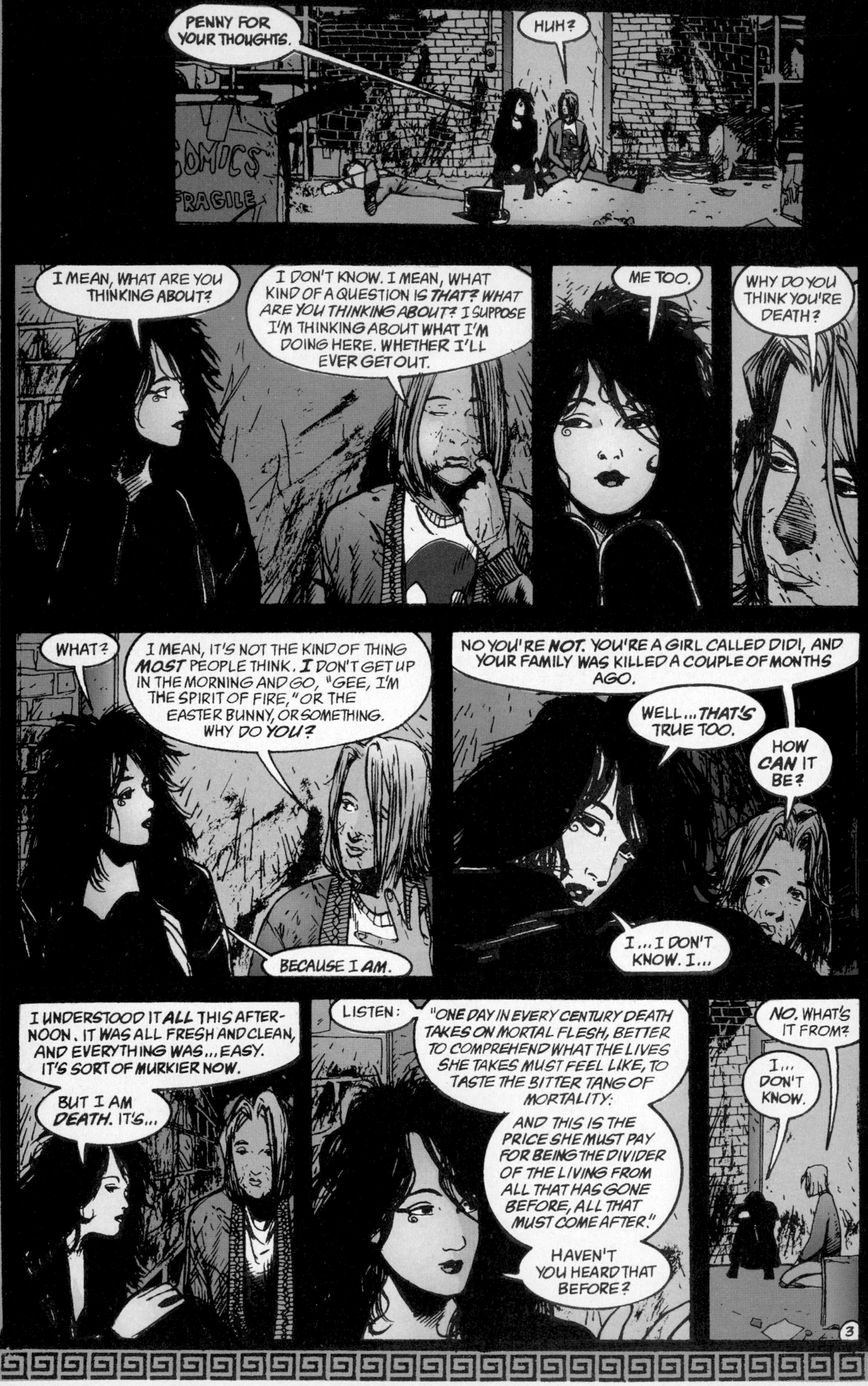
PENNY FOR YOUR THOUGHTS.
HUH?
COMICS
FRAGILE
I MEAN, WHAT ARE YOU THINKING ABOUT?
I DON'T KNOW. I MEAN, WHAT KIND OF A QUESTION IS THAT? WHAT ARE YOU THINKING ABOUT? I SUPPOSE I'M THINKING ABOUT WHAT I'M DOING HERE. WHETHER I'LL EVER GET OUT.
ME TOO.
WHY DO YOU THINK YOU'RE DEATH?
WHAT?
I MEAN, IT'S NOT THE KIND OF THING MOST PEOPLE THINK. I DON'T GET UP IN THE MORNING AND GO, "GEE, I'M THE SPIRIT OF FIRE," OR THE EASTER BUNNY, OR SOMETHING. WHY DO YOU?
BECAUSE I AM.
NO YOU'RE NOT. YOU'RE A GIRL CALLED DIDI, AND YOUR FAMILY WAS KILLED A COUPLE OF MONTHS AGO.
WELL... THAT'S TRUE TOO.
HOW CAN IT BE?
I... I DON'T KNOW. I...
I UNDERSTOOD IT ALL THIS AFTERNOON. IT WAS ALL FRESH AND CLEAN, AND EVERYTHING WAS... EASY. IT'S SORT OF MURKIER NOW.
BUT I AM DEATH. IT'S...
LISTEN:
"ONE DAY IN EVERY CENTURY DEATH TAKES ON MORTAL FLESH, BETTER TO COMPREHEND WHAT THE LIVES SHE TAKES MUST FEEL LIKE, TO TASTE THE BITTER TANG OF MORTALITY:
AND THIS IS THE PRICE SHE MUST PAY FOR BEING THE DIVIDER OF THE LIVING FROM ALL THAT HAS GONE BEFORE, ALL THAT MUST COME AFTER."
HAVEN'T YOU HEARD THAT BEFORE?
NO. WHAT'S IT FROM?
I... DON'T KNOW.

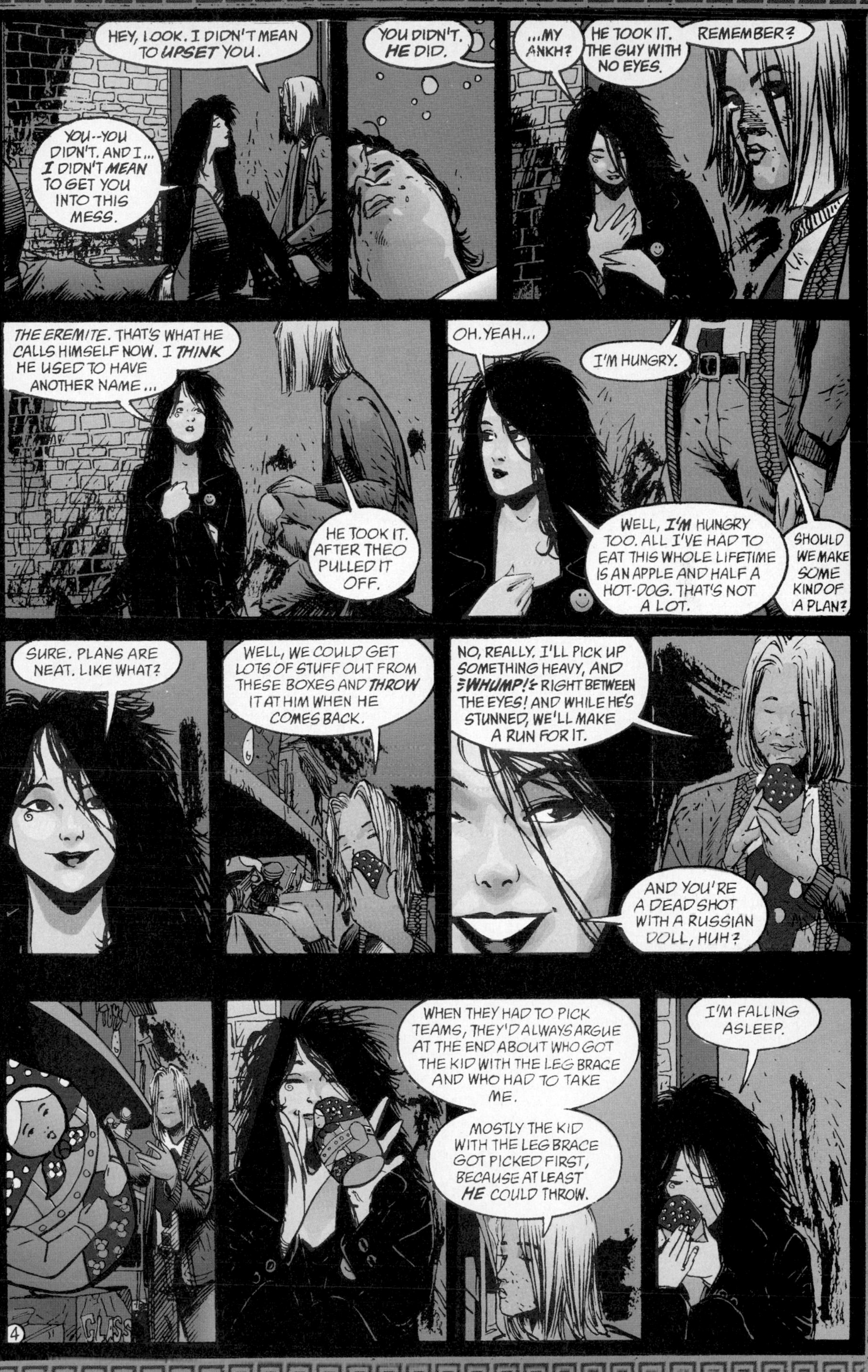
HEY, LOOK. I DIDN'T MEAN TO UPSET YOU.
YOU--YOU DIDN'T. AND I... I DIDN'T MEAN TO GET YOU INTO THIS MESS.
YOU DIDN'T. HE DID.
...MY ANKH?
HE TOOK IT. THE GUY WITH NO EYES.
REMEMBER?
THE EREMITE. THAT'S WHAT HE CALLS HIMSELF NOW. I THINK HE USED TO HAVE ANOTHER NAME...
HE TOOK IT. AFTER THEO PULLED IT OFF.
OH. YEAH...
I'M HUNGRY.
WELL, I'M HUNGRY TOO. ALL I'VE HAD TO EAT THIS WHOLE LIFETIME IS AN APPLE AND HALF A HOT-DOG. THAT'S NOT A LOT.
SHOULD WE MAKE SOME KIND OF A PLAN?
SURE. PLANS ARE NEAT. LIKE WHAT?
WELL, WE COULD GET LOTS OF STUFF OUT FROM THESE BOXES AND THROW IT AT HIM WHEN HE COMES BACK.
NO, REALLY. I'LL PICK UP SOMETHING HEAVY, AND WHUMP! RIGHT BETWEEN THE EYES! AND WHILE HE'S STUNNED, WE'LL MAKE A RUN FOR IT.
AND YOU'RE A DEAD SHOT WITH A RUSSIAN DOLL, HUH?
WHEN THEY HAD TO PICK TEAMS, THEY'D ALWAYS ARGUE AT THE END ABOUT WHO GOT THE KID WITH THE LEG BRACE AND WHO HAD TO TAKE ME.
MOSTLY THE KID WITH THE LEG BRACE GOT PICKED FIRST, BECAUSE AT LEAST HE COULD THROW.
I'M FALLING ASLEEP.
GLASS

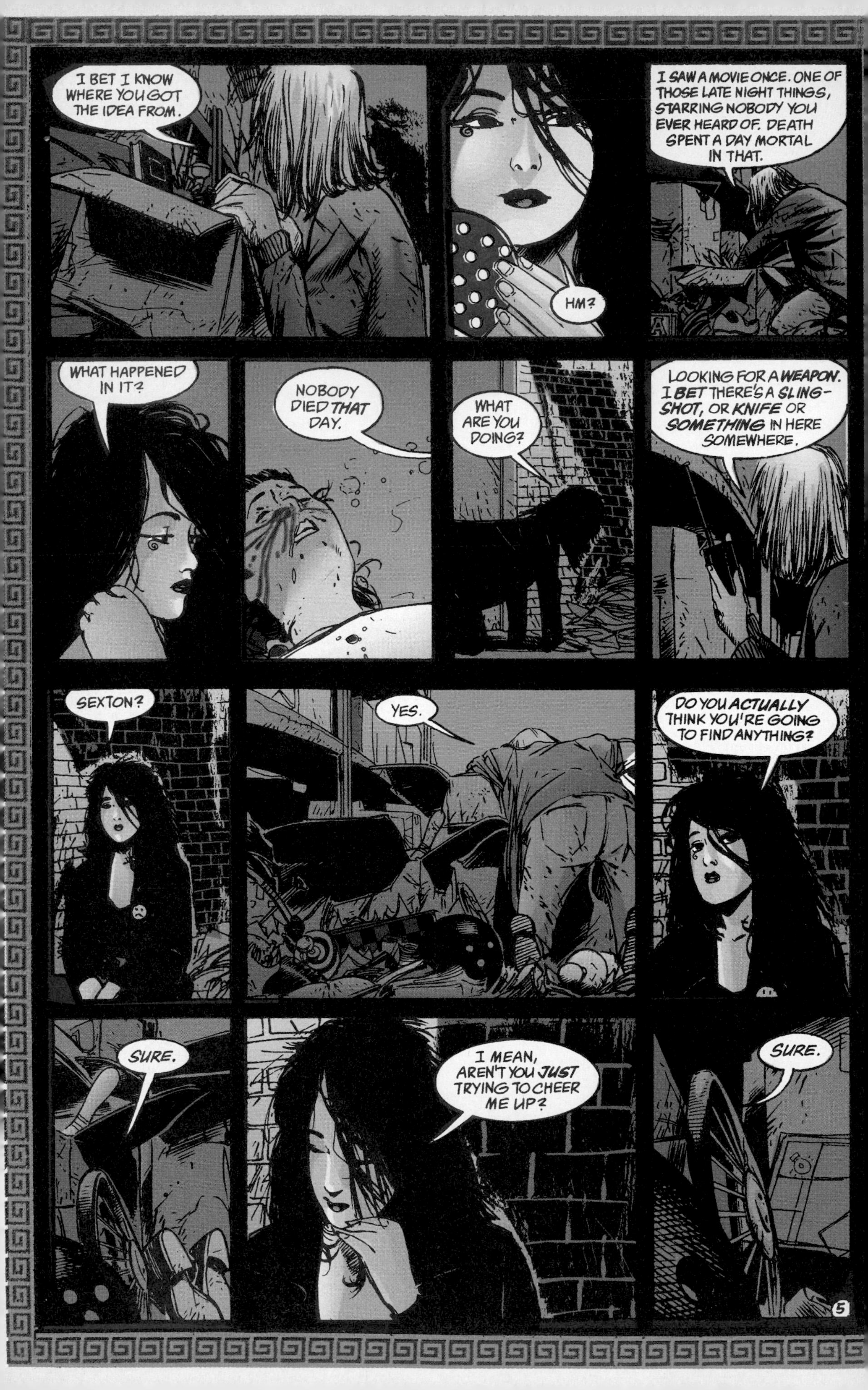
I BET I KNOW WHERE YOU GOT THE IDEA FROM.
I SAW A MOVIE ONCE. ONE OF THOSE LATE NIGHT THINGS, STARRING NOBODY YOU EVER HEARD OF. DEATH SPENT A DAY MORTAL IN THAT.
HM?
WHAT HAPPENED IN IT?
NOBODY DIED THAT DAY.
WHAT ARE YOU DOING?
LOOKING FOR A WEAPON. I BET THERE'S A SLING-SHOT, OR KNIFE OR SOMETHING IN HERE SOMEWHERE.
SEXTON?
YES.
DO YOU ACTUALLY THINK YOU'RE GOING TO FIND ANYTHING?
SURE.
I MEAN, AREN'T YOU JUST TRYING TO CHEER ME UP?
SURE.
5

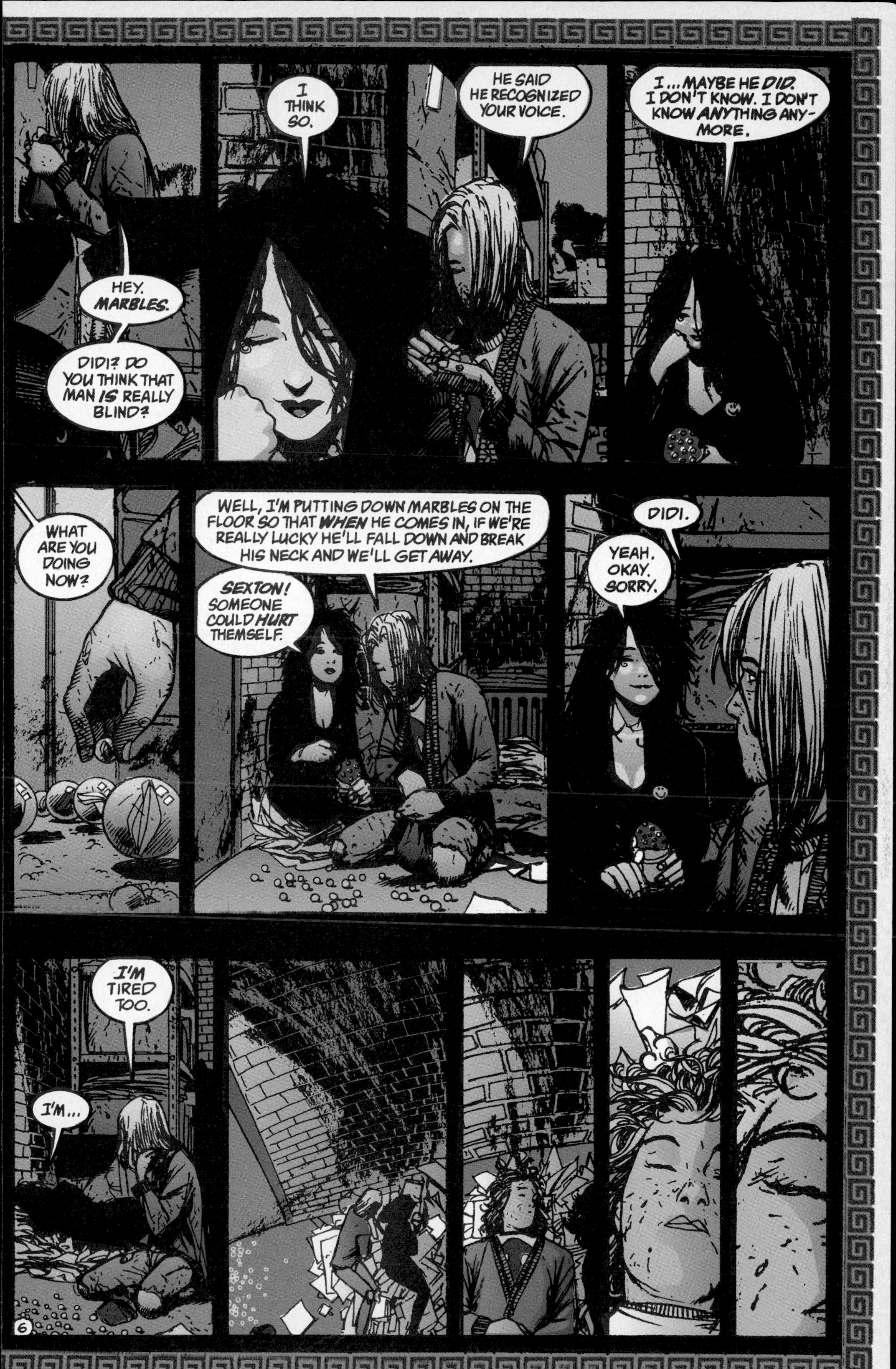
I THINK SO.
HE SAID HE RECOGNIZED YOUR VOICE.
I... MAYBE HE DID. I DON'T KNOW. I DON'T KNOW ANYTHING ANYMORE.
HEY. MARBLES.
DIDI? DO YOU THINK THAT MAN IS REALLY BLIND?
WHAT ARE YOU DOING NOW?
WELL, I'M PUTTING DOWN MARBLES ON THE FLOOR SO THAT WHEN HE COMES IN, IF WE'RE REALLY LUCKY HE'LL FALL DOWN AND BREAK HIS NECK AND WE'LL GET AWAY.
SEXTON! SOMEONE COULD HURT THEMSELF.
DIDI.
YEAH. OKAY. SORRY.
I'M TIRED TOO.
I'M...
6

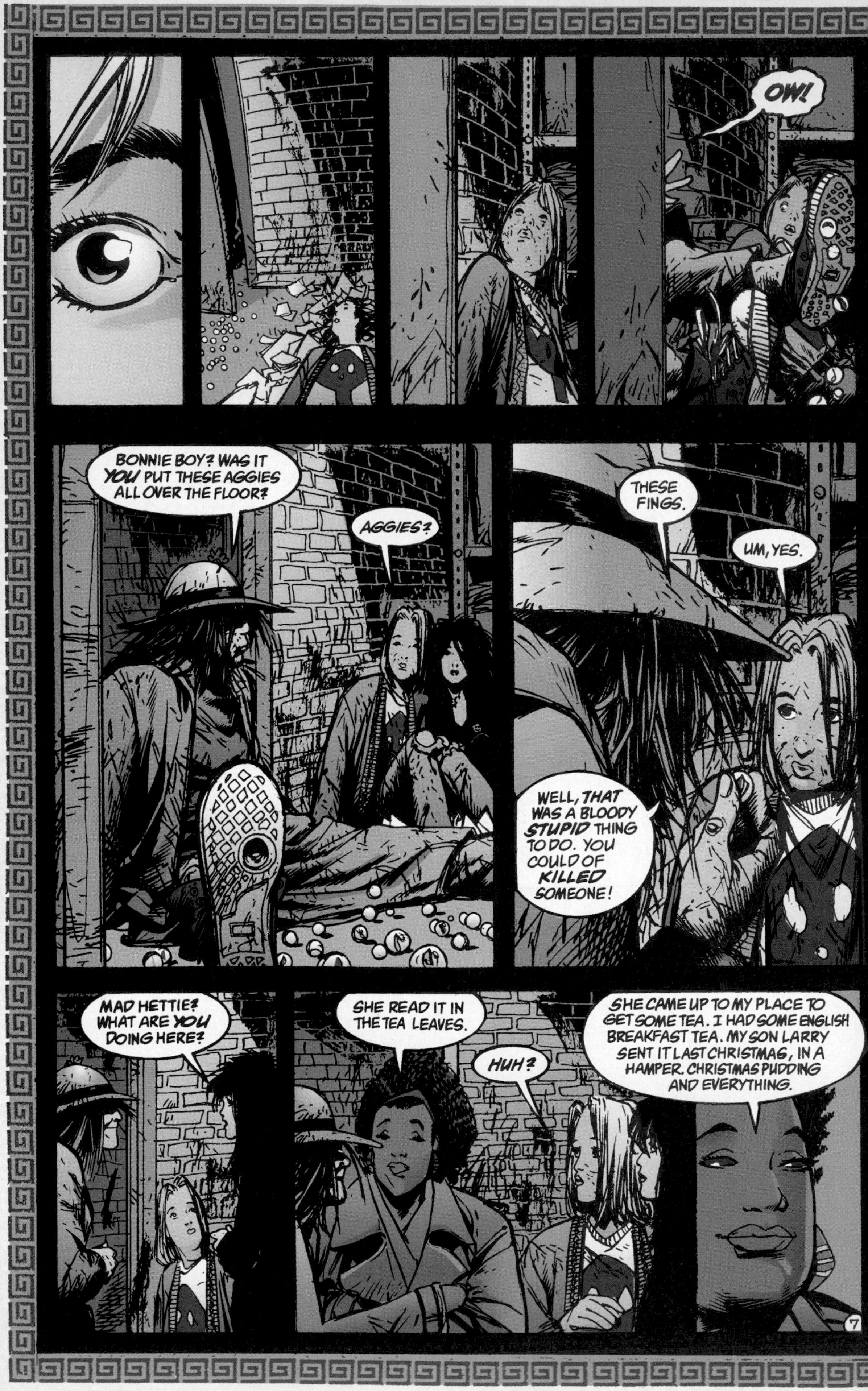
OW!
BONNIE BOY? WAS IT YOU PUT THESE AGGIES ALL OVER THE FLOOR?
AGGIES?
THESE FINGS.
UM, YES.
WELL, THAT WAS A BLOODY STUPID THING TO DO. YOU COULD OF KILLED SOMEONE!
MAD HETTIE? WHAT ARE YOU DOING HERE?
SHE READ IT IN THE TEA LEAVES.
HUH?
SHE CAME UP TO MY PLACE TO GET SOME TEA. I HAD SOME ENGLISH BREAKFAST TEA. MY SON LARRY SENT IT LAST CHRISTMAS, IN A HAMPER. CHRISTMAS PUDDING AND EVERYTHING.
7

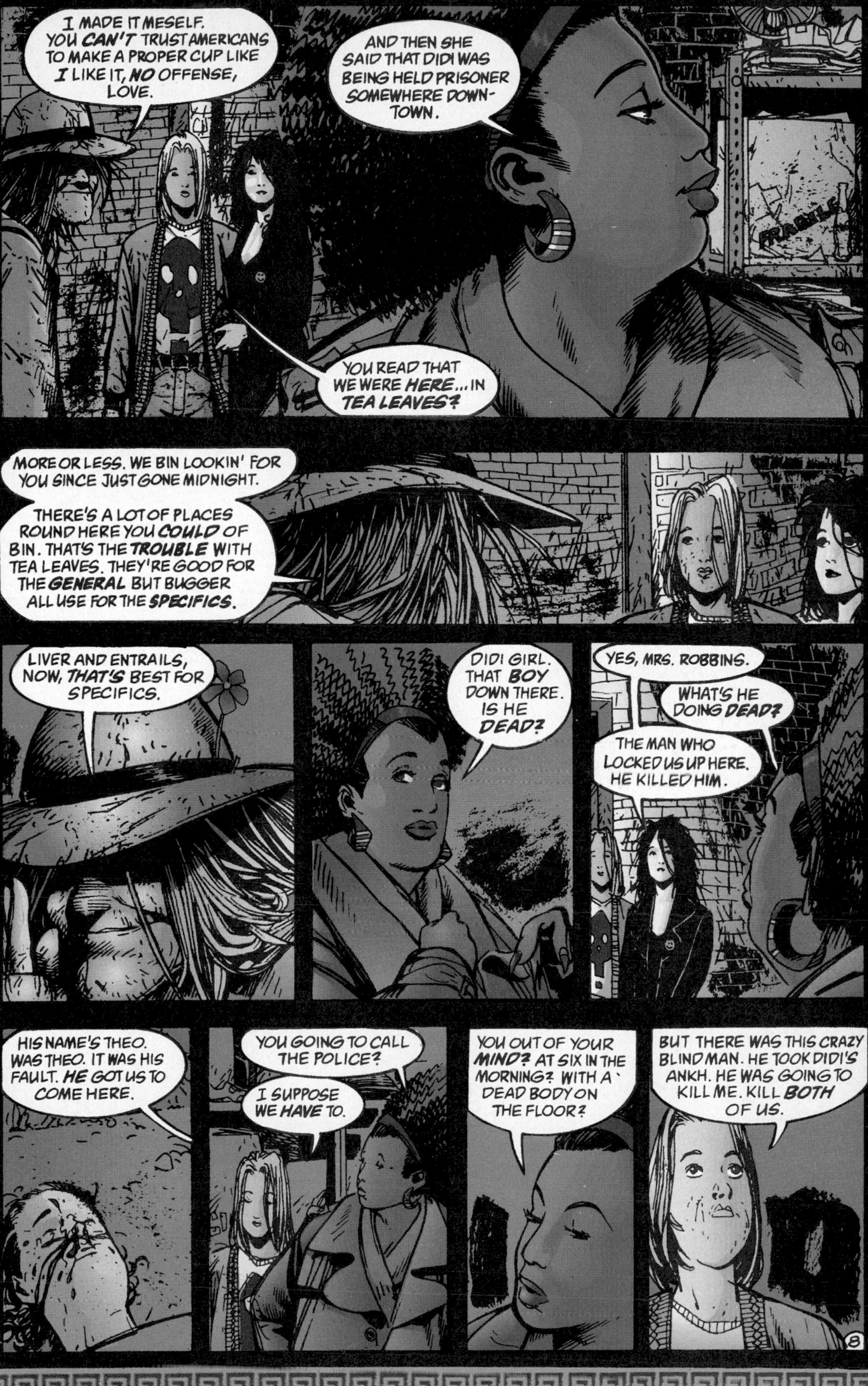

I MADE IT MESELF. YOU CAN'T TRUST AMERICANS TO MAKE A PROPER CUP LIKE I LIKE IT, NO OFFENSE, LOVE.
AND THEN SHE SAID THAT DIDI WAS BEING HELD PRISONER SOMEWHERE DOWN-TOWN.
YOU READ THAT WE WERE HERE... IN TEA LEAVES?
FRAGILE
MORE OR LESS. WE BIN LOOKIN' FOR YOU SINCE JUST GONE MIDNIGHT.
THERE'S A LOT OF PLACES ROUND HERE YOU COULD OF BIN. THAT'S THE TROUBLE WITH TEA LEAVES. THEY'RE GOOD FOR THE GENERAL BUT BUGGER ALL USE FOR THE SPECIFICS.
LIVER AND ENTRAILS, NOW, THAT'S BEST FOR SPECIFICS.
DIDI GIRL. THAT BOY DOWN THERE. IS HE DEAD?
YES, MRS. ROBBINS.
WHAT'S HE DOING DEAD?
THE MAN WHO LOCKED US UP HERE. HE KILLED HIM.
HIS NAME'S THEO. WAS THEO. IT WAS HIS FAULT. HE GOT US TO COME HERE.
YOU GOING TO CALL THE POLICE?
I SUPPOSE WE HAVE TO.
YOU OUT OF YOUR MIND? AT SIX IN THE MORNING? WITH A DEAD BODY ON THE FLOOR?
BUT THERE WAS THIS CRAZY BLIND MAN. HE TOOK DIDI'S ANKH. HE WAS GOING TO KILL ME. KILL BOTH OF US.
8

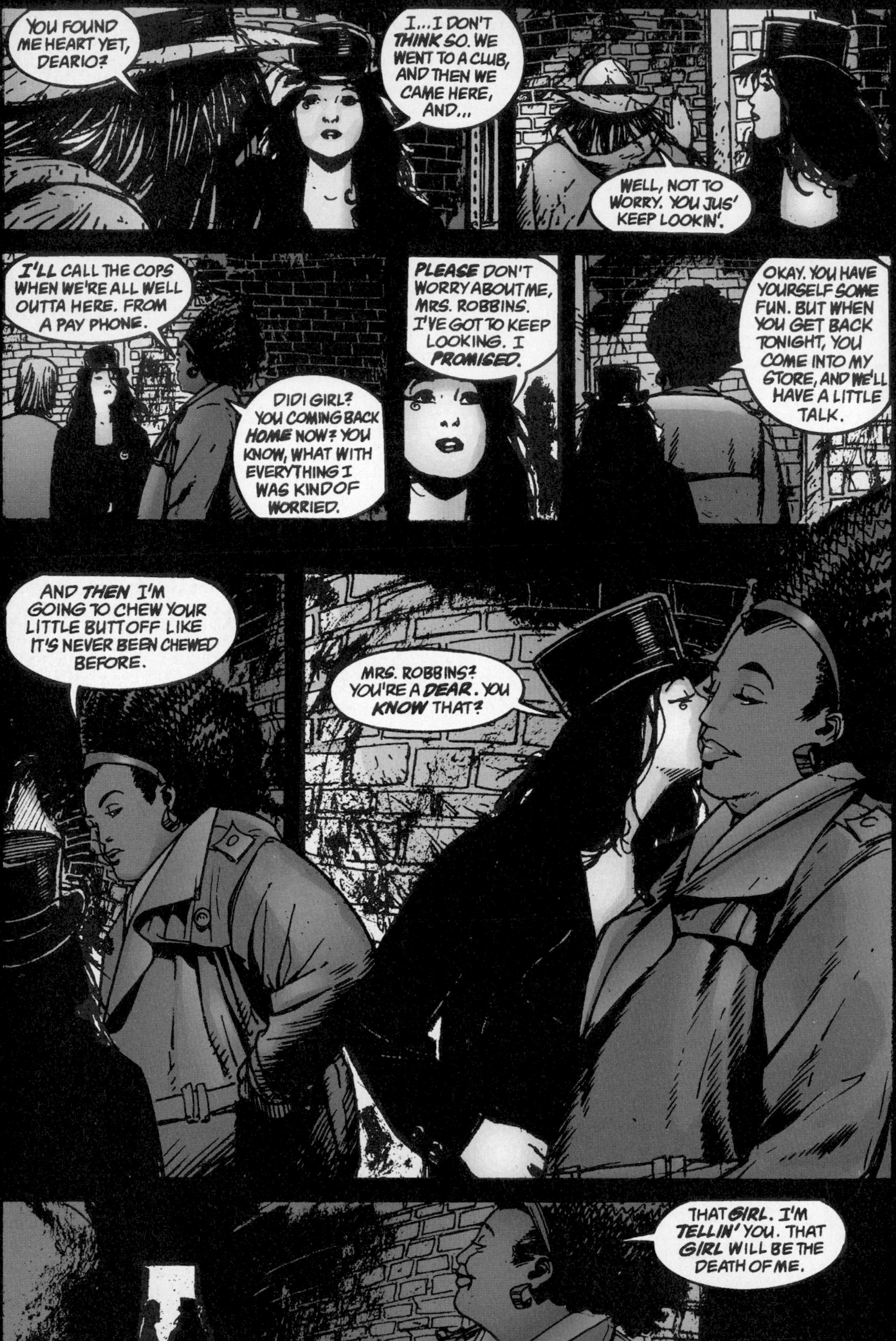
YOU FOUND ME HEART YET, DEARIO?
I...I DON'T THINK SO. WE WENT TO A CLUB, AND THEN WE CAME HERE, AND...
WELL, NOT TO WORRY. YOU JUS' KEEP LOOKIN'.
I'LL CALL THE COPS WHEN WE'RE ALL WELL OUTTA HERE. FROM A PAY PHONE.
DIDI GIRL? YOU COMING BACK HOME NOW? YOU KNOW, WHAT WITH EVERYTHING I WAS KIND OF WORRIED.
PLEASE DON'T WORRY ABOUT ME, MRS. ROBBINS. I'VE GOT TO KEEP LOOKING. I PROMISED.
OKAY. YOU HAVE YOURSELF SOME FUN. BUT WHEN YOU GET BACK TONIGHT, YOU COME INTO MY STORE, AND WE'LL HAVE A LITTLE TALK.
AND THEN I'M GOING TO CHEW YOUR LITTLE BUTT OFF LIKE IT'S NEVER BEEN CHEWED BEFORE.
MRS. ROBBINS? YOU'RE A DEAR. YOU KNOW THAT?
THAT GIRL. I'M TELLIN' YOU. THAT GIRL WILL BE THE DEATH OF ME.

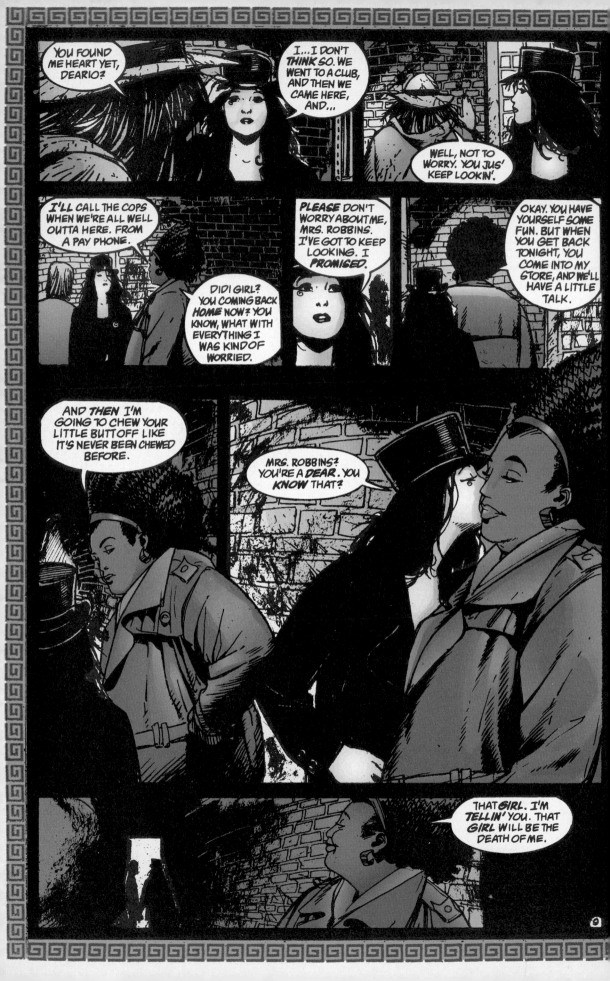

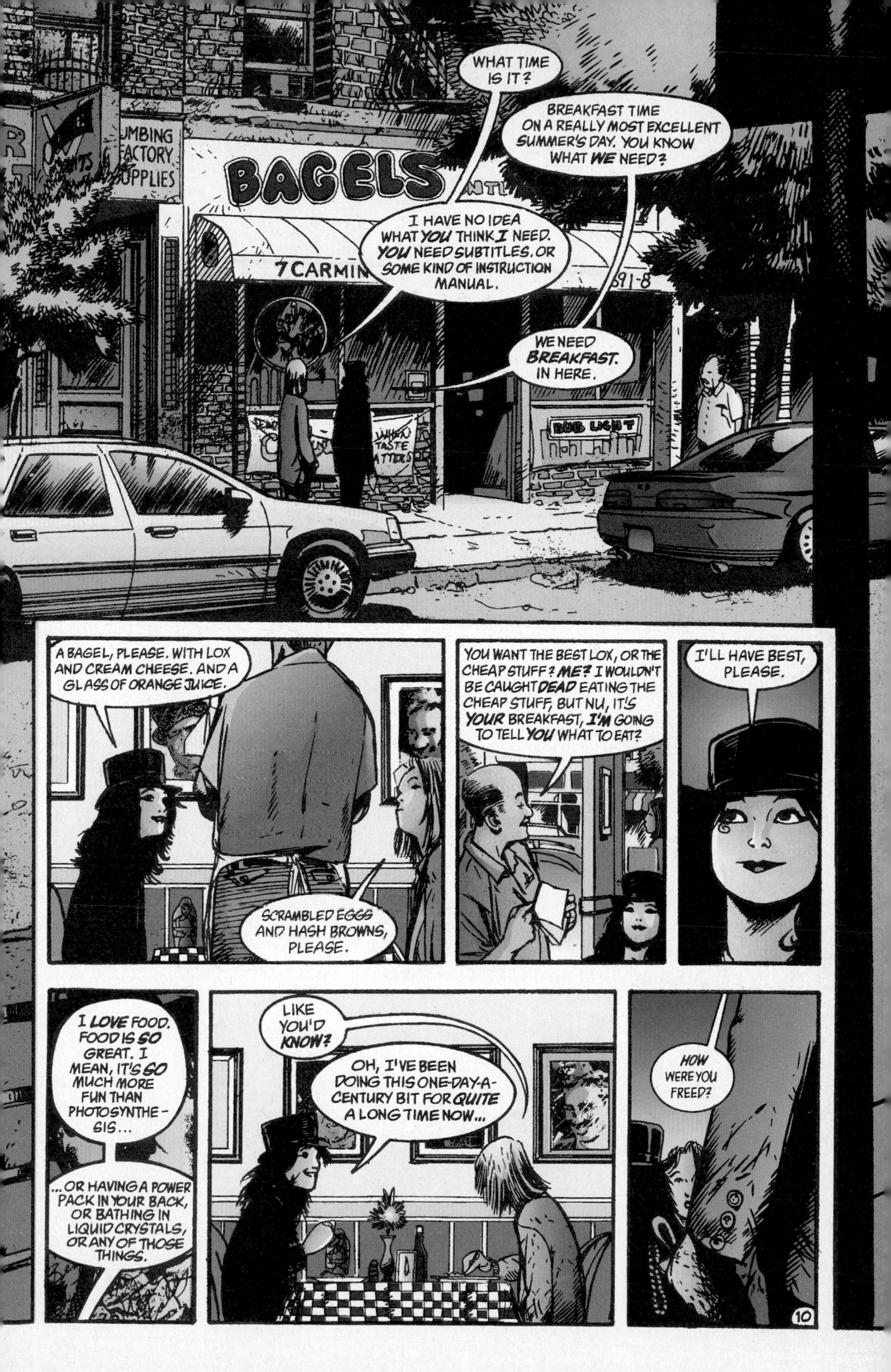

UMBING FACTORY SUPPLIES
BAGELS
7 CARMIN
WHAT TIME IS IT?
BREAKFAST TIME ON A REALLY MOST EXCELLENT SUMMER'S DAY. YOU KNOW WHAT WE NEED?
I HAVE NO IDEA WHAT YOU THINK I NEED. YOU NEED SUBTITLES. OR SOME KIND OF INSTRUCTION MANUAL.
WE NEED BREAKFAST. IN HERE.
BUD LIGHT
WHEN TASTE MATTERS
A BAGEL, PLEASE. WITH LOX AND CREAM CHEESE. AND A GLASS OF ORANGE JUICE.
SCRAMBLED EGGS AND HASH BROWNS, PLEASE.
YOU WANT THE BEST LOX, OR THE CHEAP STUFF? ME? I WOULDN'T BE CAUGHT DEAD EATING THE CHEAP STUFF, BUT NU, IT'S YOUR BREAKFAST, I'M GOING TO TELL YOU WHAT TO EAT?
I'LL HAVE BEST, PLEASE.
I LOVE FOOD. FOOD IS SO GREAT. I MEAN, IT'S SO MUCH MORE FUN THAN PHOTOSYNTHE-SIS...
...OR HAVING A POWER PACK IN YOUR BACK, OR BATHING IN LIQUID CRYSTALS, OR ANY OF THOSE THINGS.
LIKE YOU'D KNOW?
OH, I'VE BEEN DOING THIS ONE-DAY-A-CENTURY BIT FOR QUITE A LONG TIME NOW...
HOW WERE YOU FREED?
10

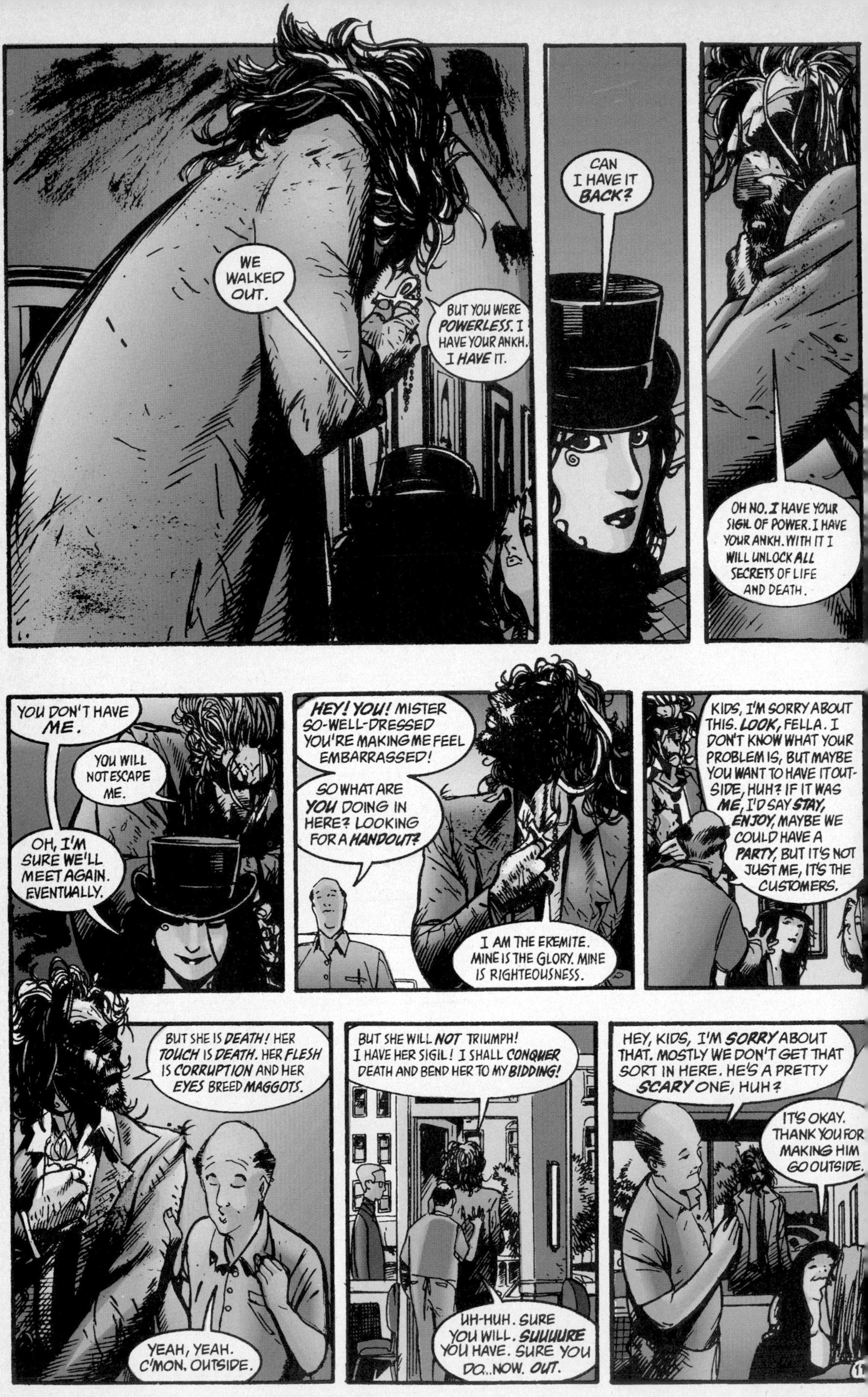
WE WALKED OUT.
BUT YOU WERE POWERLESS. I HAVE YOUR ANKH. I HAVE IT.
CAN I HAVE IT BACK?
OH NO. I HAVE YOUR SIGIL OF POWER. I HAVE YOUR ANKH. WITH IT I WILL UNLOCK ALL SECRETS OF LIFE AND DEATH.
YOU DON'T HAVE ME.
YOU WILL NOT ESCAPE ME.
OH, I'M SURE WE'LL MEET AGAIN. EVENTUALLY.
HEY! YOU! MISTER SO-WELL-DRESSED YOU'RE MAKING ME FEEL EMBARRASSED!
SO WHAT ARE YOU DOING IN HERE? LOOKING FOR A HANDOUT?
I AM THE EREMITE. MINE IS THE GLORY. MINE IS RIGHTEOUSNESS.
KIDS, I'M SORRY ABOUT THIS. LOOK, FELLA. I DON'T KNOW WHAT YOUR PROBLEM IS, BUT MAYBE YOU WANT TO HAVE IT OUTSIDE, HUH? IF IT WAS ME, I'D SAY STAY, ENJOY, MAYBE WE COULD HAVE A PARTY, BUT IT'S NOT JUST ME, IT'S THE CUSTOMERS.
BUT SHE IS DEATH! HER TOUCH IS DEATH. HER FLESH IS CORRUPTION AND HER EYES BREED MAGGOTS.
YEAH, YEAH. C'MON. OUTSIDE.
BUT SHE WILL NOT TRIUMPH! I HAVE HER SIGIL! I SHALL CONQUER DEATH AND BEND HER TO MY BIDDING!
UH-HUH. SURE YOU WILL. SUUUURE YOU HAVE. SURE YOU DO...NOW. OUT.
HEY, KIDS, I'M SORRY ABOUT THAT. MOSTLY WE DON'T GET THAT SORT IN HERE. HE'S A PRETTY SCARY ONE, HUH?
IT'S OKAY. THANK YOU FOR MAKING HIM GO OUTSIDE.
11

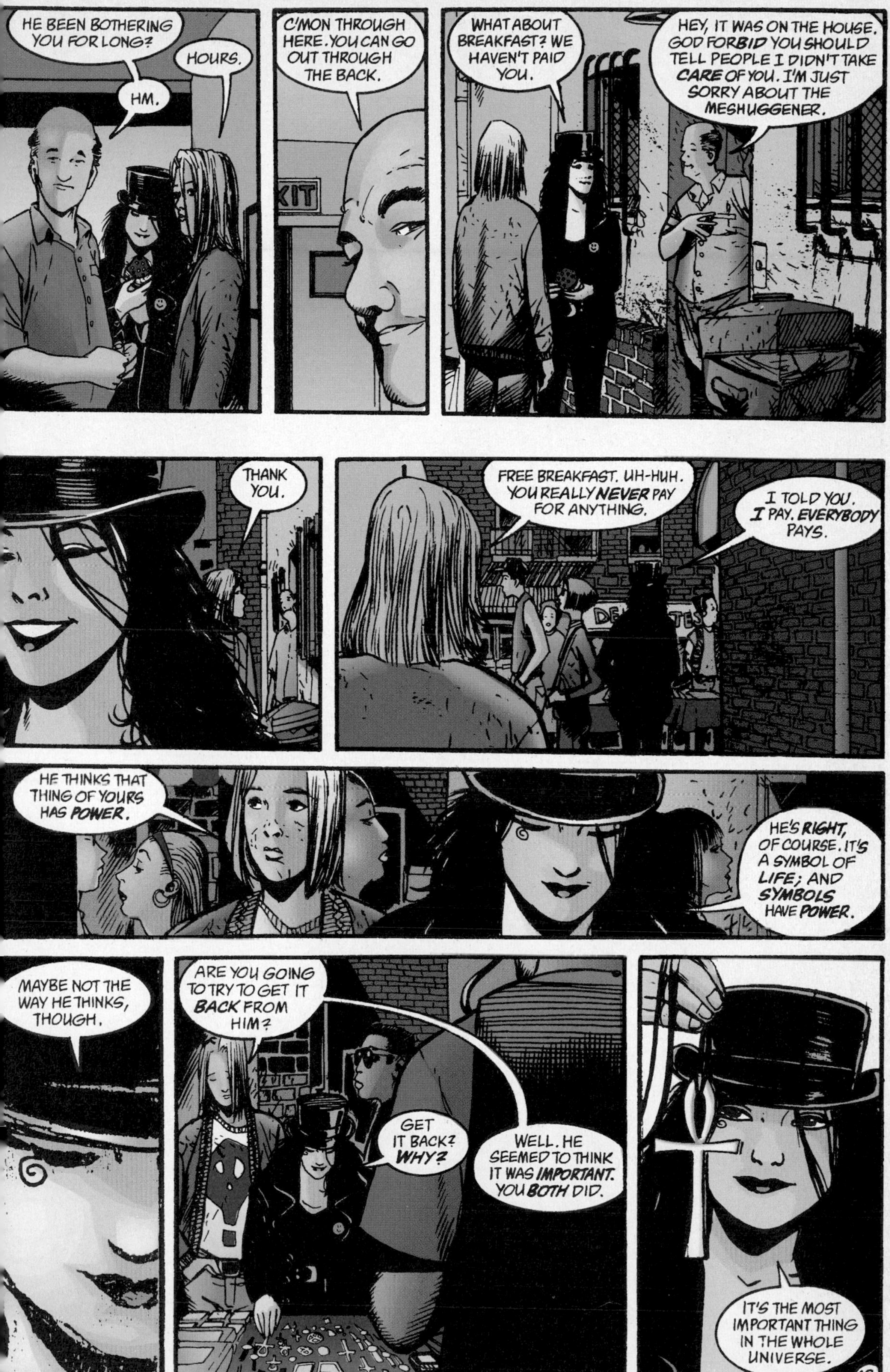
HE BEEN BOTHERING YOU FOR LONG?
HOURS.
HM.
C'MON THROUGH HERE. YOU CAN GO OUT THROUGH THE BACK.
WHAT ABOUT BREAKFAST? WE HAVEN'T PAID YOU.
HEY, IT WAS ON THE HOUSE. GOD FORBID YOU SHOULD TELL PEOPLE I DIDN'T TAKE CARE OF YOU. I'M JUST SORRY ABOUT THE MESHUGGENER.
THANK YOU.
FREE BREAKFAST. UH-HUH. YOU REALLY NEVER PAY FOR ANYTHING.
I TOLD YOU. I PAY. EVERYBODY PAYS.
HE THINKS THAT THING OF YOURS HAS POWER.
HE'S RIGHT, OF COURSE. IT'S A SYMBOL OF LIFE; AND SYMBOLS HAVE POWER.
MAYBE NOT THE WAY HE THINKS, THOUGH.
ARE YOU GOING TO TRY TO GET IT BACK FROM HIM?
GET IT BACK? WHY?
WELL. HE SEEMED TO THINK IT WAS IMPORTANT. YOU BOTH DID.
IT'S THE MOST IMPORTANT THING IN THE WHOLE UNIVERSE.

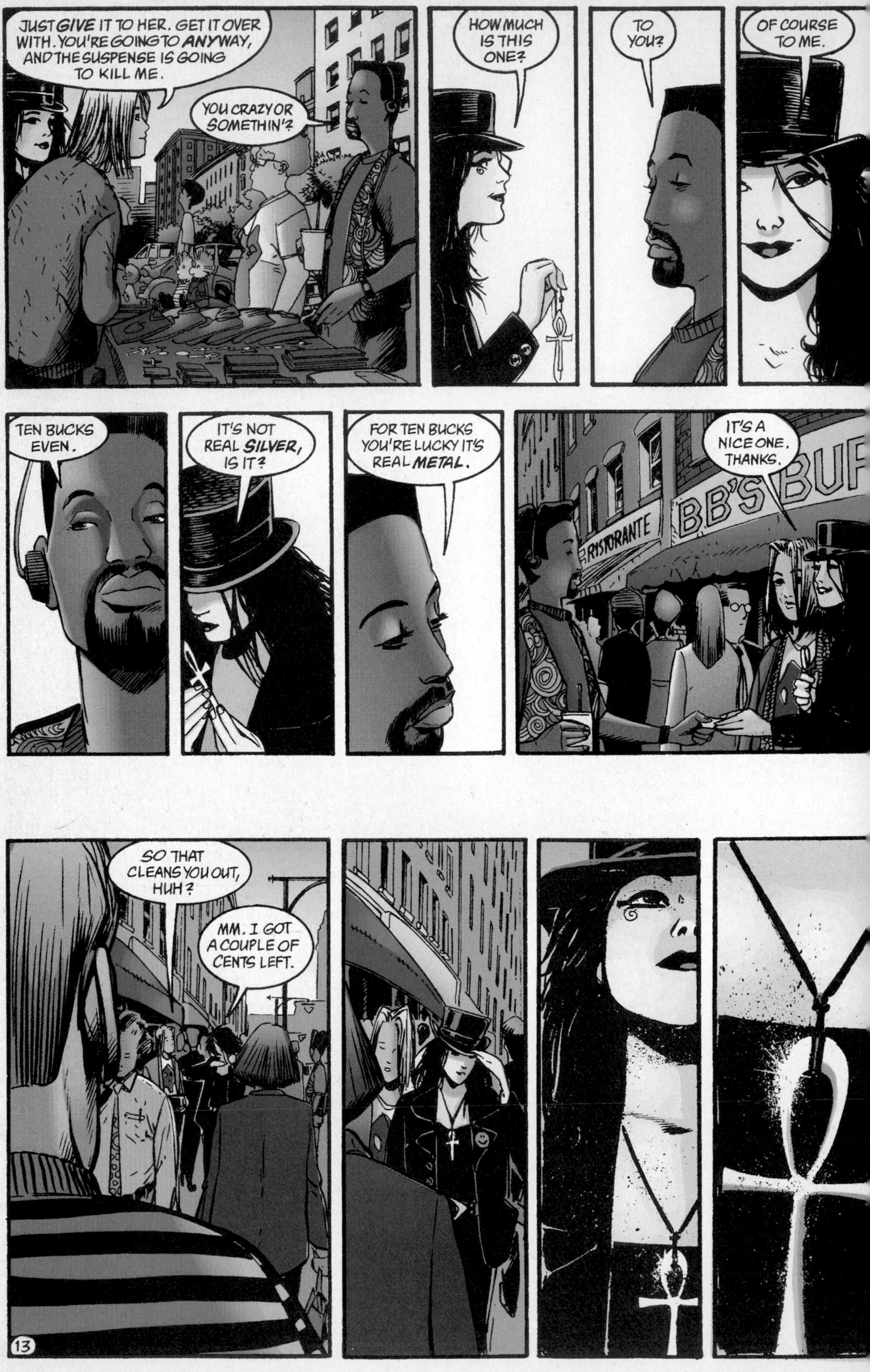

JUST GIVE IT TO HER. GET IT OVER WITH. YOU'RE GOING TO ANYWAY, AND THE SUSPENSE IS GOING TO KILL ME.
YOU CRAZY OR SOMETHIN'?
HOW MUCH IS THIS ONE?
TO YOU?
OF COURSE TO ME.
TEN BUCKS EVEN.
IT'S NOT REAL SILVER, IS IT?
FOR TEN BUCKS YOU'RE LUCKY IT'S REAL METAL.
IT'S A NICE ONE. THANKS.
RISTORANTE
BB'S BUF
SO THAT CLEANS YOU OUT, HUH?
MM. I GOT A COUPLE OF CENTS LEFT.

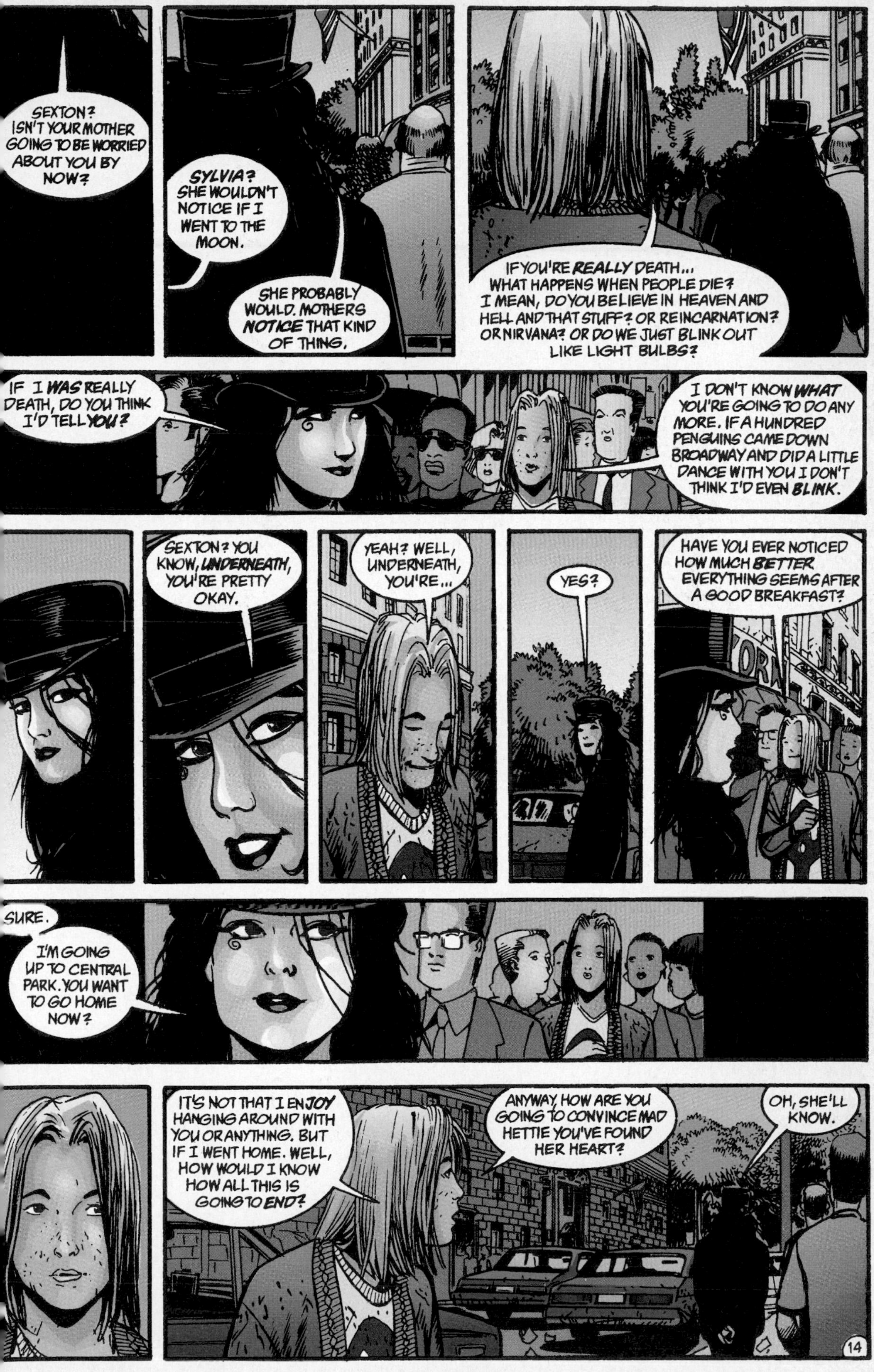
SEXTON? ISN'T YOUR MOTHER GOING TO BE WORRIED ABOUT YOU BY NOW?
SYLVIA? SHE WOULDN'T NOTICE IF I WENT TO THE MOON.
SHE PROBABLY WOULD. MOTHERS NOTICE THAT KIND OF THING.
IF YOU'RE REALLY DEATH... WHAT HAPPENS WHEN PEOPLE DIE? I MEAN, DO YOU BELIEVE IN HEAVEN AND HELL AND THAT STUFF? OR REINCARNATION? OR NIRVANA? OR DO WE JUST BLINK OUT LIKE LIGHT BULBS?
IF I WAS REALLY DEATH, DO YOU THINK I'D TELL YOU?
I DON'T KNOW WHAT YOU'RE GOING TO DO ANY MORE. IF A HUNDRED PENGUINS CAME DOWN BROADWAY AND DID A LITTLE DANCE WITH YOU I DON'T THINK I'D EVEN BLINK.
SEXTON? YOU KNOW, UNDERNEATH, YOU'RE PRETTY OKAY.
YEAH? WELL, UNDERNEATH, YOU'RE...
YES?
HAVE YOU EVER NOTICED HOW MUCH BETTER EVERYTHING SEEMS AFTER A GOOD BREAKFAST?
SURE.
I'M GOING UP TO CENTRAL PARK. YOU WANT TO GO HOME NOW?
IT'S NOT THAT I ENJOY HANGING AROUND WITH YOU OR ANYTHING. BUT IF I WENT HOME. WELL, HOW WOULD I KNOW HOW ALL THIS IS GOING TO END?
ANYWAY, HOW ARE YOU GOING TO CONVINCE MAD HETTIE YOU'VE FOUND HER HEART?
OH, SHE'LL KNOW.
14

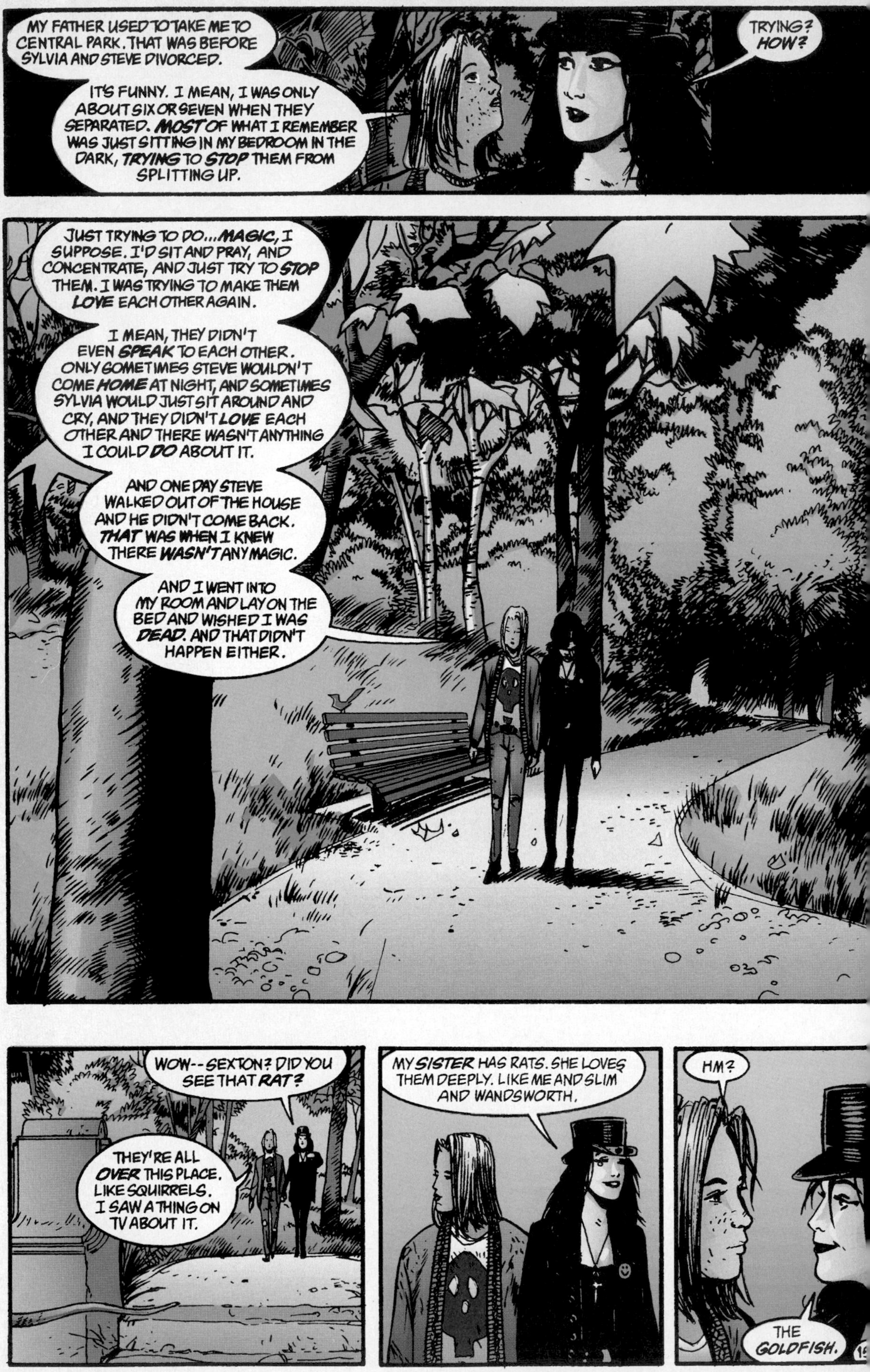
MY FATHER USED TO TAKE ME TO CENTRAL PARK. THAT WAS BEFORE SYLVIA AND STEVE DIVORCED.
IT'S FUNNY. I MEAN, I WAS ONLY ABOUT SIX OR SEVEN WHEN THEY SEPARATED. MOST OF WHAT I REMEMBER WAS JUST SITTING IN MY BEDROOM IN THE DARK, TRYING TO STOP THEM FROM SPLITTING UP.
TRYING? HOW?
JUST TRYING TO DO... MAGIC, I SUPPOSE. I'D SIT AND PRAY, AND CONCENTRATE, AND JUST TRY TO STOP THEM. I WAS TRYING TO MAKE THEM LOVE EACH OTHER AGAIN.
I MEAN, THEY DIDN'T EVEN SPEAK TO EACH OTHER. ONLY SOMETIMES STEVE WOULDN'T COME HOME AT NIGHT, AND SOMETIMES SYLVIA WOULD JUST SIT AROUND AND CRY, AND THEY DIDN'T LOVE EACH OTHER AND THERE WASN'T ANYTHING I COULD DO ABOUT IT.
AND ONE DAY STEVE WALKED OUT OF THE HOUSE AND HE DIDN'T COME BACK. THAT WAS WHEN I KNEW THERE WASN'T ANY MAGIC.
AND I WENT INTO MY ROOM AND LAY ON THE BED AND WISHED I WAS DEAD. AND THAT DIDN'T HAPPEN EITHER.
WOW-- SEXTON? DID YOU SEE THAT RAT?
THEY'RE ALL OVER THIS PLACE. LIKE SQUIRRELS. I SAW A THING ON TV ABOUT IT.
MY SISTER HAS RATS. SHE LOVES THEM DEEPLY. LIKE ME AND SLIM AND WANDSWORTH.
HM?
THE GOLDFISH.

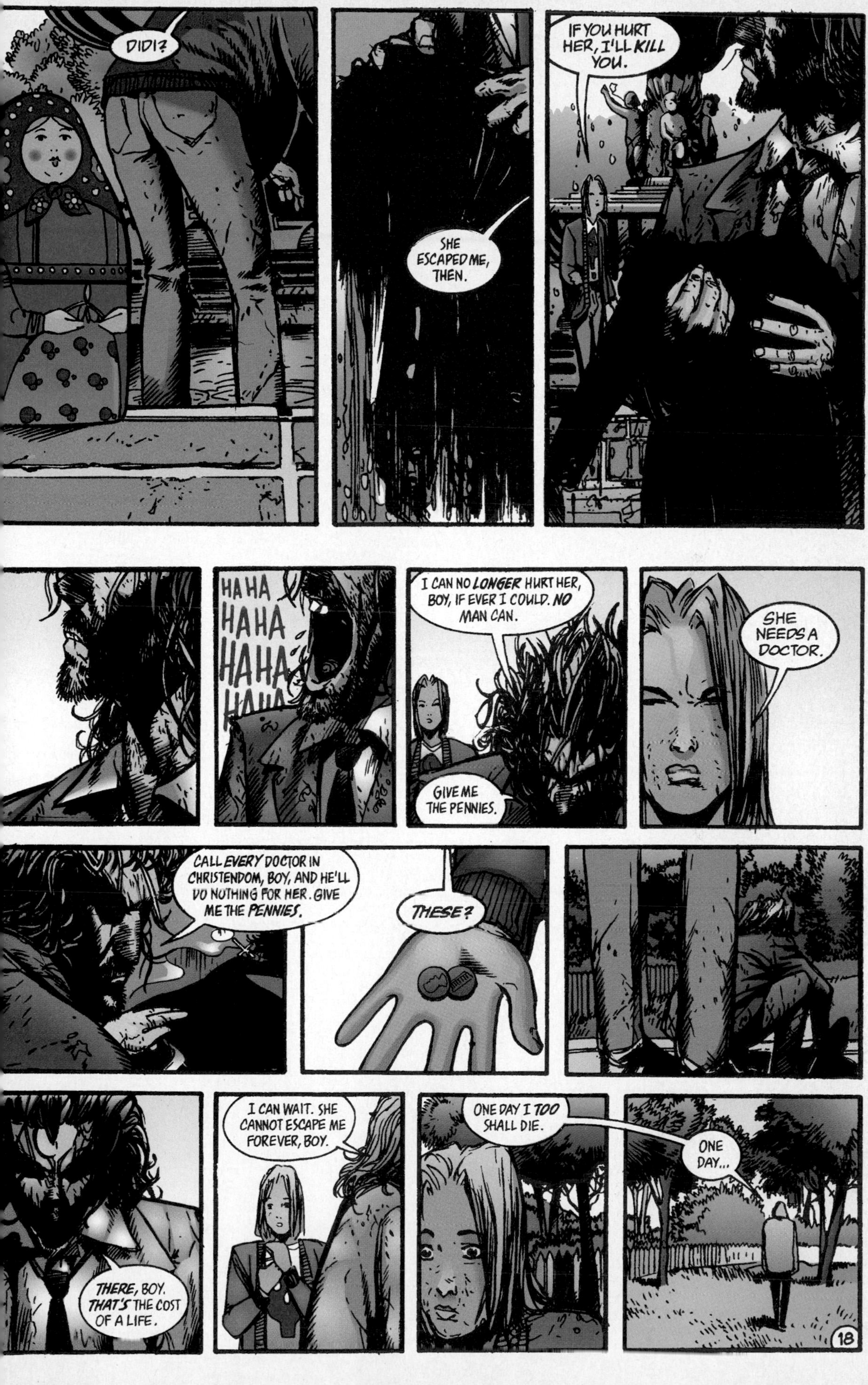
DIDI?
SHE ESCAPED ME, THEN.
IF YOU HURT HER, I'LL KILL YOU.
HA HA HA HA HA HA HA
I CAN NO LONGER HURT HER, BOY, IF EVER I COULD. NO MAN CAN.
GIVE ME THE PENNIES.
SHE NEEDS A DOCTOR.
CALL EVERY DOCTOR IN CHRISTENDOM, BOY, AND HE'LL DO NOTHING FOR HER. GIVE ME THE PENNIES.
THESE?
THERE, BOY. THAT'S THE COST OF A LIFE.
I CAN WAIT. SHE CANNOT ESCAPE ME FOREVER, BOY.
ONE DAY I TOO SHALL DIE.
ONE DAY...

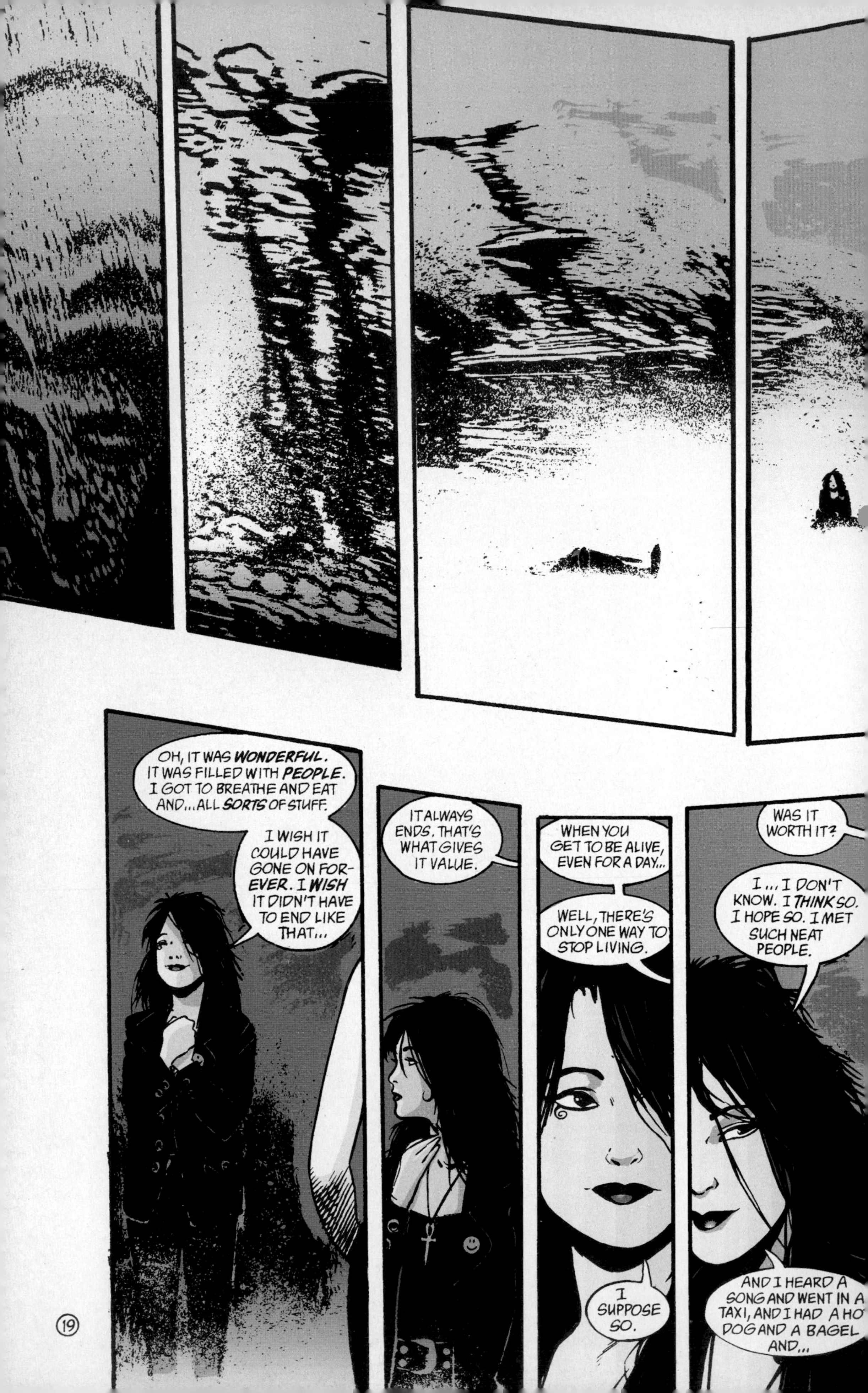

OH, IT WAS WONDERFUL. IT WAS FILLED WITH PEOPLE. I GOT TO BREATHE AND EAT AND... ALL SORTS OF STUFF.
I WISH IT COULD HAVE GONE ON FOREVER. I WISH IT DIDN'T HAVE TO END LIKE THAT...
IT ALWAYS ENDS. THAT'S WHAT GIVES IT VALUE.
WHEN YOU GET TO BE ALIVE, EVEN FOR A DAY...
WELL, THERE'S ONLY ONE WAY TO STOP LIVING.
I SUPPOSE SO.
WAS IT WORTH IT?
I... I DON'T KNOW. I THINK SO. I HOPE SO. I MET SUCH NEAT PEOPLE.
AND I HEARD A SONG AND WENT IN A TAXI, AND I HAD A HO DOG AND A BAGEL AND...

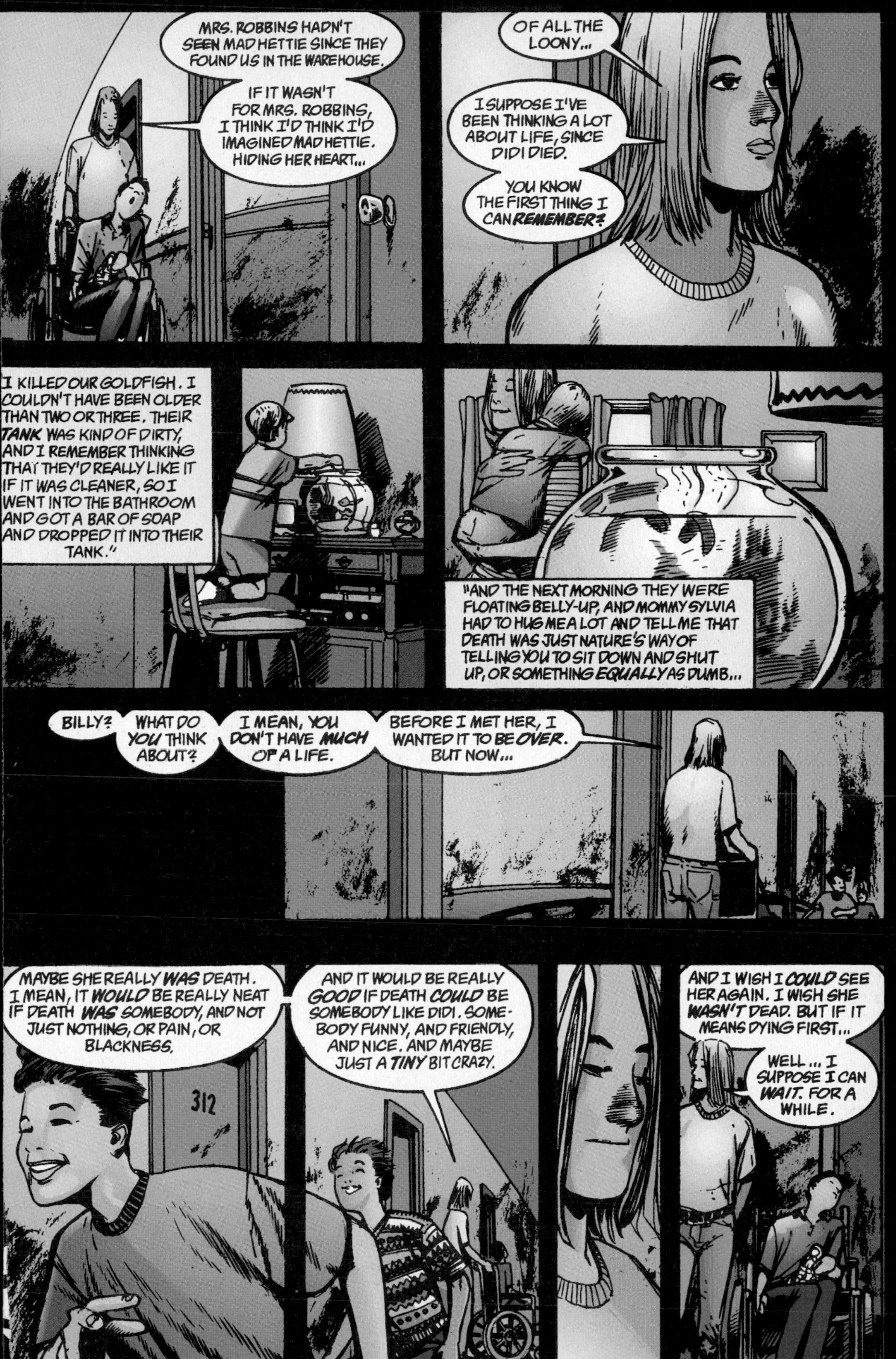
MRS. ROBBINS HADN'T SEEN MAD HETTIE SINCE THEY FOUND US IN THE WAREHOUSE.
IF IT WASN'T FOR MRS. ROBBINS, I THINK I'D THINK I'D IMAGINED MAD HETTIE. HIDING HER HEART...
OF ALL THE LOONY...
I SUPPOSE I'VE BEEN THINKING A LOT ABOUT LIFE, SINCE DIDI DIED.
YOU KNOW THE FIRST THING I CAN REMEMBER?
"I KILLED OUR GOLDFISH. I COULDN'T HAVE BEEN OLDER THAN TWO OR THREE. THEIR TANK WAS KIND OF DIRTY, AND I REMEMBER THINKING THAT THEY'D REALLY LIKE IT IF IT WAS CLEANER, SO I WENT INTO THE BATHROOM AND GOT A BAR OF SOAP AND DROPPED IT INTO THEIR TANK."
"AND THE NEXT MORNING THEY WERE FLOATING BELLY-UP, AND MOMMY SYLVIA HAD TO HUG ME A LOT AND TELL ME THAT DEATH WAS JUST NATURE'S WAY OF TELLING YOU TO SIT DOWN AND SHUT UP, OR SOMETHING EQUALLY AS DUMB...
BILLY?
WHAT DO YOU THINK ABOUT?
I MEAN, YOU DON'T HAVE MUCH OF A LIFE.
BEFORE I MET HER, I WANTED IT TO BE OVER. BUT NOW...
MAYBE SHE REALLY WAS DEATH. I MEAN, IT WOULD BE REALLY NEAT IF DEATH WAS SOMEBODY, AND NOT JUST NOTHING, OR PAIN, OR BLACKNESS.
312
AND IT WOULD BE REALLY GOOD IF DEATH COULD BE SOMEBODY LIKE DIDI. SOMEBODY FUNNY, AND FRIENDLY, AND NICE. AND MAYBE JUST A TINY BIT CRAZY.
AND I WISH I COULD SEE HER AGAIN. I WISH SHE WASN'T DEAD. BUT IF IT MEANS DYING FIRST...
WELL... I SUPPOSE I CAN WAIT. FOR A WHILE.

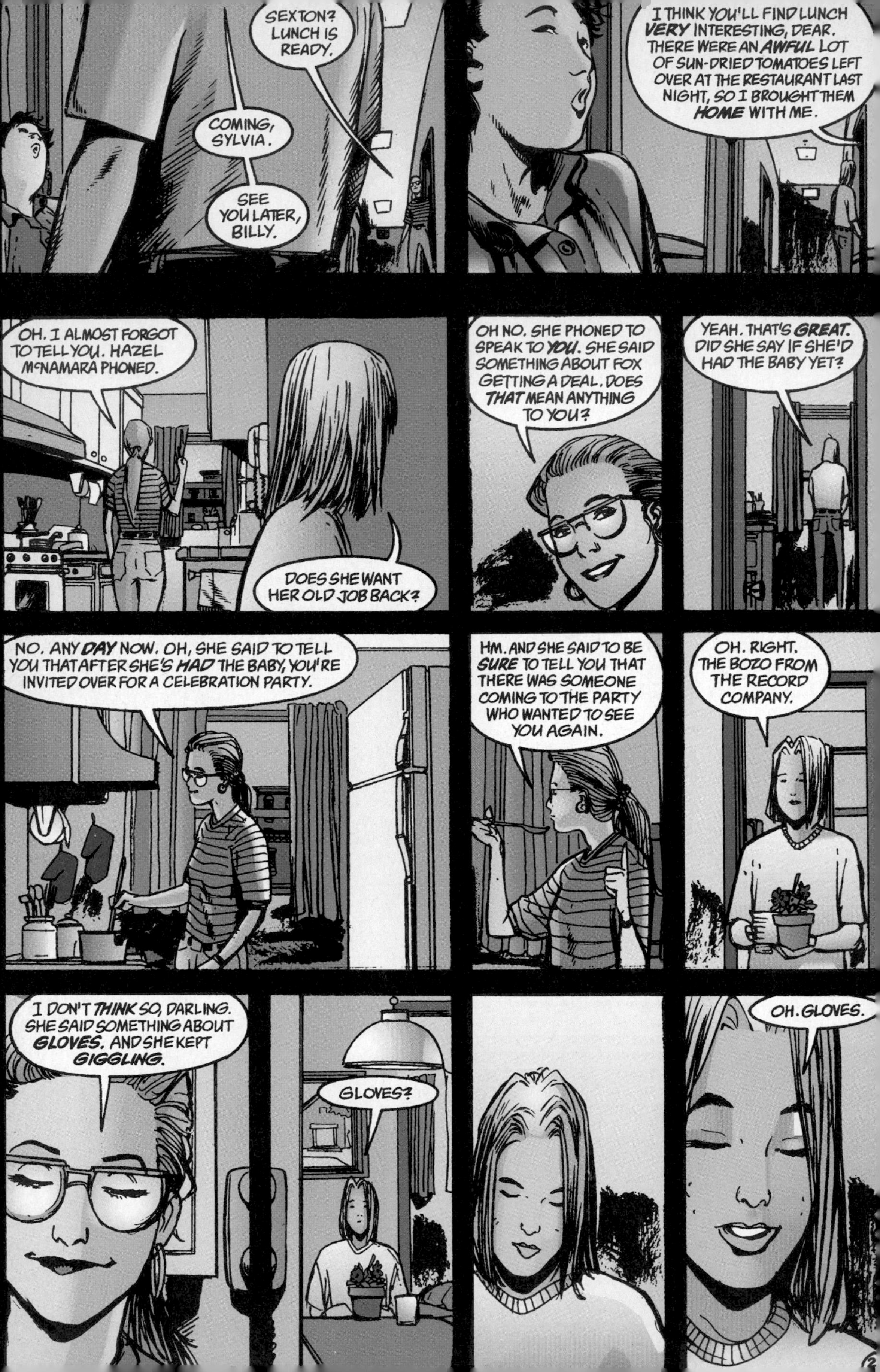

SEXTON? LUNCH IS READY.
COMING, SYLVIA.
SEE YOU LATER, BILLY.
I THINK YOU'LL FIND LUNCH VERY INTERESTING, DEAR. THERE WERE AN AWFUL LOT OF SUN-DRIED TOMATOES LEFT OVER AT THE RESTAURANT LAST NIGHT, SO I BROUGHT THEM HOME WITH ME.
OH. I ALMOST FORGOT TO TELL YOU. HAZEL McNAMARA PHONED.
DOES SHE WANT HER OLD JOB BACK?
OH NO. SHE PHONED TO SPEAK TO YOU. SHE SAID SOMETHING ABOUT FOX GETTING A DEAL. DOES THAT MEAN ANYTHING TO YOU?
YEAH. THAT'S GREAT. DID SHE SAY IF SHE'D HAD THE BABY YET?
NO. ANY DAY NOW. OH, SHE SAID TO TELL YOU THAT AFTER SHE'S HAD THE BABY, YOU'RE INVITED OVER FOR A CELEBRATION PARTY.
HM. AND SHE SAID TO BE SURE TO TELL YOU THAT THERE WAS SOMEONE COMING TO THE PARTY WHO WANTED TO SEE YOU AGAIN.
OH. RIGHT. THE BOZO FROM THE RECORD COMPANY.
I DON'T THINK SO, DARLING. SHE SAID SOMETHING ABOUT GLOVES. AND SHE KEPT GIGGLING.
GLOVES?
OH. GLOVES.

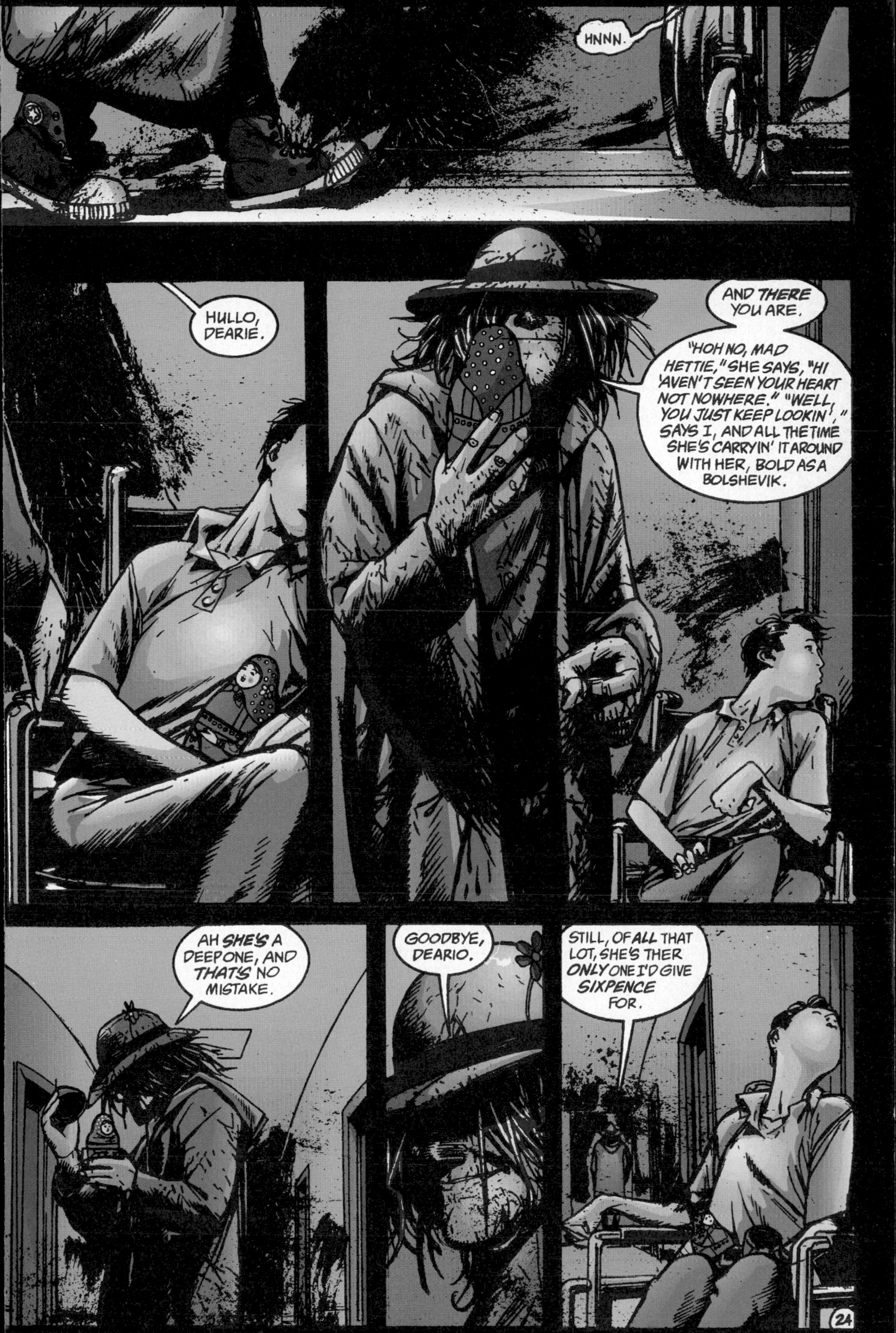
HNNN.
HULLO, DEARIE.
AND THERE YOU ARE.
"HOH NO, MAD HETTIE," SHE SAYS, "HI 'AVEN'T SEEN YOUR HEART NOT NOWHERE." "WELL, YOU JUST KEEP LOOKIN'," SAYS I, AND ALL THE TIME SHE'S CARRYIN' IT AROUND WITH HER, BOLD AS A BOLSHEVIK.
AH SHE'S A DEEP ONE, AND THAT'S NO MISTAKE.
GOODBYE, DEARIO.
STILL, OF ALL THAT LOT, SHE'S THER ONLY ONE I'D GIVE SIXPENCE FOR.

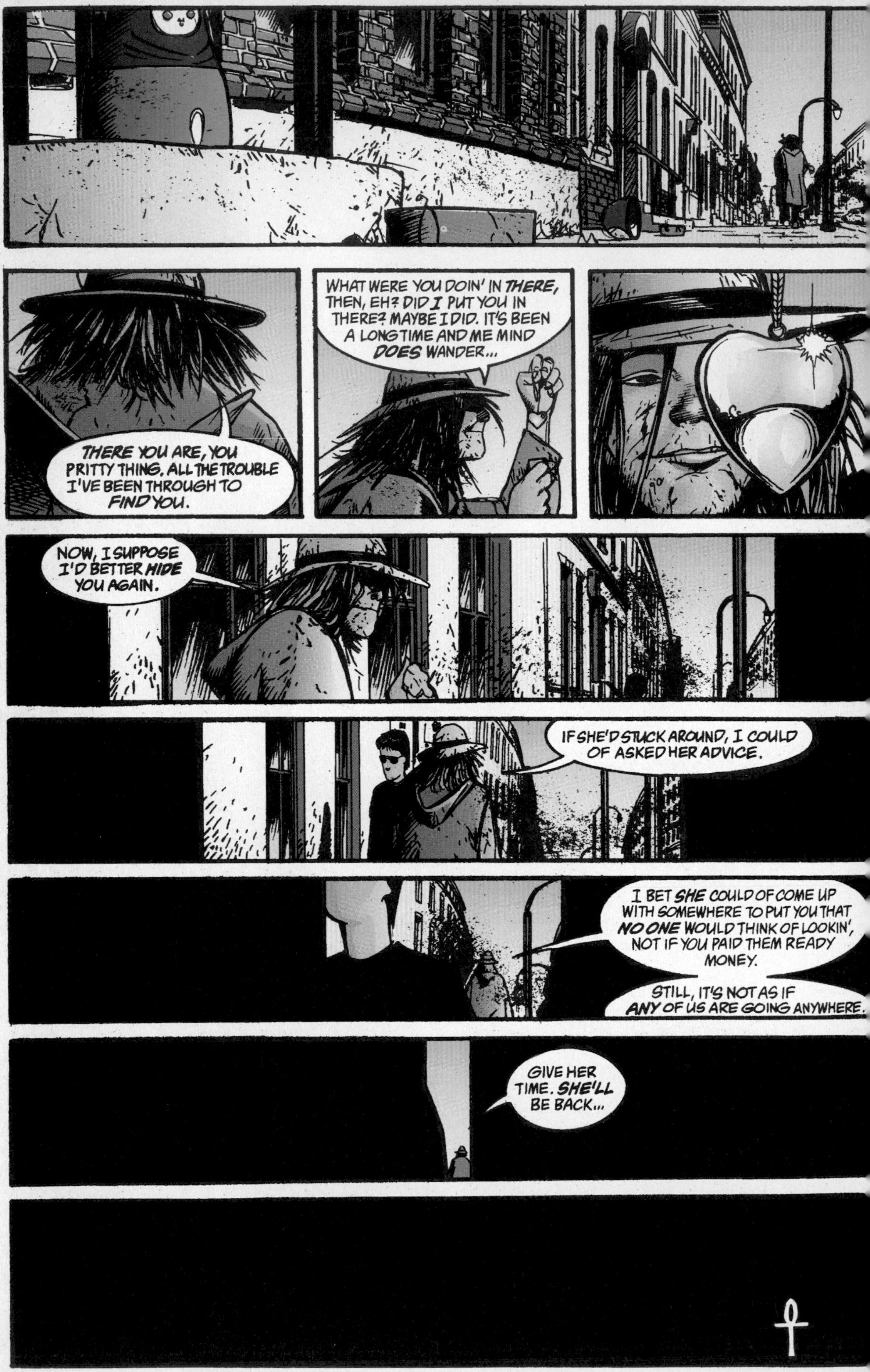

THERE YOU ARE, YOU PRITTY THING. ALL THE TROUBLE I'VE BEEN THROUGH TO FIND YOU.
WHAT WERE YOU DOIN' IN THERE, THEN, EH? DID I PUT YOU IN THERE? MAYBE I DID. IT'S BEEN A LONG TIME AND ME MIND DOES WANDER...
NOW, I SUPPOSE I'D BETTER HIDE YOU AGAIN.
IF SHE'D STUCK AROUND, I COULD OF ASKED HER ADVICE.
I BET SHE COULD OF COME UP WITH SOMEWHERE TO PUT YOU THAT NO ONE WOULD THINK OF LOOKIN', NOT IF YOU PAID THEM READY MONEY.
STILL, IT'S NOT AS IF ANY OF US ARE GOING ANYWHERE.
GIVE HER TIME. SHE'LL BE BACK...

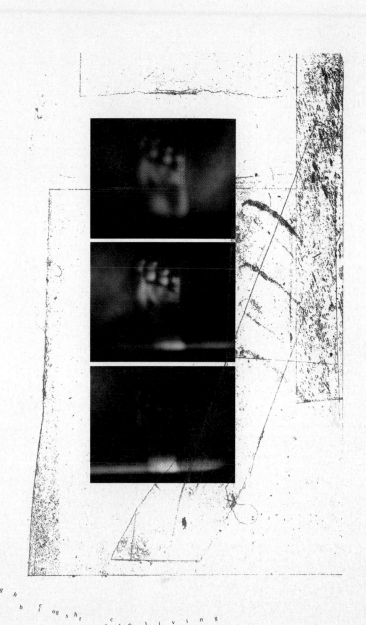

the high
the h f o g s h t c o f o l i v i n g
                  s t   o f   l i v i n g

the   high   cost   of
                                    l i v i n g

on't think of her so much

n fact never. I never just say

i when the sun is on my

ongue and my belly's all warm

n bad days I talk to

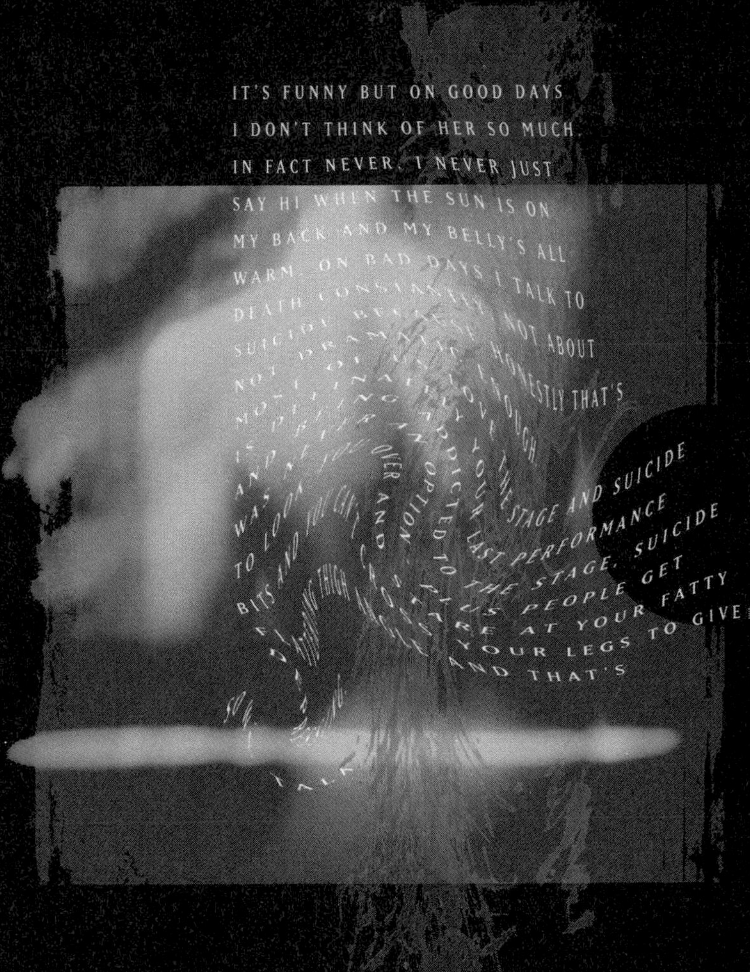
IT'S FUNNY BUT ON GOOD DAYS
I DON'T THINK OF HER SO MUCH.
IN FACT NEVER. I NEVER JUST
SAY HI WHEN THE SUN IS ON
MY BACK AND MY BELLY'S ALL
WARM. ON BAD DAYS I TALK TO
NOT ABOUT
HONESTLY THAT'S
STAGE AND SUICIDE
LAST PERFORMANCE
THE STAGE, SUICIDE
PEOPLE GET
AT YOUR FATTY
YOUR LEGS TO GIVE
AND THAT'S

he says things no one else see

o come up with like let's hav

hotdog and then it's like

nothing's impossible

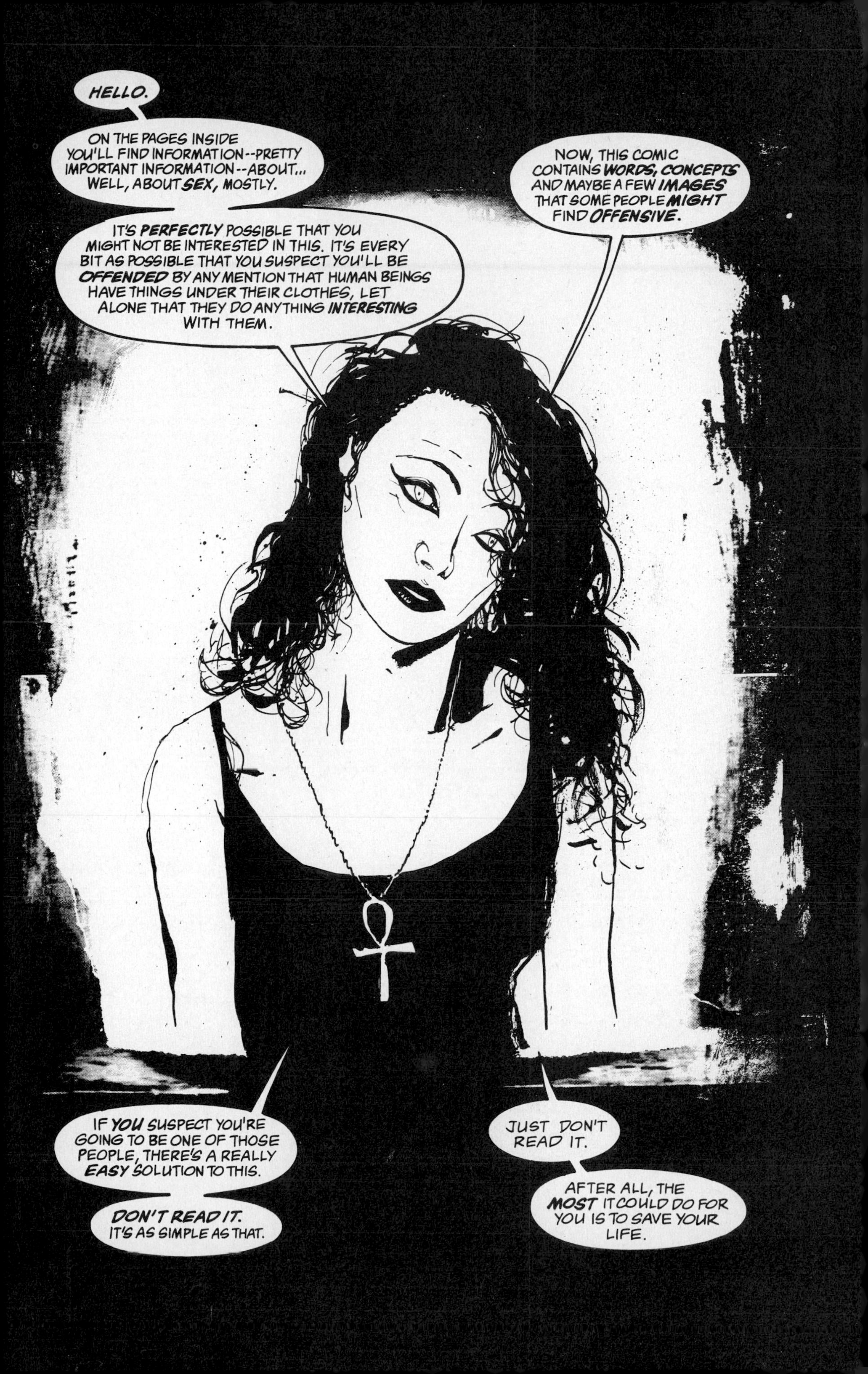
HELLO.
ON THE PAGES INSIDE YOU'LL FIND INFORMATION--PRETTY IMPORTANT INFORMATION--ABOUT... WELL, ABOUT SEX, MOSTLY.
IT'S PERFECTLY POSSIBLE THAT YOU MIGHT NOT BE INTERESTED IN THIS. IT'S EVERY BIT AS POSSIBLE THAT YOU SUSPECT YOU'LL BE OFFENDED BY ANY MENTION THAT HUMAN BEINGS HAVE THINGS UNDER THEIR CLOTHES, LET ALONE THAT THEY DO ANYTHING INTERESTING WITH THEM.
NOW, THIS COMIC CONTAINS WORDS, CONCEPTS AND MAYBE A FEW IMAGES THAT SOME PEOPLE MIGHT FIND OFFENSIVE.
IF YOU SUSPECT YOU'RE GOING TO BE ONE OF THOSE PEOPLE, THERE'S A REALLY EASY SOLUTION TO THIS.
DON'T READ IT. IT'S AS SIMPLE AS THAT.
JUST DON'T READ IT.
AFTER ALL, THE MOST IT COULD DO FOR YOU IS TO SAVE YOUR LIFE.

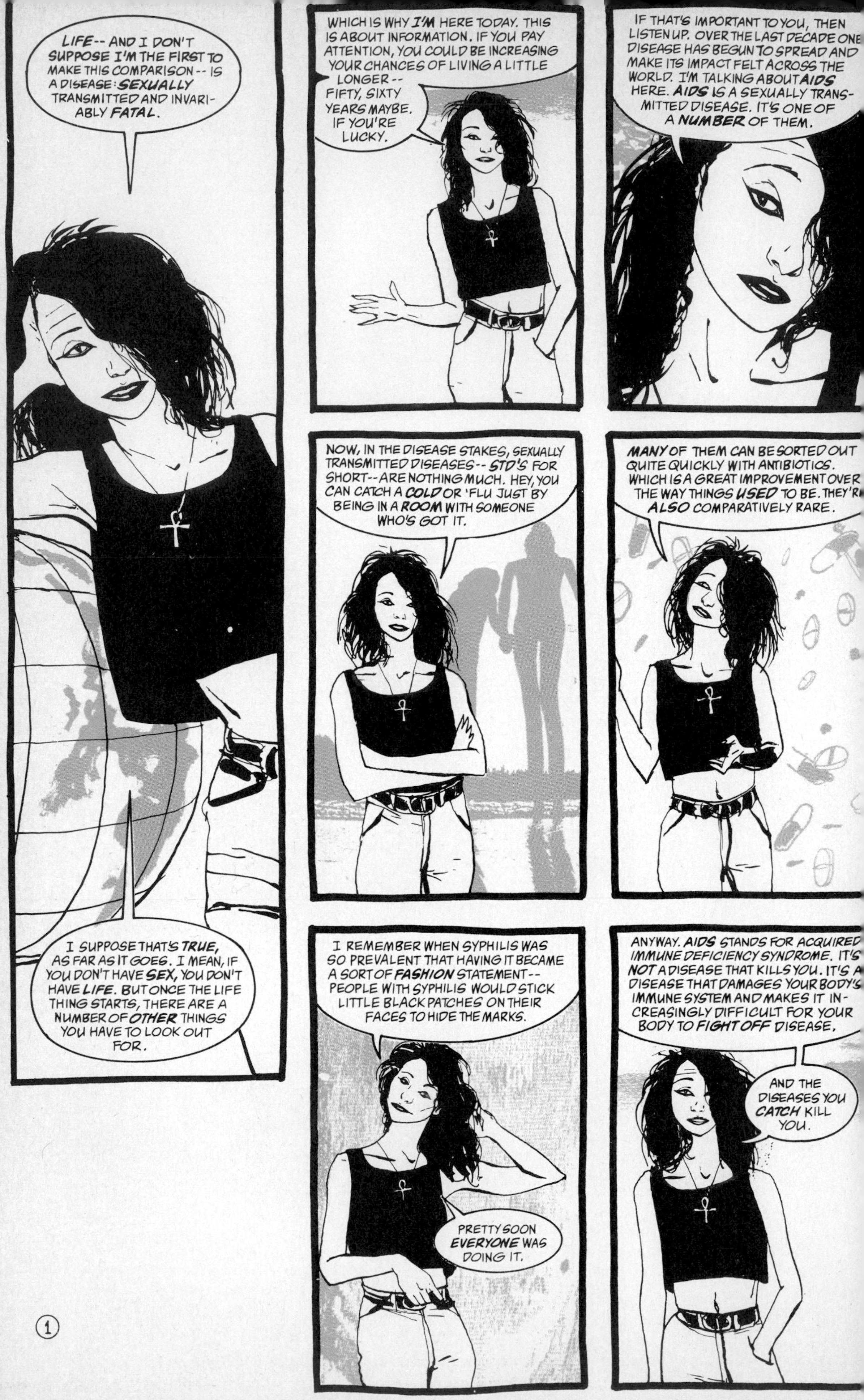
LIFE-- AND I DON'T SUPPOSE I'M THE FIRST TO MAKE THIS COMPARISON -- IS A DISEASE: SEXUALLY TRANSMITTED AND INVARIABLY FATAL.
I SUPPOSE THAT'S TRUE, AS FAR AS IT GOES. I MEAN, IF YOU DON'T HAVE SEX, YOU DON'T HAVE LIFE. BUT ONCE THE LIFE THING STARTS, THERE ARE A NUMBER OF OTHER THINGS YOU HAVE TO LOOK OUT FOR.
WHICH IS WHY I'M HERE TODAY. THIS IS ABOUT INFORMATION. IF YOU PAY ATTENTION, YOU COULD BE INCREASING YOUR CHANCES OF LIVING A LITTLE LONGER -- FIFTY, SIXTY YEARS MAYBE. IF YOU'RE LUCKY.
IF THAT'S IMPORTANT TO YOU, THEN LISTEN UP. OVER THE LAST DECADE ONE DISEASE HAS BEGUN TO SPREAD AND MAKE ITS IMPACT FELT ACROSS THE WORLD. I'M TALKING ABOUT AIDS HERE. AIDS IS A SEXUALLY TRANSMITTED DISEASE. IT'S ONE OF A NUMBER OF THEM.
NOW, IN THE DISEASE STAKES, SEXUALLY TRANSMITTED DISEASES -- STD'S FOR SHORT -- ARE NOTHING MUCH. HEY, YOU CAN CATCH A COLD OR 'FLU JUST BY BEING IN A ROOM WITH SOMEONE WHO'S GOT IT.
MANY OF THEM CAN BE SORTED OUT QUITE QUICKLY WITH ANTIBIOTICS. WHICH IS A GREAT IMPROVEMENT OVER THE WAY THINGS USED TO BE. THEY'RE ALSO COMPARATIVELY RARE.
I REMEMBER WHEN SYPHILIS WAS SO PREVALENT THAT HAVING IT BECAME A SORT OF FASHION STATEMENT -- PEOPLE WITH SYPHILIS WOULD STICK LITTLE BLACK PATCHES ON THEIR FACES TO HIDE THE MARKS.
PRETTY SOON EVERYONE WAS DOING IT.
ANYWAY. AIDS STANDS FOR ACQUIRED IMMUNE DEFICIENCY SYNDROME. IT'S NOT A DISEASE THAT KILLS YOU. IT'S A DISEASE THAT DAMAGES YOUR BODY'S IMMUNE SYSTEM AND MAKES IT INCREASINGLY DIFFICULT FOR YOUR BODY TO FIGHT OFF DISEASE.
AND THE DISEASES YOU CATCH KILL YOU.

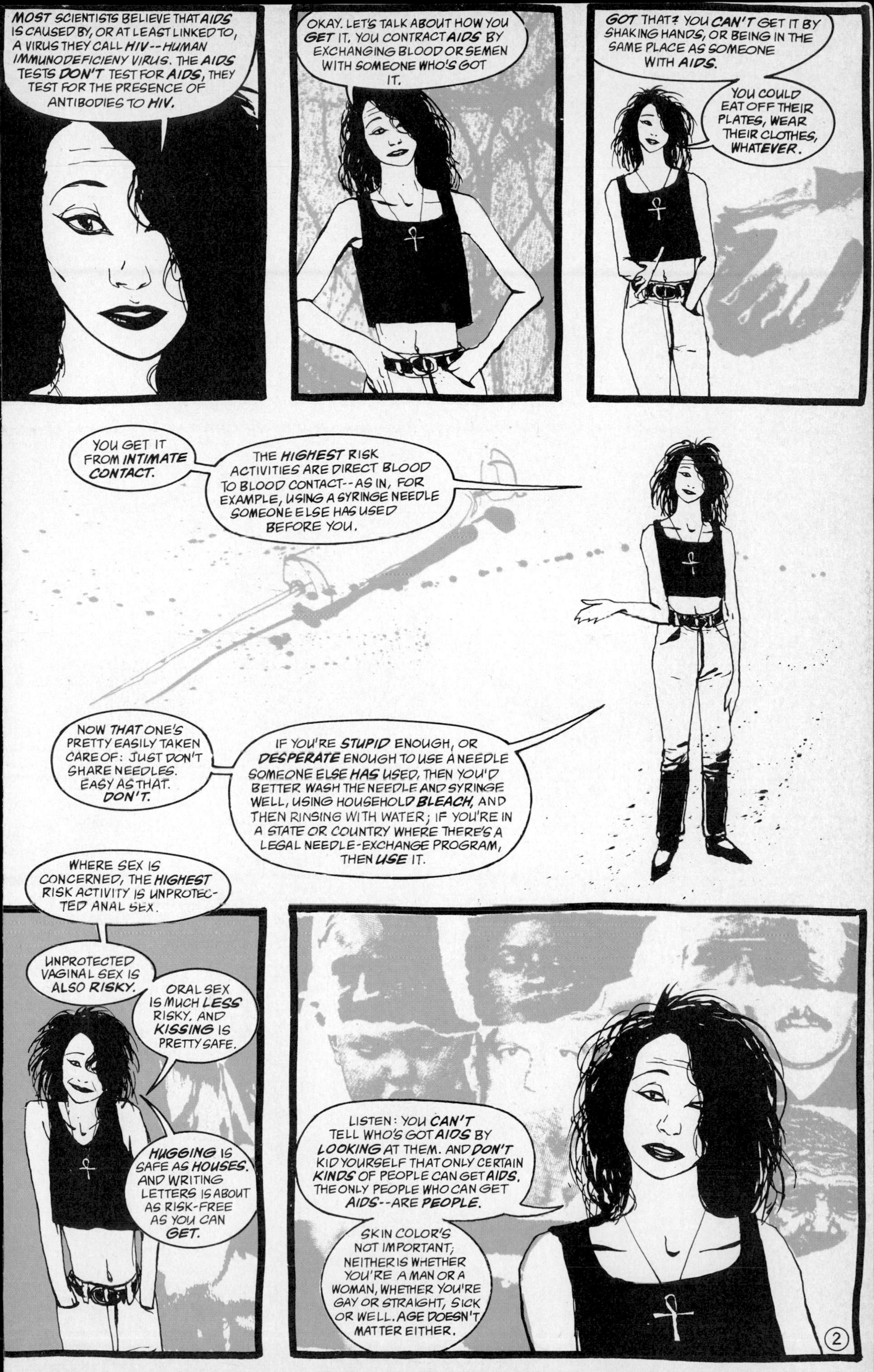
MOST SCIENTISTS BELIEVE THAT AIDS IS CAUSED BY, OR AT LEAST LINKED TO, A VIRUS THEY CALL HIV--HUMAN IMMUNODEFICIENY VIRUS. THE AIDS TESTS DON'T TEST FOR AIDS, THEY TEST FOR THE PRESENCE OF ANTIBODIES TO HIV.
OKAY. LET'S TALK ABOUT HOW YOU GET IT. YOU CONTRACT AIDS BY EXCHANGING BLOOD OR SEMEN WITH SOMEONE WHO'S GOT IT.
GOT THAT? YOU CAN'T GET IT BY SHAKING HANDS, OR BEING IN THE SAME PLACE AS SOMEONE WITH AIDS.
YOU COULD EAT OFF THEIR PLATES, WEAR THEIR CLOTHES, WHATEVER.
YOU GET IT FROM INTIMATE CONTACT.
THE HIGHEST RISK ACTIVITIES ARE DIRECT BLOOD TO BLOOD CONTACT--AS IN, FOR EXAMPLE, USING A SYRINGE NEEDLE SOMEONE ELSE HAS USED BEFORE YOU.
NOW THAT ONE'S PRETTY EASILY TAKEN CARE OF: JUST DON'T SHARE NEEDLES. EASY AS THAT. DON'T.
IF YOU'RE STUPID ENOUGH, OR DESPERATE ENOUGH TO USE A NEEDLE SOMEONE ELSE HAS USED, THEN YOU'D BETTER WASH THE NEEDLE AND SYRINGE WELL, USING HOUSEHOLD BLEACH, AND THEN RINSING WITH WATER; IF YOU'RE IN A STATE OR COUNTRY WHERE THERE'S A LEGAL NEEDLE-EXCHANGE PROGRAM, THEN USE IT.
WHERE SEX IS CONCERNED, THE HIGHEST RISK ACTIVITY IS UNPROTECTED ANAL SEX.
UNPROTECTED VAGINAL SEX IS ALSO RISKY.
ORAL SEX IS MUCH LESS RISKY, AND KISSING IS PRETTY SAFE.
HUGGING IS SAFE AS HOUSES. AND WRITING LETTERS IS ABOUT AS RISK-FREE AS YOU CAN GET.
LISTEN: YOU CAN'T TELL WHO'S GOT AIDS BY LOOKING AT THEM. AND DON'T KID YOURSELF THAT ONLY CERTAIN KINDS OF PEOPLE CAN GET AIDS. THE ONLY PEOPLE WHO CAN GET AIDS--ARE PEOPLE.
SKIN COLOR'S NOT IMPORTANT; NEITHER IS WHETHER YOU'RE A MAN OR A WOMAN, WHETHER YOU'RE GAY OR STRAIGHT, SICK OR WELL. AGE DOESN'T MATTER EITHER.
2

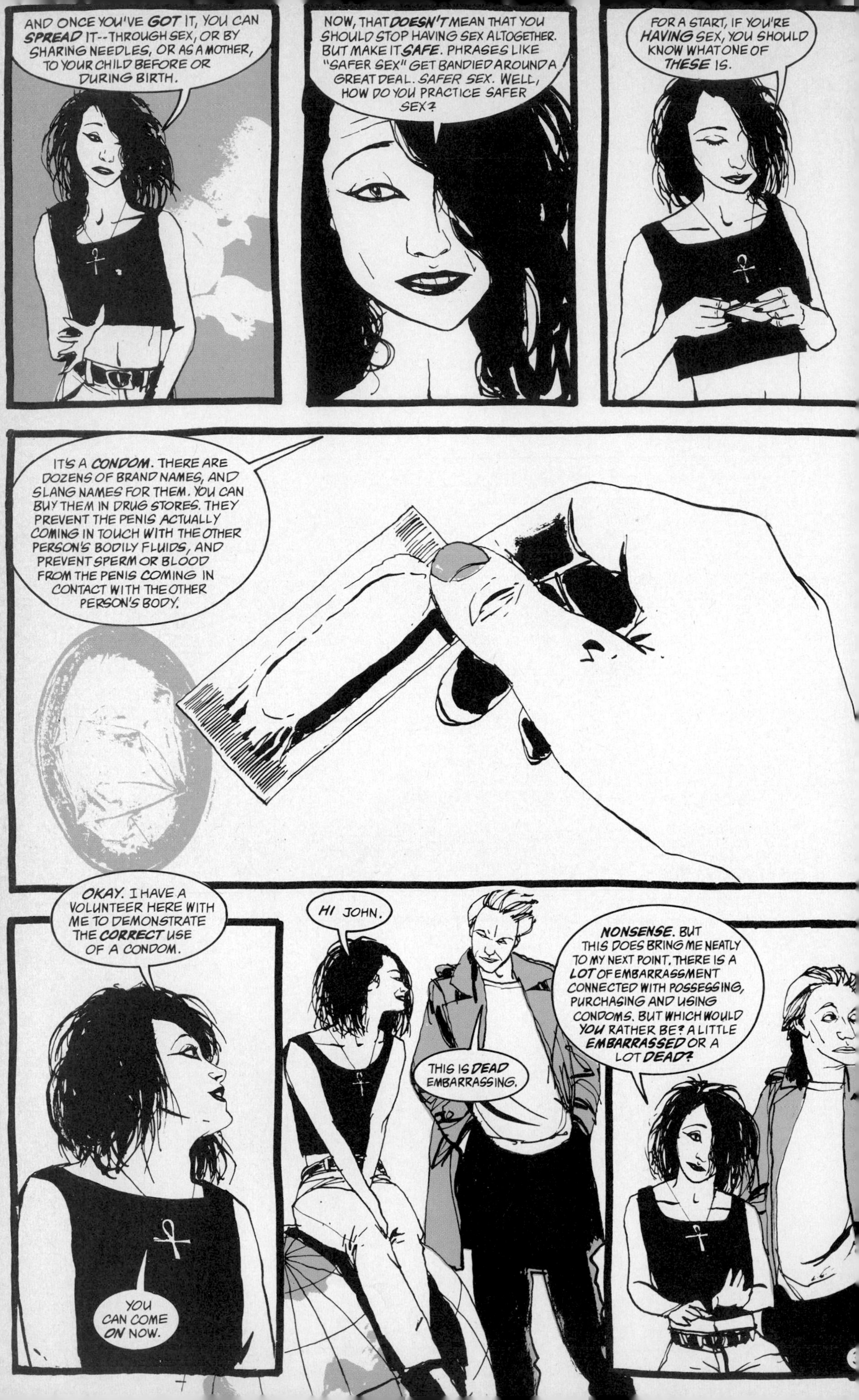
AND ONCE YOU'VE GOT IT, YOU CAN SPREAD IT--THROUGH SEX, OR BY SHARING NEEDLES, OR AS A MOTHER, TO YOUR CHILD BEFORE OR DURING BIRTH.
NOW, THAT DOESN'T MEAN THAT YOU SHOULD STOP HAVING SEX ALTOGETHER. BUT MAKE IT SAFE. PHRASES LIKE "SAFER SEX" GET BANDIED AROUND A GREAT DEAL. SAFER SEX. WELL, HOW DO YOU PRACTICE SAFER SEX?
FOR A START, IF YOU'RE HAVING SEX, YOU SHOULD KNOW WHAT ONE OF THESE IS.
IT'S A CONDOM. THERE ARE DOZENS OF BRAND NAMES, AND SLANG NAMES FOR THEM. YOU CAN BUY THEM IN DRUG STORES. THEY PREVENT THE PENIS ACTUALLY COMING IN TOUCH WITH THE OTHER PERSON'S BODILY FLUIDS, AND PREVENT SPERM OR BLOOD FROM THE PENIS COMING IN CONTACT WITH THE OTHER PERSON'S BODY.
OKAY. I HAVE A VOLUNTEER HERE WITH ME TO DEMONSTRATE THE CORRECT USE OF A CONDOM.
YOU CAN COME ON NOW.
HI JOHN.
THIS IS DEAD EMBARRASSING.
NONSENSE. BUT THIS DOES BRING ME NEATLY TO MY NEXT POINT. THERE IS A LOT OF EMBARRASSMENT CONNECTED WITH POSSESSING, PURCHASING AND USING CONDOMS. BUT WHICH WOULD YOU RATHER BE? A LITTLE EMBARRASSED OR A LOT DEAD?

OKAY, JOHN. LET'S *DO* IT.

I *STILL* THINK THIS IS EMBARRASSING.

FOR DEMONSTRATION PURPOSES, THIS IS A *BANANA*, BY THE WAY. NOT AN ERECT PENIS.

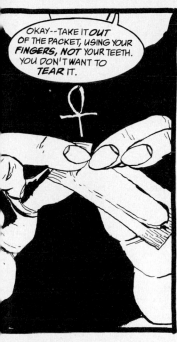

OKAY--TAKE IT *OUT* OF THE PACKET, USING YOUR *FINGERS, NOT* YOUR TEETH. YOU DON'T WANT TO *TEAR* IT.

HOLD IT AT THE *TIP,* SQUEEZING BETWEEN YOUR THUMB AND FOREFINGER, WHILE ROLLING THE CONDOM *DOWN* THE BANANA. UM. *PENIS.*

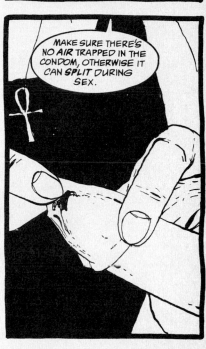

MAKE SURE THERE'S NO *AIR* TRAPPED IN THE CONDOM, OTHERWISE IT CAN *SPLIT* DURING SEX.

YOU WANT *LATEX* CONDOMS, BY THE WAY. OTHER KINDS ARE NO GOOD FOR DISEASE PREVENTION.

OKAY? YOU *GOT* ALL THAT?

THANK YOU, JOHN.

YEAH. ANY TIME.

NOW, SOME PEOPLE DON'T *LIKE* CONDOMS. BUT IF SOMEONE DOESN'T CARE ENOUGH ABOUT YOU TO *WEAR* A CONDOM -- OR TO LET *YOU* WEAR A CONDOM -- THEY PROBABLY DON'T CARE ENOUGH ABOUT YOU TO BE WORTH HAVING *SEX* WITH. YOU *KNOW?*

4

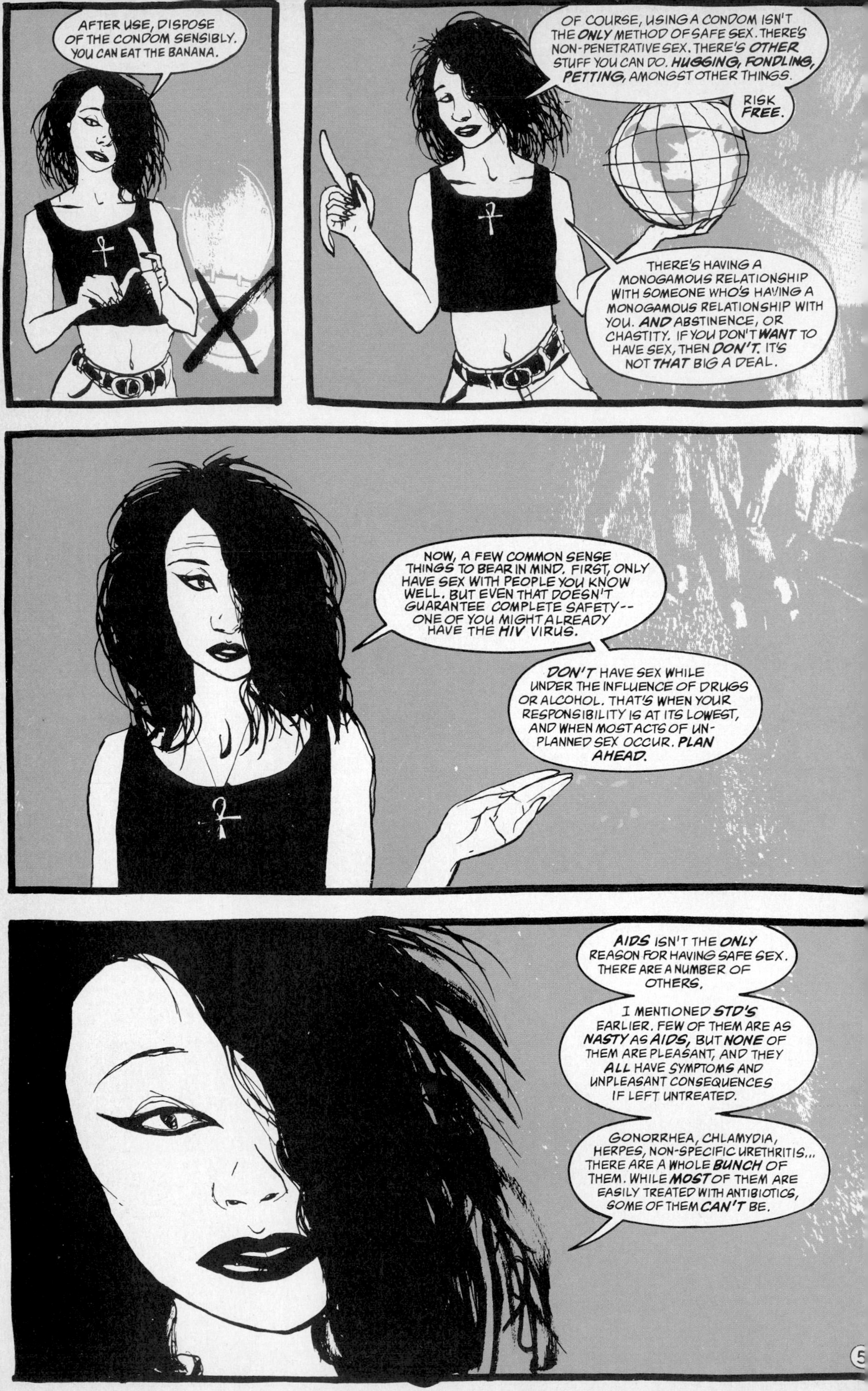
AFTER USE, DISPOSE OF THE CONDOM SENSIBLY. YOU CAN EAT THE BANANA.
OF COURSE, USING A CONDOM ISN'T THE ONLY METHOD OF SAFE SEX. THERE'S NON-PENETRATIVE SEX. THERE'S OTHER STUFF YOU CAN DO. HUGGING, FONDLING, PETTING, AMONGST OTHER THINGS.
RISK FREE.
THERE'S HAVING A MONOGAMOUS RELATIONSHIP WITH SOMEONE WHO'S HAVING A MONOGAMOUS RELATIONSHIP WITH YOU. AND ABSTINENCE, OR CHASTITY. IF YOU DON'T WANT TO HAVE SEX, THEN DON'T. IT'S NOT THAT BIG A DEAL.
NOW, A FEW COMMON SENSE THINGS TO BEAR IN MIND. FIRST, ONLY HAVE SEX WITH PEOPLE YOU KNOW WELL. BUT EVEN THAT DOESN'T GUARANTEE COMPLETE SAFETY-- ONE OF YOU MIGHT ALREADY HAVE THE HIV VIRUS.
DON'T HAVE SEX WHILE UNDER THE INFLUENCE OF DRUGS OR ALCOHOL. THAT'S WHEN YOUR RESPONSIBILITY IS AT ITS LOWEST, AND WHEN MOST ACTS OF UN-PLANNED SEX OCCUR. PLAN AHEAD.
AIDS ISN'T THE ONLY REASON FOR HAVING SAFE SEX. THERE ARE A NUMBER OF OTHERS.
I MENTIONED STD'S EARLIER. FEW OF THEM ARE AS NASTY AS AIDS, BUT NONE OF THEM ARE PLEASANT, AND THEY ALL HAVE SYMPTOMS AND UNPLEASANT CONSEQUENCES IF LEFT UNTREATED.
GONORRHEA, CHLAMYDIA, HERPES, NON-SPECIFIC URETHRITIS... THERE ARE A WHOLE BUNCH OF THEM. WHILE MOST OF THEM ARE EASILY TREATED WITH ANTIBIOTICS, SOME OF THEM CAN'T BE.

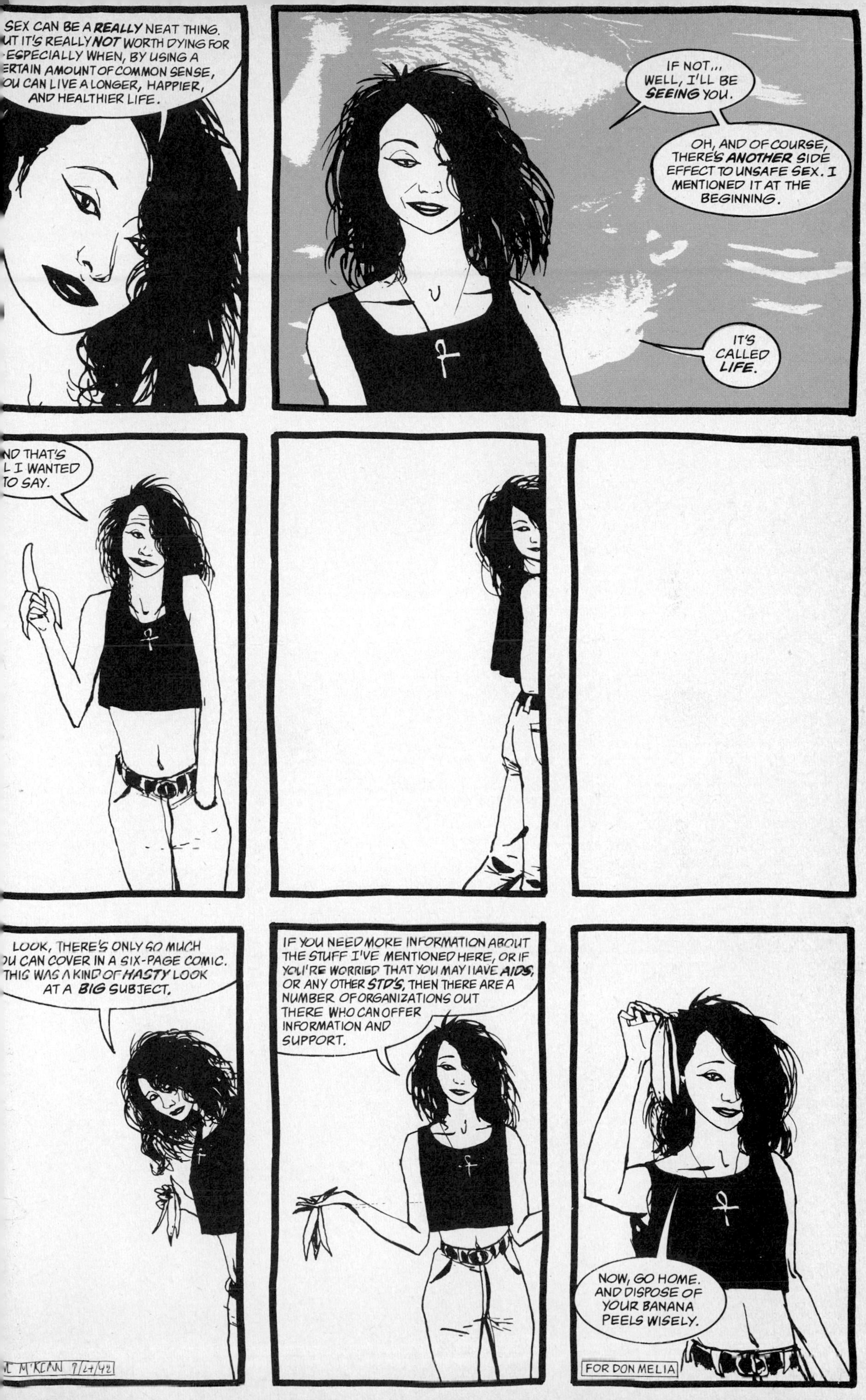
SEX CAN BE A REALLY NEAT THING. UT IT'S REALLY NOT WORTH DYING FOR ESPECIALLY WHEN, BY USING A ERTAIN AMOUNT OF COMMON SENSE, OU CAN LIVE A LONGER, HAPPIER, AND HEALTHIER LIFE.
IF NOT... WELL, I'LL BE SEEING YOU.
OH, AND OF COURSE, THERE'S ANOTHER SIDE EFFECT TO UNSAFE SEX. I MENTIONED IT AT THE BEGINNING.
IT'S CALLED LIFE.
ND THAT'S L I WANTED TO SAY.
LOOK, THERE'S ONLY SO MUCH OU CAN COVER IN A SIX-PAGE COMIC. THIS WAS A KIND OF HASTY LOOK AT A BIG SUBJECT.
IF YOU NEED MORE INFORMATION ABOUT THE STUFF I'VE MENTIONED HERE, OR IF YOU'RE WORRIED THAT YOU MAY HAVE AIDS, OR ANY OTHER STD'S, THEN THERE ARE A NUMBER OF ORGANIZATIONS OUT THERE WHO CAN OFFER INFORMATION AND SUPPORT.
NOW, GO HOME. AND DISPOSE OF YOUR BANANA PEELS WISELY.
FOR DON MELIA

The woman you've just met isn't called Death just because the tuff-sounding name complements her heavy eye makeup and black jeans.

She really *is* Death, the reaper, the one who takes you away when you've had it. It turns out the cloak and the scythe and the skeleton are just bad press; there's nothing grim about her after all.

I MUST CONFESS, I HAVE ALWAYS WONDERED WHAT LAY BEYOND LIFE, MY DEAR.
YEAH, EVERYBODY WONDERS. AND SOONER OR LATER EVERYBODY GETS TO FIND OUT.

Discriminating readers have known this since 1989, when she first appeared in her younger brother Dream's monthly comic book, THE SANDMAN. The title had already been making waves as an intelligent, involving adult fantasy series when writer Neil Gaiman and artists Mike Dringenberg and Malcolm Jones III twisted reader expectations by casting dream-weaver Morpheus as the grim, pale, gaunt one and Death as his cheerful foil.

a brief history of death

The two are members of the Endless, a loose-knit family of seven who embody their respective realms of Dream, Desire, Despair, Destiny, Delirium, Destruction and Death. Roughly as old as time, they are not merely gods or patron saints; they are the things themselves, personified.

That initial story, "The Sound of Her Wings," first printed in SANDMAN #8, went something like this: feeding pigeons in the park, Dream broods after recovering his domain in the wake of a major setback. His problems had given him a sense of purpose; now that they're largely solved, that sense is gone. Death quotes Mary Poppins — *Death quotes Mary Poppins!* — and draws her brother's feelings out before angrily refusing to indulge his self-pity. Permitting him to tag along as she casually and graciously collects the dead, she cheers him up by sheer example: if she can find satisfaction in her everyday routine, so can he.

Generously displaying her Sunday school sweetness and her rock-club looks over what amounted to 24 pages of sibling interaction (an unusually quiet theme for comics, to say the least), "The Sound of Her Wings" instantly made Death even more popular than the book's title character. Still one of the best-received Sandman stories to date, you can find it in not one but *two* paperback collections: SANDMAN: THE DOLL'S HOUSE and SANDMAN: PRELUDES & NOCTURNES.

ANYWAY: I'M NOT BLESSED, OR MERCIFUL. I'M JUST ME. I'VE GOT A JOB TO DO, AND I DO IT.
LISTEN: EVEN AS WE'RE TALKING, I'M THERE FOR OLD AND YOUNG, INNOCENT AND GUILTY, THOSE WHO DIE TOGETHER AND THOSE WHO DIE ALONE.

Fans demanding to see Death again had to wait a mere four months for SANDMAN #12's "Men of Good Fortune," by Gaiman and artists Michael Zulli and Steve Parkhouse. Here we learned that Death doesn't always take her job completely seriously. Observing tavern life in 14th-century London, she and Dream take special notice of Hob Gadling, a soldier who boasts that his stubborn refusal to die will keep him alive forever. Amused by his impertinence, Death grants him immortality. Over the ensuing centuries, Dream strikes up a fond friendship with this mortal who can't die. Again, Death's light heart enriches what might otherwise be a bleak existence for her brother. "Men of Good Fortune" can be found in the collected SANDMAN: THE DOLL'S HOUSE.

BUT... IS THAT ALL THERE WAS? IS THAT ALL I GET?
YES, I'M AFRAID SO.

Death next appeared in SANDMAN #20, in "Façade," the tragic story of a woman trapped by life, by Gaiman and artists Colleen Doran and Malcolm Jones III. Urania Blackwell wants to kill herself, but a magical artifact of the Egyptian god Ra transformed her into the super-hero Element Girl, and no one can kill Element Girl. When danger threatens, she transmutes into an appropriately defensive element... voluntarily or not. When Death claims her neighbor, Urania begs to be taken, but Death cannot oblige. She does, however, take pity on Element Girl, and helps Urania find her own solution. "Façade" is available in SANDMAN: DREAM COUNTRY.

By now, we've seen Death's devotion to her work, her refusal to take it too seriously, her flippant humor, and, again surprisingly, a hint of a social worker's bleeding heart. Her next appearances, collected in SANDMAN: SEASON OF MISTS, display her willingness to stand against her brother when he is wrong (#21, by Gaiman and Dringenberg) and an unexpectedly flexible approach to her job when circumstances warrant. The latter is apparent in SANDMAN #25, as Gaiman and Jones are accompanied by penciller Matt Wagner. Hell has given up its dead, and a harried, aerobics-outfitted Death has her hands full restoring the proper balance. We see her attempting to collect 13-year-old Charles Rowland and simply giving up when he refuses to come along, preferring to see what life has to offer with his fellow dead boy Edwin Paine.

tom peyer

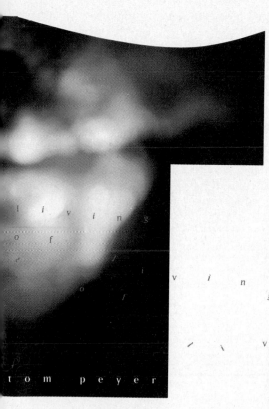

In SANDMAN SPECIAL #1, by Gaiman and Bryan Talbot, Death exempts another: Dream's son, the Orpheus of myth, who wishes to enter the realm of the dead unscathed to rescue his beloved Eurydice. As an unintended result of her boon, Orpheus survives his own beheading by centuries. This and SANDMAN #31, in which Gaiman and artist Shawn McManus introduce us to Death's favorite king, can be found in SANDMAN: FABLES AND REFLECTIONS.

Nearly every SANDMAN collection contains an appearance by Death, and she continues to appear frequently in his ongoing monthly title (most recently in #53). Her popularity has given her a life beyond Sandman stories, chiefly with the material on view here. The original publication of DEATH: THE HIGH COST OF LIVING helped launch DC's VERTIGO line of comics for mature readers with a remarkable critical and commercial response. "Death Talks About Life" ran as an insert in several pre-VERTIGO titles and met with a tide of interest in its message, causing it to be rereleased later as a public service pamphlet.

The point being: after you've read this book and you find yourself smiling when you think about Death, there's more about her out there.

ANYWAY, CONDEMNING HER TO AN ETERNITY IN HELL, JUST BECAUSE SHE TURNED YOU DOWN...
...THAT'S A REALLY SHITTY THING TO DO.
OKAY, I'VE FINISHED. YOU CAN SHOUT AT ME NOW.
Is this how you feel? Truly? That I have not behaved fittingly? That I have been unjust?
YES.

SUPERCALIFRAGILISTICEXPIALIDOCIOUS!

BIOGRAPHIES

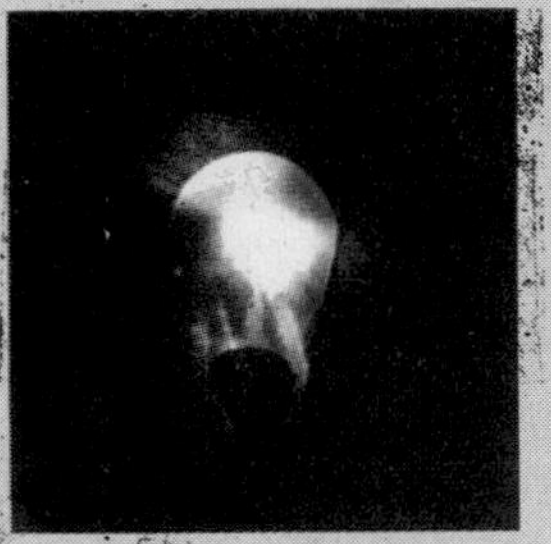

Neil Gaiman *(writer)*

Neil Gaiman is probably best known as the author of the monthly SANDMAN series. His shorter prose work has recently been collected in *Angels & Visitations* (DreamHaven Press). Forthcoming work includes *Mr. Punch* (with Dave McKean) and the BRIEF LIVES Sandman collection.
His house is huge and gothic and a little scary. He mostly writes late at night. He has grandiose plans about answering all his mail but, at present, he probably owes you a letter. If he told you how much he enjoyed working with everyone involved in THE HIGH COST OF LIVING you'd think he was making stuff up again.

Christopher Bachalo *(penciller, DEATH: the high cost of living)*

Chris is a native of glamorous Portage La Prairie, Canada, host of the infamous World Curling Championships. Driven to draw after a close encounter of the fifth kind while harvesting wheat, Chris says DEATH: THE HIGH COST OF LIVING was a labor of love. "I had been a longtime fan of SANDMAN and Neil Gaiman, so drawing DEATH was both a pleasure and an honor for me." Eclectic is a good word for this artist's work and personality. His personal likes include Metallica, Rachmaninoff and Neil Diamond, while his work ranges from mystic SHADE, THE CHANGING MAN to Vertigo's CHILDREN'S CRUSADE. When asked to describe his work, Chris simply replied: "Refreshingly different."

Mark Buckingham *(inker, DEATH: the high cost of living)*

After a brief flirtation with animation followed by a design degree course at Staffordshire University, Mark Buckingham made his comics debut on HELLBLAZER (1988), first as an inker and later as a penciller.
Best known at DC for his inking work on DR. FATE, SHADE, THE CHANGING MAN, THE HACKER FILES, SANDMAN and DEATH: THE HIGH COST OF LIVING, Mark has simultaneously been developing his career as an artist in his own right. As well as joining Neil Gaiman on Miracleman, he has also contributed to SECRET ORIGINS, *Killing Stroke, 2000 AD, Ghost Rider* and SWAMP THING.
Mark has co-created *Immortalis* with Nick Vince. Mark's most recent project, *Ghost Rider 2099*, reunites him with his favorite penciller, Chris Bachalo.
Mark and his wife, Gail, currently reside in the seaside town of Clevedon, England.

Dave McKean *(covers and design, DEATH: the high cost of living; art, DEATH TALKS ABOUT LIFE)*

Dave McKean has illustrated four comics including ARKHAM ASYLUM (DC) and *Signal to Noise* (Gollancz/Dark Horse). He is currently writing and illustrating *Cages (Kitchen Sink)*, a 500-page comic novel about belief, creativity and cats. He has produced all the covers for the ongoing SANDMAN series, is a regular contributor to *The New Yorker* and has done many CD and book covers.
He lives in the Kent countryside with partner Clare and goblin Yolanda.

Steve Oliff *(colorist, Death: the high cost of living)*

Steve discovered color theory and Marvel Comics in 1963, color theory by mixing Play-Doh® and being given a full set of Prismacolor pencils (a far cry from crayons). His career was set. Steve has worked for Marvel, Eclipse, Pacific, Byron Preiss Visual Productions, The Dragon, DC, Dark Horse and Image, has colored thousands of pages and has won several comics industry awards. Steve lives in a converted water tower and is the former mayor of Point Arena, California.

Todd Klein *(letterer)*

Todd Klein is one of the most versatile and accomplished letterers in comics. He has more than 200 logo designs to his credit, among them THE HECKLER and THE ATLANTIS CHRONICLES for DC. He has also written for comics, including DC's THE OMEGA MEN. Todd is a collector of books, magazines and stamps. He doesn't seem to know why. He also is compelled to keep lists of bird species seen and has been known to travel thousands of miles to see new ones. He and his wife, Ellen, currently reside in rural Southern New Jersey.